Scandal in a Digital Age

Hinda Mandell • Gina Masullo Chen
Editors

# Scandal in a Digital Age

*Editors*
Hinda Mandell
School of Communication
Rochester Institute of Technology
Rochester, New York, USA

Gina Masullo Chen
School of Journalism
The University of Texas at Austin, USA

ISBN 978-1-137-59773-1 (hardcover)    ISBN 978-1-137-59545-4 (eBook)
ISBN: 978-1-137-59774-8 (softcover)
DOI 10.1057/978-1-137-59545-4

Library of Congress Control Number: 2016946335

This Palgrave Macmillan imprint is published by Springer Nature
The registered company is Nature America Inc. New York

*To mom and dad, the originators of it all, and to Jacob, Becky, Matt, and Mirabelle who continue the story.*
*—Hinda*

*To Peter, Ian, Chloe, and Phoebe for giving me the space to think, to write, to dream.*
*—Gina*

# FOREWORD

"Who steals my purse steals trash," wrote Shakespeare. "But he that filches from me my good name robs me of that which not enriches him and makes me poor indeed."

These are prescient words from the world's most famous bard. But in the field of computer security—where I lay my research hat—we have hardly even begun to think about how to defend ourselves against the kinds of digital breaches that rob us of our good names—the incidents that ruin careers and marriages, that send us all rushing to our computer screens, in the privacy of our own homes, to look up the latest batch of misguided tweets, or leaked nude photos, or personal emails, or would-be adulterers.

Scandal, of course, is not new, but as the authors in this interdisciplinary collection point out, the Internet changes the nature of scandal in significant and distinctly unsettling ways. The existence of permanent online communication records—and especially photos that can be instantly shared worldwide—can make scandals more immediate and vivid, not to mention more prolonged, trailing their subjects forever as the eternal responses to online search queries. Digital media can make celebrity scandals more graphic—both literally and figuratively—but it can also make us a little more sympathetic to the plight of those celebrities as we realize how easily any of our lives could be upturned by an ill-advised mouse click or unlucky data breach.

Perhaps what is most remarkable about scandal in a digital age is that we are all vulnerable—a completely unknown person who takes a mocking photo or posts an ignorant tweet can become the subject of intense international scrutiny and anger. And thousands more whose indignities never make it onto the front page have to contend with smaller but still utterly devastating scandals in their private lives. We saw this in the aftermath of large-scale data dumps like those directed at Ashley Madison or Sony, where spouses found email addresses of their intimate partners registered on an adultery website, or—in the case of Sony—where bosses and friends could read through snarky emails now made public.

In the wake of such breaches, it is hard not to feel, *There but for the grace of God...* Yes, it can be delicious savoring the details of someone else's sordid personal life, but it can also be a grim reminder of the fragility of our own privacy. Who among us has not sent an email that could rupture an important relationship or cost us our jobs? Who has not visited a website we would rather everyone else not know we viewed, or looked up a slightly embarrassing medical condition or sexual conundrum? The Internet gives us more scandal than ever before—and more vivid, well-documented scandal, to boot—but it also gives us a certain uneasiness about our appetite for this non-stop flood of titillating photographs, embarrassing emails, and displays of digital infidelity.

The authors in this collection untangle the conflicting perspectives running through our various roles in these scandals—as spectators, as Internet users, as victims, as journalists—and explore the ways in which the advent of digital communications both has and has not fundamentally changed the ways we experience and react to scandal. What an important set of issues this is to be addressing at a moment when digital scandals are regular staples of front page news, from the public shaming of politicians whose private sexts are made public to the release of executives' personal email exchanges or website accounts. This book—which offers lessons for security technologists, media producers and consumers, and policy-makers alike—seriously considers the questions of what is at stake when the scale and scope of scandal explodes in a digital age, and what we can—and should—do about it.

In the area of computer security and defense, which is my research corner, we often focus on the financial and physical consequences of security breaches, trying to devise mechanisms to ensure that even if a computer system is compromised, it will still be difficult for an attacker to use it to steal money or affect any physical damage. We do this in part because we assume that the real damage—that can be measured, that can kill people and shut down businesses, and that we most need to defend against—is the physical and financial damage, not the digital damage. After all, how much harm can the transmission of some bits, all on its own, really do?

But we also focus on defending against physical and financial harm because the digital elements are extremely difficult to prevent. It is really hard to lock down all the sensitive or personal data in the world, so instead we do our best, assume that some of it will likely be breached, and put in place safeguards like credit card cancellation, identity theft monitoring, and in-person authorization for critical services, to make sure that when those breaches do occur we have ways of limiting the resulting damage. But we have no comparable lines of defense against the attacks that are aimed not at stealing money or causing physical harm but rather at generating scandal and media attention. We do not even really know what it would mean to defend against the damage they cause after breaches occur—how to characterize or measure that damage, how to understand its impact, how to weigh it against the value of freedom of speech and the imperative of an open Internet. The best we can do, in the absence of fool-proof data protection measures, is advise people not to take naked photos, not to sign up for an extramarital affair using their real email address, not to send emails they would not want to see published on the front page of *The New York Times*. But we also acknowledge that people are not programmable robots—and while communication in a digital age can leave one open to a host of vulnerabilities, it remains difficult to legislate human behavior. It is for that reason that this book is a valuable, groundbreaking look at the costs of this crucial class of incidents, how they impact our society, and what we stand to lose if we do not figure out better modes of defense.

Public Policy and Computing Security                                    Josephine Wolff
Rochester Institute of Technology,
Rochester, NY, USA

Berkman Center for Internet and Society
Harvard University, Cambridge, MA, USA

# Acknowledgments

Thank you to the contributors whose hard work, dedication to this project, and incisive thinking have—quite literally—made this book possible. We are grateful to our editor at Palgrave Macmillan, Shaun Vigil, who believed in our book even in its earliest stage. Thank you for shepherding the book through to publication.

We extend our appreciation and gratitude to the School of Communication and the College of Liberal Arts at Rochester Institute of Technology for the funding that helped bring to life a number of essays within this book.

We also thank Deepa Fadnis and Paromita Pain for their assistance with the references for this book.

# Contents

# List of Contributors

**Neal Allen, PhD** is Assistant Professor of Political Science at Wichita State University, Kansas, USA, and he writes about civil rights, American politics, and the politics of race. His articles have appeared in *American Political Thought*, *Oklahoma Politics*, and the *National Political Science Review*. He is the author of Citizens Respond to Civil Rights: Letters to Members of Congress in the 1960s, forthcoming from the University Press of Kansas.

**Steve Almond** is the author of *Against Football: A Reluctant Manifesto*, *Candyfreak*, a *New York Times* bestseller, and *My Life in Heavy Metal*. The author of eight books his short fiction has appeared in *The Best American Short Stories* and Pushcart Prize anthologies, and his story collection *God Bless America* won the Paterson Prize for fiction. He is a regular contributor to *The New York Times Magazine* and *The Boston Globe*. He is the co-host of the WBUR podcast "Dear Sugar Radio," and he pens the advice column, Heavy Meddle, for the Cognoscenti, the commentary site for Boston's NPR station.

**Diana York Blaine, PhD** is Professor of Writing and Gender Studies at the University of Southern California, USA. She researches representations of the gendered body in mainstream media and popular discourse.

**Gina Masullo Chen, PhD** is an assistant professor in the School of Journalism at The University of Texas at Austin, USA. She spent 20 years as a print and online newspaper reporter and editor before becoming a professor. Her research focuses on online interaction and how it influences social, civic, and political engagement. Her research articles have appeared in peer-reviewed academic journals, such as *Communication Research*, *New Media & Society*, *Mass Communication & Society*, and *Computers in Human Behavior*.

**Joan L. Conners, PhD** is Professor of Communication Studies at Randolph-Macon College, Virginia, USA. Her past research on political cartoons includes analyses of Anthony Weiner's sexting scandal and resignation, portrayals of presidential candidates, and enemy representations of Saddam Hussein.

**Grant Cos, PhD** is an associate professor and Director of Graduate Programs in the School of Communication at Rochester Institute of Technology, New York, USA. His research interests include issues in political rhetoric and freedom of expression, and his articles have appeared in *Free Speech Yearbook*, *Canadian Journal of Rhetoric*, and *American Behavioral Scientist*.

**David Dahl** is Deputy Managing Editor at *The Boston Globe*. He edits page one stories and is the senior editor in charge in the evening. Previously, he was the editor of *The Boston Globe*'s regional editions and the "Your Town" hyperlocal websites and served as a political editor.

**Deepa Fadnis, MA** is a doctoral student at the School of Journalism at The University of Texas at Austin, USA. Her primary research interests are at the crossroads between international gender studies, popular culture, and cultural activism and digitally supported social movements. Her research has been presented at the Association for Education in Mass Communication and Journalism's annual conference.

**Romayne Smith Fullerton, PhD** teaches in the Media Studies and Journalism Programs at the University of Western Ontario, Canada. Her recent research interests focus on journalism ethics and international comparisons of crime coverage.

**Joshua Gamson, PhD** is Professor of Sociology at the University of San Francisco, USA. He is the author of *Claims to Fame: Celebrity in Contemporary America* (1994), *Freaks Talk Back: Tabloid Talk Shows and Sexual Nonconformity* (1998), *The Fabulous Sylvester* (2005), and *Modern Families: Stories of Extraordinary Journeys to Kinship* (2015), along with numerous articles on social movements, sexualities, and popular culture.

**Susan Keith, PhD** is an associate professor in the Department of Journalism and Media Studies at Rutgers University in New Brunswick, New Jersey, USA. She worked as a journalist for 16 years before becoming a professor, gaining experience that informs her research on transitions in journalism, media ethics and law, and media and collective memory.

**Kathleen M. Kuehn, PhD** is Lecturer in Media Studies at Victoria University of Wellington, New Zealand. Her research interests center on the political economy of digital media, cultural production, and surveillance.

**Hinda Mandell, PhD** is an assistant professor in the School of Communication at Rochester Institute of Technology, New York, USA. She researches news coverage of scandal, and her articles on the topic have appeared in the *Los Angeles Times, Chicago Tribune, USA Today, Boston Herald, Palm Beach Post, Politico*, and in academic journals, including *Women's Studies in Communication, Visual Communication Quarterly*, and *Explorations in Media Ecology*. She blogs on scandal and gender at omghinda.com.

**Erin Matson** is a feminist writer and organizer. She is co-founder and co-director of Reproaction, a direct action group that works to increase access to abortion and advance reproductive justice. She previously served as an editor at large for *RH Reality Check*, as well as a vice president of the National Organization for Women.

**Brian Moritz, PhD** is Assistant Professor of Digital Media and Online Journalism at SUNY Oswego, New York, USA. A former newspaper sports journalist, his research focuses on the social construction of sports journalism. His work has been published in the *International Journal of Sports Communication, Computers in Human Behavior*, and *Media, War & Conflict*. He also blogs about sports media issues at sportsmediaguy.com.

**Paromita Pain, MA** is a doctoral student in the School of Journalism at The University of Texas at Austin, USA. She spent a decade writing long-form stories on human rights and gender for *The Hindu* national newspaper in India. Her research focuses on participatory media, gender, and community empowerment. Her research article has appeared in *Journalism and Mass Communication Educator*, and she has presented her work at the annual conferences of the Association for Education in Mass Communication and Journalism and the Midwest Association for Public Opinion Research.

*Gemma Richardson, PhD* is a Program Coordinator and Professor in the Bachelor of Digital Communications and Bachelor of Journalism programs at Humber College in Toronto, Canada. Her research interests include media coverage of suicide, journalism ethics and media coverage of protest movements.

*J. Richard Stevens, PhD* is an associate professor in Media Studies at the University of Colorado Boulder, USA. Stevens' research delves into the intersection of ideological formation and media message dissemination, comprising studies such as how cultural messages are formed and passed through popular culture, how technology infrastructure affects the delivery of media messages, communication technology policy, and related studies in how media and technology platforms are changing American public discourse.

*Mark Ward Sr., PhD* is Associate Professor of Communication at the University of Houston-Victoria, Texas, USA. He is editor of the recent multi-volume series *The Electronic Church in the Digital Age: Cultural Impacts of Evangelical Mass Media* (2016); he has authored two histories of religious broadcasting, published numerous journal articles on evangelical culture and media, and received the 2014 Article of the Year Award from the Religious Communication Association.

*Josephine Wolff, PhD* is Assistant Professor of Public Policy and a member of the extended faculty in Computing Security at Rochester Institute of Technology, New York, USA. Her research focuses on measuring the impact of computer security policies and understanding the complementary roles of social, technical, and policy-based defense mechanisms for protecting computer systems. She is a faculty associate at the Harvard Berkman Center for Internet & Society and her articles have appeared in *Slate*, *The Atlantic*, *Scientific American*, *The New Republic*, *Newsweek*, and *The New York Times*.

# PART I

# Historical Perspectives on Scandal

# CHAPTER 1

# Introduction: Scandal in an Age of Likes, Selfies, Retweets, and Sexts

## Hinda Mandell and Gina Masullo Chen

It was the day before Valentine's, and one congressman was clearly besotted with a blonde bikini model—so much so that he could not keep his attention on the president's "State of the Union" address. Congressman Steve Cohen (D-TN), representing a district that includes Memphis, Tennessee, was spotted picking up his phone amid his peers in Congress. He felt compelled to send that special someone a private message on Twitter.

Except he sent it publicly as a tweet.

"nice to know you were watchin SOTU(state of the union). Happy Valentines beautiful girl. ilu," wrote Congressman Cohen, as President Barack Obama addressed the nation in 2013 about the country's issues surrounding the longtime debt crisis, tax reform, and Medicare.

Cut to the news media's perspective:

America's economic vitality? B-O-R-I-N-G!
A sex scandal that stars a 64-year-old politician and a 24-year-old woman? Now we are talking.

Across the land, editors snapped their fingers and journalists pounced on Congressman Cohen, ready to uncover a naughty relationship. Cohen deleted the tweets within minutes, adding to an air of illicit mystery. The next day, the congressman—who is not married—came clean as he spoke with reporters in his office: The bikini model was actually his long-lost daughter. The tweets were "fatherly rather than flirtatious," wrote the New York *Daily News* the

H. Mandell (✉)
School of Communication, Rochester Institute of Technology, Rochester, NY, USA

G.M. Chen
School of Journalism, The University of Texas at Austin, TX, USA

© The Editor(s) (if applicable) and The Author(s) 2016
H. Mandell, G.M. Chen (eds.), *Scandal in a Digital Age*,
DOI 10.1057/978-1-137-59545-4_1

following day.[1] During this private news conference, Cohen said he learned of his paternal relationship to this woman only three years ago, and they were both attempting to establish a father–daughter bond. Cohen said, according to NBC News:

> When she let me know she was watching the State of the Union address, I was thrilled that she wanted Steve Cohen to be part of her. I had such joy, that I couldn't hold back from tweeting her.[2]

Meanwhile, five months after the SOTU Twitter incident, a DNA test revealed that the young model was *not* actually Cohen's daughter—saddening Cohen[3]—and marking "case closed" on what began as a congressman's cryptic tweets to a comely woman.[4]

The Cohen kerfuffle emphasizes that if a politician tweets—and then deletes—messages to an attractive woman, the nature of their relationship can only be one thing: scandalous. But in this instance, the truth revealed itself to be far less salacious than the facts originally seemed.

This book represents an effort to probe the frenzied, knee-jerk, and titillating relationship between scandal, news, social media, and the public in a digital age.

It is dangerous out there.

For this reason, it is worth revisiting the elegantly phrased nod to discretion immortalized by Martin Lomasney—a Massachusetts politician from last century who famously said, "Never write if you can speak; never speak if you can nod; never nod if you can wink."[5] But because Lomasney was born 20 years before the invention of the telephone (The phone! Who has time to talk to someone in real time *these* days?), his guide needs a twenty-first-century approach. Here is our attempt to update Lomasney's charming—if antiquated—wisdom:

> *Don't sext when you can talk dirty offline. Don't talk when you can whisper in person. Don't whisper when you can wink. Make sure you have the consent of all those involved. Have them sign non-disclosure agreements. Don't share passwords. Know that everything's hackable. Never email. And dear lord: Put the iPhone away when the clothes come off.*

Life, indeed, was much simpler back then.

But even our amended homage to Lomasney does little to help someone who is recorded without his or her awareness—and whose actions are certainly scandalous. Consider the case of the former British Member of Parliament, Lord John Sewel, who was 69 at the time of an incident that caught him—on video—in a rather delicate and unflattering situation in 2015. Ironically, Sewel was also chairman of the Privileges and Conduct Committee, which oversees the behavior of Lords behaving badly in Parliament. Therefore, he likely did know better than to enjoy a romp with prostitutes in London while snorting coke, fondling them, and making derogatory comments about Asians.[6] But he partied anyhow, and—unfortunately for this lusty lord—the sex workers captured the rendezvous using a hidden camera. Footage, easily available through a simple Google search, shows the politician lounging in an orange brassiere and snorting three lines of coke. To Sewel, perhaps Lomasney would advise: Do not party with women who are not your wife, when you can just party with your wife. Sewel added insult to spousal injury when he "turned a framed picture of his wife face-down"[7] during the tryst. Lomasney himself never married.

This book offers a collection of essays and studies on scandal in a digital age when our misdeeds and private moments can be broadcast to a worldwide audience in less time than it takes to enjoy a cool sip of water. The scandals that we are interested in are not just any old, analog example of people behaving recklessly with wild abandon. Rather, we are interested in how the misuse of technology facilitates scandal and how technology itself can capture our most private moments and share them to an eager crowd of 7 billion and counting, ready and armed to comment, retweet, share, and like. Our scandals include politicians' misdeeds, as well as those of celebrities, journalists, religious leaders, and even private people.

Elsewhere, we have argued that scandals represent a social institution because there is the habitual way that scandals unfold in the news and there is the presence of "character" types who fulfill roles specific to their status or position.[8] When approaching scandals one at a time, the events constituting one scandal may appear distinct from the next one that comes down the line. But when scandal is viewed as a social institution—in aggregate—with set agents and patterns of behavior, then it is possible to pinpoint the repetition of processes and to identify a scandal script. In scandal, one can find a consistent narrative, which sociologist Joshua Gamson (who appears in this book) has labeled "a common script."[9] This script includes an "accusation or revelation, broadcast, denial and/or confession, and, frequently, a comeback or attempted comeback."[10]

While we have established a general scandal "script," what exactly defines a *scandal?* The simple definition is a "breach of virtue exposed" that causes public disapproval.[11] John Thompson, a sociologist at the University of Cambridge who wrote the foundational book *Political Scandal: Power and Visibility in the Media Age*, describes five qualities to scandal.[12]

1. Scandals involve the breach of "values, norms, and moral codes."[13]
2. Scandals involve secrecy or hush-hush activity.
3. People disapprove of this moral breach once it becomes public.
4. Some folks express their outrage.
5. There is the risk of a damaged reputation for those involved in the scandal.

Public revelation is central for an event to explode into one hot mess of a scandal.[14] Therefore, media play a central role in the evolution of a scandal. It is the platform that allows people to "consume" its juicy contents. If the public is not aware of the event in question, then a scandal cannot transpire. (Of course, that does not mean the scandalous event never happened. It certainly did. It is just that the public did not find out about it. The phenomenon is equivalent to that old tree in the forest, albeit with a modern twist: If a celebrity made a sex tape but never leaked it to the public, can its existence be scandalous?) Or think of it this way: "Corruption [or scandalous activity] is a constant, and scandal is a variable."[15]

But there is something distinctly different about scandal in our digital age versus the analog age: We have long been socialized to set our gaze as voyeurs upon the personal lives of others. As a routine part of our day, we have normalized online lurking and Googling and peeping into the digital footprint of strangers and friends alike. And the media enables and indulges our peccadilloes to pursue our superficial curiosity about others' private moments. Clay Calvert, the journalism scholar and author of *Voyeur Nation*, coined a term for this phenomenon: "Mediated voyeurism." It involves "the consumption of revealing images of and information about others' apparently real and unguarded lives, often yet not always for the purposes of entertainment but frequently at the expense of privacy and discourse, through the means of the mass media and Internet."[16]

Mediated voyeurism certainly facilitates our eager consumption of scandal. But it is not as if our collective interest in scandal only emerged with the digital technologies that sculpted us as voyeurs. Indeed, the historian John H. Summers writes that our proclivity to probe private details in public life has roots with the founding of the USA (and certainly, one would presume, goes back to the start of civilization!). "In the early republic and throughout the nineteenth century, American political culture subjected the sexual character of officeholders to closer, steady, and often unflattering scrutiny, as most voters insisted a man of virtue constituted 'the only safe depository of public trust.'"[17] Of course, as the republic grew up to become the USA, and as journalists emerged as polished professionals eager to embed themselves within elite circles of influence in the early twentieth century, the practice of airing private details of powerful men grew out of favor. But then the Civil Rights Movements of the twentieth century, along with the Watergate corruption scandal and the intractable Vietnam War of the 1970s, prompted journalists to reconsider their comfy-cozy relationship to those at the top of the power structure. Certainly, issues relating to one's private character inform the public persona—the logic went—so the protective cover journalists gave to public figures began to disintegrate. The Internet boom in the 1990s was a boon to the proliferation of scandal coverage, further bolstering the cut-throat rules of engagement defining 24/7 journalism that began with the cable era. Is it really a coincidence that the biggest sex scandal in US history—President Bill Clinton's relationship to the White House intern Monica Lewinsky—was first reported on a website in 1998 and not in a newspaper?

The Internet and its complementary digital tools make it so much easier for us all to scratch our lustful itch. "Contemporary society is apparently held together by a suspicion and a distaste for public life," writes Jean Seaton, a professor of media history. "Prurience has rarely been more powerful than it is at present."

In this anthology, we certainly do not blame technology for the rapid-fire move toward public disclosure of private behavior, which runs the gamut from illegal to abusive to callous to merely mortifying. Rather, we see technology as a tool that facilitates the broadcasting of scandal, not only because information about a particular scandal can be accessed by anyone with an Internet connection (i.e. The World) but also because technology itself captures these illicit moments and offers evidence.

Long gone are the days when a newspaper such as the *Miami Herald* had to pay money to send an undercover team of five journalists with two rental cars to stake out the Washington, DC, house of Gary Hart—the leading contender for the Democratic nominee for president of the USA in 1988—to catch evidence of his extramarital affair.[18] That is a lot of money, manpower, and time fueling a single gotcha-moment. These days, politicians and public figures (and mere mortals, as well) too often incriminate themselves within seconds—saving news organizations a lot of legwork—and assuring a steady diet of public titillation. With one errant click, swipe, or tap, their careers and reputations are thrown onto the garbage heap of history.

There is no shortage of examples detailing the unique pitfalls of scandal in a digital age. At the time of writing, the following events caught our attention:

- **Queen Elizabeth's Nazi salute in 1933**: *Hold up!*, you say. *I thought this book was about scandal in the digital age.* Indeed you are right, but the digital age allows some events—once privately tucked away under a historical shroud—a new airing. In 2015, news outlets broadcast home video from 1933 when the Queen of England was just 6 years old, playfully enacting the notorious salute in deference to Adolf Hitler, the year that he became chancellor of Germany. "It is disappointing that film, shot eight decades ago and apparently from (Her Majesty's) personal archive, has been obtained and exploited in this manner," said a spokesperson for Buckingham Palace.[19]
- **A political wife in the UK prone to posting selfies of her ample assets:** Karen Danczuk was the selfie-obsessed wife of a British Member of Parliament who liked to feature shots of her cleavage and bum on Twitter. These photographs, while scandalous, did not constitute a scandal in and of themselves. Instead, it was the fact that the political wife filed for divorce from her husband, the politician Simon Danczuk, and that she was alleged to have an affair with either a car salesman[20] or the personal trainer responsible for crafting her curves.[21]
- **A wife in China catches her husband having sex with her twin sister:** News outlets reported that when Ting Su—age 29 at the time of the confrontation in 2014—caught her husband having sex with her sister in a parked car at a mall parking lot, the cheating duo jumped out of the car— naked as the day they were born.[22] Su hopped inside the car and drove away, leaving her husband and sister to stand before a gawking crowd armed with smartphones. Photos of the philanderers went viral within minutes.

- **A lawmaker in Michigan orchestrates a fake sex scandal alleging he had sex with men to detract from his actual extramarital affair with a woman:** Republican lawmaker Todd Courser resigned from the Michigan Legislature in 2015 after he orchestrated a fictitious email to his political supporters. The email alleged that Courser, a married father of four children, behaved in ways contrary to his Conservative Christian values. According to the email: "He is a FREAK! He is a gun toting bible thumping cock sucking freak! His whole personalit [*sic*] is a sham!"[23] (Underlined in the original.) The purpose of that email was to cover up—albeit unsuccessfully—an actual affair that Courser had with another Republican member of the Michigan House of Representatives, Cindy Gamrat. Gamrat, a married mother of three, who is also a Conservative Christian, was expelled from her seat in September 2015. Both Courser and Gamrat ran for their legislative seats again in the November 2015 elections. And both lost by an overwhelming landslide.
- **A news organization "outs" the Chief Financial Officer of a media giant, publishing his private text messages with a gay, porn-star escort:** Gawker Media was slammed by news outlets in 2015 for publishing an exchange between David Geithner, Chief Financial Officer of Condé Nast—who is married to a woman with whom he has three children—and a male sex worker, who was granted anonymity by Gawker. The two were allegedly arranging a tryst but never met up. Geithner (brother to Timothy Geithner, the former secretary of the US Treasury) denies the authenticity of the text-message exchange and called the article—which was subsequently deleted from Gawker—a "shakedown."[24]

Before proceeding with an overview of the book, we would like to highlight a unique aspect of this book—it is a marriage of journalistic and academic writing. Within these pages, you will read insights by journalists along with scholarly inquiry by academics. This way, we hope to bring to readers the best of both worlds, the breezy, topical, and incisive writing by those reporting from the ground, along with specialized connections to the academic literature within the fields of communication, politics, sociology, rhetoric, and media studies.

## Section I: Historical Perspectives on Scandal

This section highlights the cultural function of scandal, drawing on historic examples to illustrate how scandal has developed over time. The section juxtaposes scandalous accounts from the past to those of the present in order to explain the evolution of scandal within our "always-on" digital culture.

The first contribution in this section, Chap. 2, examines "Scandal's Role in Creating a Surveillance Culture." J. Richard Stevens takes us back in time to 1890, when the first legal tort for privacy appeared in an issue of the Harvard Law Review. It addressed the rising moral panic surrounding the use of snap cameras—an emerging technology at that time—which allowed the middle and lower classes to publish photographs of elites without their permission. Suddenly, they lost control over their own image and likeness. The chapter explores the scandal that birthed American privacy law (an individual's "right to be left alone"), documenting how advances in technology continually disrupt the control elites possess over both the publicity activities that create fame and the unwanted attention to private facts that creates scandal.

In Chap. 3, Neal Allen explores how political scandal limits the power of social justice movements, focusing on the struggle for civil rights and racial justice in the USA. Attempts to "scandalize" Martin Luther King Jr. the 1965 Selma-to-Montgomery marchers, and members of the broader Civil Rights Movement represent examples of how scandal is deployed by defenders of existing social and political hierarchies against those fighting for progress.

In Chap. 4, Grant Cos asks us to revisit the 1960s. Amid a backdrop of political assassinations that stole the lives of President John F. Kennedy, US Senator Robert Kennedy, and Civil Rights leader Martin Luther King Jr. Senator Edward M. Kennedy faced issues of his own political survival. Late one July night in 1969, after partying on Chappaquiddick Island in Massachusetts, Edward M. Kennedy, who was married at the time, drove off a bridge—leaving to die his lone passenger, a young woman who was not his wife. Cos revisits Kennedy's televised address to the people of Massachusetts, one week after the car accident, and demonstrates how Kennedy's attempt at apologia impacted the narrative of scandal for decades to come.

In Chap. 5, Mark Ward Sr. explores why the sex scandals of televangelists Jim Bakker and Jimmy Swaggart stole headlines in the 1980s, while the national media took a pass in 2010 when televangelist Marcus Lamb confessed adultery and alleged a multimillion-dollar extortion plot against him. Yet a sex scandal in 2015 involving reality TV star Josh Duggar, a then-emerging evangelical leader, went viral overnight. The chapter illustrates how the proliferation of media platforms has fragmented audiences so that some scandals—which might have been big news a generation ago—now circulate only within special interest communities, yet social media magnifies cases like Duggar's.

Next up, in Chap. 6, journalist David Dahl imagines how a world besotted with social media would have shaped the President Bill Clinton mega-scandal—of cigar and blue-dress notoriety—if it unfolded today. Dahl ruminates over what it means for the world's most famous intern, Monica Lewinsky, to be the Internet's first victim of public shaming when the story originated online in 1998, after the esteemed legacy magazine, *Newsweek*, delayed the story.

## SECTION II: WHEN PRIVATES GO PUBLIC

Today's digitized world has erased the former distinction between the public and private self in the social sphere. In the past, a firm line separated what was private—and personal—from what was public and knowable. At that time, scandals—even among politicians and other public figures—were often seen as personal affairs, and the press did not write about them for publication. This contrasts with today's world where even seemingly minor events involving the private lives of public people blast into the social consciousness. In this section, we draw on German philosopher Jürgen Habermas' concept of the public sphere, as both a form of open discussion about matters of common concern and the physical space—in this case a digital space—where these conversations take place.[25] This section draws from both current and historic examples to illustrate this transition.

In Chap. 7, Joshua Gamson examines the evolution of sexting scandals, which first emerged in news coverage back in 2009. He focuses on two events in particular—scandals belonging to NFL quarterback Brett Favre in 2010 and New York Congressman Anthony Weiner in 2011—where sexting itself generated the sensational media frenzy. While sexting technology may be new(ish), Gamson argues that the media narratives proceeded according to existing scandal scripts.

In Chap. 8, essayist Steve Almond excoriates the modern media system—and the public, as its voracious scandal consumers—for making news out of oversexed guys who make stupid mistakes. Focusing on former New York politician Anthony Weiner and the two rounds of his sext-tweeting scandal in 2011 and 2013, the author rails against a system that deems indiscretions newsworthy.

And in Chap. 9 we hear from Diana York Blaine, who personally recounts what happened when pictures of her bare chest were broadcast on the nightly news. The pictures garnered more than 1 million views, catapulting her into a public scandal. She explains how she weathered the storm, standing for her freedom despite raging pundits and scolding administrators.

In Chap. 10, Kathleen M. Kuehn offers a case study of what happens when two people have sex in a space they think is private, but their intimacy is publicly viewed and recorded. The convergence of mobile technologies, participatory media, and the birth of the "digital witness" have given rise to the democratization of scandal—where anyone can get caught in humiliating circumstances and evidence of the incident is circulated publicly. Through an analysis of the 2014 Christchurch, New Zealand, "office sex romp," this chapter explores the relationship between social media, surveillance, and scandal to contemplate "public privacy" in an era where all actions have the potential to be visually captured and circulated at any time, without our knowledge or consent.

Next up, in Chap. 11, Gina Masullo Chen along with Paromita Pain and Deepa Fadnis explore the clash between public and private on Facebook by drawing on the experience of South Carolina Congressman Mark Sanford. The chapter analyzes more than 300 comments that people posted on his Facebook wall in 2014 after Sanford detailed battles with his ex-wife, who had divorced him after Sanford's much-publicized affair in 2009 when he was governor of that state. The analysis reveals a public consciousness that questions politicians using social media to air private quarrels, even amid the voracious public appetite for these tidbits of personal news about those with political power.

In Chap. 12, Gemma Richardson and Romayne Smith Fullerton analyze Canadian media coverage of the 2013 scandal surrounding the former mayor of Toronto, Rob Ford, who was caught on a cell-phone video smoking crack cocaine. According to the authors, the backlash against investigative journalists who broke this story reveals a public that is deeply lacking in knowledge of newsroom conduct and highly skeptical of media coverage of scandal, often questioning the authenticity of digital media that captures scandalous conduct.

## SECTION III: DIGITAL SURVEILLANCE

This section contemplates scandal's anatomy and how we maneuver through a world where every moment, no matter how intimate or illicit, is potentially watched, recorded, documented, and shared through digital media. We define digital surveillance as the potential eyes of everyone with Internet access to see all the titillating tidbits that are placed online. Our definition, therefore, is not limited to merely the computer infrastructure[26] that makes these data available but also includes the way the public spreads these saucy snippets online. This section focuses on a variety of scandals that touch on the world of celebrity, sport, and journalism to illustrate how our interconnected, digitized culture reveals all—often to our regret.

In Chap. 13, Susan Keith explores the 2015 revelations that NBC Nightly News anchor Brian Williams and Fox News opinion show host Bill O'Reilly exaggerated their war reporting experiences, highlighting problems with the promotional culture of US broadcast journalism. These scandals demonstrate the difficulty journalists face to maintain their credibility within legacy journalism as opportunities grow for the public surveillance of journalists and their digital footprints.

In Chap. 14, Joan L. Conners is our guide into the world of political cartoons, focusing on how the medium framed the National Security Agency (NSA) snooping and wiretap scandal of 2013. She found that when political cartoonists attacked NSA's domestic spying tactics, the cartoonists spared no one: not the agency nor Edward Snowden, who leaked the NSA files, or President Barack Obama. Political cartoons targeted the NSA for its intrusive Big-Brother-like practices; the Obama administration was skewered for its tepid response about these tactics; and even US citizens were lampooned for their lack of concern into their own violations of privacy.

In Chap. 15, Brian Moritz traces media coverage of the 2014 Ray Rice domestic violence and football scandal to probe how a scandal's narrative can change over time. The chapter argues that journalistic routines and the social construction of news altered the nature of the Ray Rice scandal from an athlete accused of domestic violence into a much larger story of institutional corruption and fact-dodging within the NFL.

Activist and writer Erin Matson offers a personal approach to investigating the impact of the Ray Rice scandal in Chap. 16. The aftermath of this media frenzy saw the emergence of the feminist-inspired Twitter hashtag

#WhyIStayed. Its goal was to challenge common (mis)perceptions of domestic violence, including the view that women who experience it should be subject to public probing and judgment. This chapter also explores how feminists promote story sharing as a powerful tool to restore voice and agency to women who have been shamed.

Finally, in Chap. 17, we conclude by pointing to new directions for scandal research and predict what the scandal environment might look like in the decades to come, especially as new technologies, apps, and devices become integrated into our lives.

For better or worse, the prevalence of scandal gives us much juicy material to gnaw on: There are prevailing and shifting norms to dissect, discourses to analyze, and cultural practices to ponder. Editing a book on scandal has kept us busy. But we (likely) would not protest if a steep decline in scandal's occurrence had the effect of muting our research area.

Does the prevalence of scandal and the erosion of privacy rewire our brain to expect increasingly personal information from people? We will leave that question for other researchers to test in the future. But we do have a hunch that there must be some type of social effect when device-connected voyeurs dominate the cultural system. As a scandal-consuming army of billions, we are outfitted with the capability to instantly and broadly publicize private and scandalous moments belonging to ourselves and others. It is clear there is no longer a distinction between online and "In Real Life" modalities of living. There is just "life," which merges our tech and offline selves. We should all be wary of the fact that none of us are free of the proverbial skeleton in the closet. Let us just keep a smartphone out of its hands.

## NOTES

1. Kristen A. Lee, "Congressman's Tweets to Bombshell Blonde Lead to Bombshell Announcement—She's His Daughter!" *Daily News*, February 14, 2013 http://www.nydailynews.com/news/politics/congressman-flirty-tweets-college-student-raise-eyebrows-article-1.1264230.
2. Breanna Edwards, "Rep. Cohen Reveals Secret Daughter," *Politico*, February 14, 2013 http://www.politico.com/story/2013/02/woman-cohen-tweeted-is-daughter-087694.
3. Ron Kampeas, "Lawmaker Cohen 'Dismayed' Model Victoria Brink is Not His Daughter," *JTA*, July 21, 2013 http://www.jta.org/2013/07/21/news-opinion/the-telegraph/cohen-dismayed-victoria-brink-is-not-his-daughter.
4. Amy Argetsinger, "Re. Steve Cohen's 'Secret Daughter' is Not His Daughter, DNA Tests Show," *The Washington Post*, July 18, 2013 https://www.washingtonpost.com/news/reliable-source/wp/2013/07/18/rep-steve-cohens-secret-daughter-is-not-his-daughter-dna-tests-show/.
5. Roy Greene, "The Life, Legend and Lessons of Martin Lomasney: Ward Boss, West End Icon," *The Boston Globe*, June 5, 2012 http://www.boston.com/yourtown/news/beacon_hill/2012/06/the_life_legend_and_lessons_of.html.

6. Brendan Carlin, Ian Gallagher, and Emma Glanfield, "Pictured: Moment Disgraced Lord was Caught Snorting Cocaine with £200-a-Night Prostitute During Sordid Romp. Peer Resigns and Faces Police Probe but He Can STILL Claim £300-a-Day Allowance," *The Daily Mail*, July 25, 2015 http://www.dailymail.co.uk/news/article-3174689/Lord-Snorty-Blair-crony-responsible-behaviour-peers-filmed-taking-cocaine-200-night-prostitute-s-breasts-romp-two-escorts-discounted-flat.html.

7. Carlin, Gallagher, and Glanfield, "Pictured: Moment Disgraced Lord was Caught Snorting Cocaine with £200-a-Night Prostitute During Sordid Romp. Peer Resigns and Faces Police Probe but He Can STILL Claim £300-a-Day Allowance."

8. Hinda Mandell, "Political Wives and Scandal: Reading Agency in Silence at Press Conferences," *Catalan Journal of Communication & Cultural Studies* 4, no. 2 (2012): 203–220; Peter L. Berger and Thomas Luckmann, *The social construction of reality. A treatise in the sociology of knowledge*, (New York: Anchor Books, 1966), 53.

9. Joshua Gamson, "Normal Sins: Sex Scandal Narratives as Institutional Morality Tales," *Social Problems* 48, no. 2 (2001): 18–205.

10. Gamson, "Normal Sins," 40.

11. Andrei S. Markovits and Mark Silverstein, eds, *The Politics of Scandal: Power and Process in Liberal Democracies* (New York: Holmes & Meier, 1988) vii.

12. John B. Thompson, *Political Scandal: Power and Visibility in the Media Age.* (Cambridge: Blackwell Publishers, 2000).

13. Thompson, *Political Scandal*, 13.

14. Paul Apostolidis and Juliet A. Williams, *Public Affairs: Politics in the Age of Sex Scandals* (Durham, NC: Duke, 2004); Mark West, *Secrets, Sex, and Spectacle: The Rules of Scandal in Japan and the United States* (Chicago: University of Chicago Press, 2006).

15. Theodore J. Lowi, "Power and Corruption: Political Competition and the Scandal Market," in Public Affairs: Politics in the Age of Sex Scandals, ed. Paul Apostolidis and Juliet A. Williams in Apostolidis & Williams (Durham, NC: Duke University Press, 2004), 70.

16. Clay Calvert, *Voyeur Nation: Media, Privacy, and Peering in Modern Culture* (Boulder, CO: Westview Press, 2000), 2.

17. John H. Summers, "What Happened to Sex Scandals? Politics and Peccadilloes, Jefferson to Kennedy," *The Journal of American History* 87, no. 3 (2000): 825.

18. Matt Bai, "How Gary Hart's Downfall Forever Changed American Politics," *The New York Times Magazine*, September 18, 2014 http://www.nytimes.com/2014/09/21/magazine/how-gary-harts-downfall-forever-changed-american-politics.html.

19. Laura Smith-Spark and Radina Gigova, "UK Newspaper Publishes Footage of Queen Giving Nazi Salute as Child," *CNN*, July 18, 2015 http://www.cnn.com/2015/07/18/europe/uk-queen-nazi-salute-footage/.

20. Tania Steere and Sara Smyth, "Selfie Queen 'Cheated on MP Husband with Car Salesman': Claims Karen Danczuk Told Man She was in Love with Him and Posed in Lingerie on Marital Bed," *The Daily Mail*, July 9, 2015 http://www.dailymail.co.uk/news/article-3155650/Selfie-queen-cheated-MP-husband-car-salesman-Claims-Karen-Danczuk-told-man-love-posed-lingerie-marital-bed.html.

21. Natalie Clarke, "As the Queen of Selfies Ditches Her MP Hubby, Has Karen Danczuk Set Her Sights on Her Personal Trainer?" *Daily Mail*, June 29, 2015 http://www.dailymail.co.uk/news/article-3143958/As-Queen-Selfies-ditches-MP-hubby-Karen-Danczuk-set-sights-personal-trainer.html.

22. QMI Agency, "Wife Catches Hubby Having Sex with Her Twin, Strands Them Naked in Parking Lot," *The Toronto Sun*, December 19, 2014 http://www.torontosun.com/2014/12/18/wife-catches-hubby-having-sex-with-her-twin-strands-them-naked-in-parking-lot; "This Woman Caught Her Husband Banging Her Twin," *Cosmopolitan*, December 19, 2014 http://www.cosmopolitan.com.au/relationships/relationship-advice/2014/12/chinese-woman-catches-husband-having-sex-with-her-twin-in-car/; Ryan Barrell, "Woman, Ting Sun, Finds Husband Cheating with Her Own Twin, Gets Spectacular Revenge," *The Huffington Post*, December 18, 2014, http://www.huffingtonpost.co.uk/2014/12/18/cheating-husband-left-naked_n_6346994.html.

23. Brandon Hall, "Read Todd Courser's Full False Flag Email Uncensored (Warning: Explicit Content)," *West Michigan Politics* (blog), August 7, 2015 http://west-mipolitics.blogspot.com/2015/08/read-todd-coursers-full-false-flag.html.

24. Lloyd Grove, "Gawker Got in Bed with the Wrong Escort and Civil War Ensues," *The Daily Beast*, July 17, 2015 http://www.thedailybeast.com/articles/2015/07/17/gawker-got-in-bed-with-the-wrong-escort-and-civil-war-ensues.html.

25. Jeffrey M. Berry and Sarah Sobieraj, *The Outrage Industry: Political Opinion Media and the New Incivility*, (New York, NY: Oxford University Press, 2014); Jürgen Habermas, *The Structural Transformation of the Public Sphere* (Cambridge, MA: MIT Press, 1991).

26. Christian Fuchs, "New Media, Web 2.0 and Surveillance," *Sociology Compass* 5, no. 2: 134–147.

# CHAPTER 2

# Scandal's Role in Creating a Surveillance Culture

## *J. Richard Stevens*

Media scandals represent that curious intersection between our interest in prominent people and the limits we impose upon access to information in our lives. As private citizens, we trust that details of our personal affairs will be shared only with those closest to us and that boundaries we erect to guard against the roving attention of strangers will be respected. At the same time, we also revel in the disclosure of that same information by prominent people, public officials, and celebrities. This contradiction leads to frequent litigation concerning disputes about invasions of privacy for famous people, and those conflicts often result in rulings that erode the protections granted to news media under the First Amendment.[1]

The increased coverage devoted to the actions and choices of public figures and those within celebrity culture—people that historian Daniel J. Boorstin[2] calls the "well known for their well-knownness"—in the early twenty-first century appears to be a function of the expansion of communication technology (perhaps most notably, social media platforms and cell phone cameras) and a changing media culture that is more permissive of such content. Traditional news media outlets are featuring more of this content, and a large number of newer media sources have emerged that focus upon it. In that sense, the current increase in attention to elites is similar to the rise in interest in the last decade of the nineteenth century and the beginning of the twentieth century. Each era featured the rapid introduction of communication technologies and dramatic changes to the standard practices of media outlets.

Of course, general curiosity about the lives of others has been an American trait. In 1807, British Writer Charles Williams Janson remarked:

J.R. Stevens (✉)
Media Studies, University of Colorado, Boulder, Boulder, CO, USA

> If the Americans have any national trait ... it is this intrusive curiosity. Nor is it to acquire useful information that these people pester strangers; it is habit, for they act in the same manner towards each other; and on meeting, they propose ... in one breath, a long string of questions to each other.[3]

Scandals involving prominent people or celebrity culture and the commercial interest in reputation promotion come into a curious intersection with the limitations we have imposed upon information access to our lives. In his book about celebrity culture, film historian Richard Schnickel observed that the line between news and gossip about famous people has evaporated, because the ever-intruding gaze into the private lives of others "heightens our sense of false intimacy with celebrated people."[4] Our attitudes toward these connections despite our own reservations about surveillance may seem contradictory, but in fact questions concerning control of one's reputation are inherently interlinked and have been since the dawn of the twentieth century. The origins of American privacy law (the "right to be left alone") and the laws regulating control of one's commercial image (the right to publicity) both draw their arguments and justifications from the same source: an 1890 reaction to invasions of prominent people by the rising middle class.

This chapter explores the dual nature of the desire by media elites to control their image: both by controlling access against unwanted disclosures and by providing greater control over the publicity generated around a person's actions. These competing functions represent the awkward space in which media scandals occur, where elites try to hide embarrassing personal events and promote the images that support their desired celebrity narrative. By looking back at the environment that spawned the seminal functions for each form of control, this chapter examines the forces at work that changed the relationships between elites and the middle and lower classes as well as the changing culture of media institutions. One of the reasons media scandals today are so compelling involves the boundary questions regarding changes in technology access and personal voice. These same tensions were present in urban America in the late nineteenth century, as America experienced the effects of the Industrial Revolution upon the social sphere. A similar shift is occurring in America today, as the forces behind the Digital Revolution are disrupting the social mores and controls from the last century even as they enable elites to craft complex media identities. To understand the scope of the dramatic changes American society is currently experiencing because of the tools and abilities afforded by digital technologies, it is helpful to understand how the previous norms were formed around the emergence of mechanical technologies. Given the nature of the digital language, some of the changes in the twenty-first century will likely be unique. But many of the early reactions and claims made by media elites about media scandals pose an eerie similarity to those made by the elites experiencing technological upheaval in the nineteenth century.

The first legal tort for privacy did not emerge until 1890 and was a curious product of the changes to the newspaper industry, erosion of the American class system, and technological advances. In short, privacy became a concern for (wealthy) Americans because of the changes wrought by the Industrial Revolution, and the impetus for privacy came from the rising interest in scandal. In fact, it may have been a particular invasion born of class warfare that birthed the codification of the "right to be left alone."

Prior to 1890, privacy was not a codified legal right, nor had Americans apparently considered that it should be. Unlike other core legal and philosophical concepts in the American system, privacy was completely ignored by the great liberal thinkers whose philosophies influenced the formation of American society.[5] In fact, as privacy scholar Alan Westin[6] noted, the contemporary justifications for a right of privacy are derived almost solely from inferences from John Locke's philosophy of private property, and these inferences were not applied to our social and legal framework until more than 100 years after the creation of the country. Nor does any clause in the US Constitution contain the word "privacy." Though it has been argued that the Americans present at the ratification of the Constitution understood privacy as an intrinsic part of liberty, the documents themselves did not articulate privacy as a concept. Nor did subsequent federal or state laws written within the first 100 years of the nation's history create a legal conception of privacy for the American citizenry.

The Americans who were adapting to the dramatic changes imposed by the Industrial Revolution looked very different than the population does today. Though it had been more than two decades since the American Civil War had established once and for all that national policy and culture would supersede local and state culture, the changes to social structures were less obvious. From 1868 to 1890, America's major political parties were balanced so tightly that neither party could exert its will into law. Partisan politics froze into gridlock, and little changed politically in either the parties or the federal law itself. The stagnation that had followed the Civil War soon began to yield to a new age of commerce, technological innovation, and industrialization. It was in the midst of the shift from the American Victorian era to the progressive era that a need for legal privacy was born.

Part of the need came from the shifting focus of America's newspapers. In the 1840s, James Gordon Bennett had created America's first gossip column in the *New York Herald* to show that American upper-class life was as dazzling as European aristocracy.[7] The *Herald* was considered by elites and members of the newspapers serving elites as a salacious "very bad paper,"[8] but the kind of content offerings that spurred comments like these became increasingly common as more and more papers emerged to meet the demands of middle- and lower-class readers.

As the nineteenth century advanced, newspapers became a true mass medium, and millions of average Americans were beginning to read them. The expanding scope of the audience created a new market for printed media, and that market affected what the paper presented as news. Entertainment was a chief goal, alongside the mission to educate and inform, and that led to a rising trend toward sensationalism, gossip, and scandal. Interviewing became an accepted practice, and the rise in human-interest topics changed the focus of stories. Interest in the activities of elites was increasing.

Bennett's reporters began to follow elites around the country, both the wealthy and those who became of interest to the public, the group that would eventually become known as "celebrities." In 1882, when Lillie Langry returned to America after she was discarded as the Prince of Wales' mistress, James Gordon Bennett Jr. assigned a reporter to follow her 24 hours a day to report on her activities.

Such activity became a trend, and particularly during the intense circulation war between William Randolph Hearst newspapers and those of Joseph Pulitzer, content increasingly focused on society happenings among the wealthy—their dinners, balls, and weddings filled society pages—which in turn increased the demand for photographs. Socialites objected to coverage because "to submit to this kind of surveillance is getting to be intolerable."[9]

The other force driving the changes was the rapid introduction of several key communication technologies that changed the way individual Americans thought about themselves and their relationship to society. Among the emergent technologies were the typewriter in 1873, the telephone in 1876, the first sound recording device in 1876, the fountain pen in 1884, the linotype that allowed high-speed typesetting by newspapers in 1886, and the Kodak "snap" camera in 1888.

During this period, journalism became an increasingly valued and esteemed occupation in urban America.[10] Between 1870 and 1890, the value of newsgathering increased and—as a result—the salaries of professional reporters doubled.[11] An increasing number of journalists entered the profession with college degrees, raising the level of writing and the standards of ethics in the industry as a whole. The increase of newspaper circulation coincided with a wave of rising population and a trend toward urbanization: In 1820, there were 124,000 New Yorkers, but there were more than a million by 1880.

As the professional ties and camaraderie drew individual reporters to survey each other's work, reporters began to compete against each other, scrambling for the next big story. Soon, individual reporters began to be publicly identifiable by their personalities, and their adventurous exploits captured the attention of an ever-widening audience.[12] To hold attention, journalists began mixing cold, hard facts into an exciting narrative style that fed the reader's taste for entertainment, and social investigation became the new newspaper genre. For some papers, the mandate of the professional journalist became to root out hypocrisy and corruption in society. As historian Gunther Barth wrote, the rise of the metropolitan press was largely brought about by a "shift in public values that replaced the minister with the editor as the conscience of the community."[13]

It is difficult to underplay the role of mass media in the rise of social norms and cultural change. As media scholar Michael Schudson explained:

The media are a central institution—one might even claim *the* central institution—in the cultural construction of American nationhood and cityhoods and communityhoods across the land. The 18th-century newspapers were key instruments of commercial and, later, political integration. The 19th-century newspapers were key instruments of urbanization, providing not only the advertising forum that made new institutions like department stores possible, but also providing a community identity that held a city together when it was no longer a face-to-face community or even a "walking city."[14]

By the late nineteenth century, most urban areas supported several papers, with papers reaching different demographics of people. Though some papers that focused on upper class concerns continued to cover the high-brow interests of their audience, an increasing number of papers focused on reaching the common man were born. Enterprising publishers such as Joseph Pulitzer and William Randolph Hearst began to base their financial model of publication on sales and advertising rather than political party contribution. As a result, many newspapers began to play down their party ties and began to think about providing a less partisan coverage of news in order to appeal to a larger audience.[15]

To maintain attention, such papers often resorted to sensational headlines and stories. This "yellow journalism" (so named because of the Yellow Kid editorial cartoons used by both Hearst and Pulitzer) of the mass papers targeted at the lower-class audiences was derided by the upper classes as the promotion of the vulgar in public discourse. As this trend continued, new sections of newspapers were introduced to cover sports, fashion, and comics. In addition, social commentary and gossip about prominent citizens began to be prominently featured in the papers of the lower classes, and the audience seemed to accept this with a gleeful empowerment they had not previously experienced.

Elite papers did not witness these changes in silence. A publishing war broke out that pitted the upper-class newspapers (such as *The New York Times*) against the common man's press. As the sensational papers (such as Pulitzer's *New York World* and Hearst's *New York Journal*) began to move away from a rational model of journalism and toward a sensational model, conflicts over journalistic practice (including whether or not it was appropriate to publish "private" material in the newspaper) were a cover for the brewing class conflict.[16] The rising interest by the lower and middle classes in the affairs of the upper class was fueled by a sense of outrage at the growing economic divide. Two of the popular books from that era demonstrate that interest: Both Ward McAllister's 1890 *Society as I Have Found It* (which chronicled the extravagance of elites) and Jacob Riis' *How the Other Half Lives* (which offered photographs of miserable conditions of New York tenement life) were widely read.

Into this environment, one major technological innovation above others led directly to the establishment of a privacy protection for upper-class members: photography. Though photography had existed for more than half a century, the speed of early photography was rather slow, requiring 15 minutes of exposure before the image could be processed. The 15-minute exposure period meant a person being photographed would have to pose absolutely still (since movement would blur the subject's representation). As a result, photographs could not be taken without the subject's full knowledge and consent: the subject's cooperation was required for the process to be successful.

However, technological innovation in the photographic process soon changed the nature of the relationship between photographer and subject. In 1884, George Eastman filed the first patent for roll film, an improvement that allowed photographers to reduce the size and weight of their cameras, as well as to take many photos without stopping to reload their cameras between shots. In 1888, the Eastman Company simplified the process further in its "Kodak" camera, allowing photographers to shoot 100 exposures without changing film and use cameras a fraction of the size of previous camera bodies.

With the introduction of flash powder to the process, the exposure time needed for a photograph was only limited by the limitations of the mechanical hardware, and photographs could be taken in less than a single second. As a result, "snap shots" allowed a photographer take photographs without the permission or even knowledge of the subject.

The ability of photographs to capture action led to an increased interest in the activities of other people. As newspapers began to publish photographs of prominent people in compromising positions, the public's desire for this content increased, and newspapers began to serve the entertainment appetite by emphasizing scandal with renewed vigor. As *The Daily Graphic* editor David G. Croly explained in 1875,

> Human beings are very curious about one another. Nothing is more interesting to them in a newspaper than what their fellow-beings are doing. A newspaper that satisfies this desire will have a very great measure of success.[17]

## The Birth of the Legal Right to Be Left Alone

In 1890, two young lawyers from Boston decided to challenge that practice with the law. The beginning of American privacy as a legal right originated with an 1890 *Harvard Law Review* article titled "The Right to Privacy."[18] This article, by Samuel D. Warren and Louis D. Brandeis, was initially reported as prompted by Warren's outrage at the coverage of his daughter's wedding in the gossip columns of the local metropolitan paper,[19] though this account has since been disputed.[20,21,22] Brandeis' biographer Alpheus Thomas Mason attributed the article to Warren's outrage over the coverage of his own wedding on January 25, 1883.[23] Warren had married Mabel Bayard, daughter of the ambassador to Great Britain, a figure whose activities the editors of local society papers had deemed a matter of public interest. Warren was particularly outraged by photographs of his new family taken without his knowledge or permission.[24]

Journalism and law professor Amy Gajda[25] dug into more than 50 newspaper articles of media coverage involving Warren and his family over several years and suggested that the comprehensive coverage was likely building up his sense of outrage over time.

Before Warren's wedding, his stay in a Washington hotel was covered by the *Washington Post* ("Personal" December 26, 1882), as well as his attendance at a New Year's Eve Party ("Social World" December 31, 1882). The day before the wedding, the *Washington Post* chronicled Warren's arrival in Washington, DC, from Boston ("Social World" January 24, 1883).

The *New York Times* published 728 words about Warren's wedding, disclosing many details, including the naming of some guests ("Washington Society World" January 16, 1883), and *The Washington Post* published 550 words, also including indications that the mood was "anxious" before the bride and groom arrived ("A Brilliant Bridal" January 26, 1883).

Perhaps most notably, in 1886, Warren's wife would lose both her sister[26] and her mother,[27] and media coverage included detailed descriptions of the deaths,[28] responses,[29] and funeral services.[30]

In 1889, Mrs. Warren's father, former Secretary of State and Senator Thomas Francis Bayard married Mary Willing Clymer, a woman 20 years his junior. *The Washington Post*,[31] *The New York Times*,[32] and the *Boston Daily Globe*[33] all covered the engagement activities. *The Washington Post* would also run three additional stories, two of which could be considered to portray the relocated setting in derogatory terms.[34]

This was the wedding—of Warren's father in law—that Dean of the College of Law at University of California Berkeley William Prosser would later conclude was the actual impetus for *The Right to Privacy*, but considering the coverage of the preceding years, the wedding coverage can likely be considered the watershed. Warren, a relatively unknown lawyer from Boston, would probably have not been accustomed to the amount of coverage that his family received following his marriage, given the high profile of the family into which he married.

Warren had been second in his class at Harvard, but had reluctantly given up law to assume control of the family publishing business. Frustrated, he joined with Louis D. Brandeis, who had been first in his class at Harvard, and the two represented a formidable pair of legal minds.

In "The Right to Privacy," Warren and Brandeis did not attempt to establish a right of privacy from a constitutional justification, nor did they pose an argument of privacy's intrinsic value to all societies. Their argument was that as American society had evolved, a "certain level of sophistication" in society meant it was increasingly difficult for a person to retreat from external scrutiny:

Recent inventions and business methods call attention to the next step which must be taken for the protection of the person, and for securing to the individual, what Judge Cooley calls the right 'to be left alone.' Instantaneous photographs and newspaper enterprise have invaded the sacred precincts of private and domestic life; and numerous mechanical devices threaten to make good the prediction that "what is whispered in the closet shall be proclaimed from the housetops."[35]

The authors cited the development of instant flash photography and numerous other mechanical devices as threats to personal space that required a legal restriction for their use. Reacting to these devices led to their definition of the right to privacy simply as the "right to be left alone," a reference to Judge Thomas Cooley's statement concerning "personal immunity"[36] involving unwanted touching two years earlier. While elegant in its simplicity, the "right to be left alone" was of little help in the legal arena, as determining to what extent someone should be left alone has varied almost as often as the circumstances under which the right is challenged by a competing right of access.

In function, Warren and Brandeis' foundation of privacy stitches together English Common law (e.g., "[t]he common law secures to each individual the right of determining, ordinarily, to what extent his thoughts, sentiments, and emotions shall be communicated to others"[37]) and existing copyright law to form a right to withhold personal information from publication, which gave them the foundation for a right to privacy. This connection is what eventually also created a right of publicity—the control of one's image.

The authors claimed that a right of privacy is due to an individual out of respect for his or her standing and claimed that the unauthorized disclosure of private facts (the only form of violation mentioned in their article) can corrupt a society by encouraging the nation to divert its attention away from important political and economic issues ("matters of community interest"[38]). In this sense, the argument they posed sought to legally insulate the eroding class structure by privileging the values of the upper class.

One of the most significant contributions from the article is that each person possesses an "inviolable personality," an abstract collection of images, texts, and facts that when assembled forms a person's identity. This construct allowed the authors to claim that this "inviolable personality" should be controlled by the possessor, because the "common law secures to each individual the right of determining, ordinarily, to what extent his thoughts, sentiments, and emotions shall be communicated to others."[39] Functionally, they argued the precedent of copyright law makes a person the owner of his or her image, with the implied control and disposal rights granted private property.

The link between privacy and copyright law also implied that a citizen had the right to sell his or her image. "Inviolable personality" is also an abstract self composed up of images, texts, and facts, the collection of which can be sold as a commodity. In other words, Warren and Brandeis seem to have been arguing that people hold the copyright to themselves, which allowed the person to have their potential marketability of their "inviolable personality" damaged or "assaulted" (and thus in need of protection under tort law) when someone exposed them to public scrutiny without permission. Thus, this abstract self—a person's image, or the representation of reputation—soon became a commodity in its own right.

For the authors, this protection of the abstract self was based on their desire to provide a response mechanism for upper-class individuals trying to protect the sanctity of their family names and reputations. As technology empowered the lower classes in democratic fashion, the upper classes turned to law to reinforce the existing social boundaries. Literary scholar Brook Thomas[40] framed "The Right to Privacy" as a representation of "elitist, bourgeois ideology," and William Prosser[41] called it an attempt by the Boston elite to make law out of failing social custom.

But the authors had done so by connecting their objections to the promotional use of personal information, gossip columns, intrusive snooping into private life events, and the use of new technology to gain visual and audio recordings, asserting that it "both belittles and perverts. It belittles by inverting the relative importance of things, thus dwarfing the thoughts and aspirations of a people." This phrasing, intended to shame the consumers of such content, actually created the instrumentation to control the promotion of one's reputation, or the basis for regulating celebrity status. For not everyone abhorred the attention brought by the press. After all, this was the era that produced Ward McAllister's list of "the four hundred" in 1892, a list of the elites "who matter." The number 400 was derived because it was the capacity of Mrs. William Backhouse Astor Jr.'s ballroom.[42]

## The Right to Publicity

The eventual adoption of the view that a person owns the right to one's image signaled an important shift in American culture. The codification of the right to control over one's publicity occurred in 1953 with *Haelan Laboratories v. Topps Chewing Gum, Inc.*, in which a New York court found that baseball players had a "right to publicity" which included the marketing of baseball cards. This new "right to publicity" was reaffirmed in 1957 with *Hogan v. A. S. Barnes and Co., Inc*, when the judicial minds of Pennsylvania ruled that golfer Ben Hogan retained his rights of self-promotion for the purposes of profit. Hogan had sued Barnes, a book publisher, for publishing a book on golf containing photographs of him against his wishes. In his suit, Hogan actually claimed that the book violated his right of privacy.

The court disagreed with the argument, observing that

> the true theory upon which Hogan seeks to base Barnes' liability to him is the very antithesis of the right of privacy. He does not complain that his name should be withheld from public scrutiny; on the contrary, he asserts his name has great commercial value in connection with the game of golf, and that Barnes' use of his name has resulted in damage to him. We therefore decided that Hogan's right of privacy has not been violated.[43]

In effect, this line of legal progression eventually separated a person's rights to his or her public self from a person's rights to his or her private self, the very nexus of disputes involving scandals and famous individuals. This tangent of the Warren and Brandeis' article would also eventually lead to arguments for the right of intellectual property in the late twentieth century.

Both the right to privacy and the right to publicity were born from an environment of social upheaval, one in which the increasing concentration of populations in urban centers created the dense audience that fueled the circulation wars of the sensational press, and the rapid introduction of communication technologies continued the erosion of access barriers between social classes. Novelist Henry James observed the changing culture in 1879, saying that the United States had

> [n]o State, in the European sense of the word, and indeed barely a specific national name. No sovereign, no court, no personal loyalty, no aristocracy, no church, no clergy, no army, no diplomatic service, no country gentlemen, no palaces, no castles, nor manors, nor old country-houses, nor parsonages, nor thatched cottages nor ivied ruins; no cathedrals, nor abbeys, nor little Norman churches; no great Universities nor public schools—no Oxford, nor Eton, nor Harrow; no literature, no novels, no museums, no pictures, no political society, no sporting class—no Epsom nor Ascot.[44]

In this commentary on America, James pointed to the absence of socially binding institutions in the country. America had no state-established church, nor an aristocratic class to provide continuity in political leadership and an almost non-existent federal military. This lack of structure (relative to Europe) also made the collection of individuals in the upper class who were of interest more permeable. And indeed, as the twentieth century approached, the number of persons of interest that courted media attention was growing. This trend rose very quickly, as author Roger Wilkes observed:

> In the 1870s, the best-known New Yorkers were philanthropists, politicians, merchants, artistic and cultural figures. But by the 1890s, these titans had been swept aside in the public consciousness by a new elite, people celebrated not for their accomplishments but for their gossip value.[45]

In short, though our fascination with celebrity culture and its lust for intimate knowledge of famous people is usually traced back to the emergence of the film industry in the 1920s,[46] the transition toward interests in elite activities actually precedes the film industry by a few decades.

The effects stemming from *The Right to Privacy* were profound, and several of the arguments posed in the article would be cited in cases used to further develop protections of the private sphere.[47] While considered one of the most influential law articles ever written,[48] it would also serve as one of the touchstones for the regulation of promotional activities for those who seek public attention. The conditions that led to the article's writing—outrage over the mass distribution of disclosures and personal information through the use of new communication technologies—strongly represents the current environment of celebrity surveillance and scandal. In both cultural moments, technology disrupted the social expectations of media elites by providing greater access and dissemination abilities to non-elites. The elites of the late nineteenth century were accustomed to being granted a certain deference to the discussion of their public activities. Snap cameras, the linotype, and typewriters changed the speed by which someone could observe, record, and report upon a person's actions. In the twenty-first century, Americans are experiencing changes related to the tools that make social media possible. Along with the increased comfort in sharing personal information and using such tools comes an increased interest in the affairs of others and a greater appetite for the surveillance of media elites. Once again, the institutions that support the status of elites are shifting as both the audience and producers of the dissemination of personal behavior expand. In this way, advances in communication technology offer a greater ease of media use but often at the expense of the control afforded elites by virtue of their formerly more exclusive access.

The paradox of identity, the rights of individuals to conceal and promote activities and control how disclosures are communicated, has been at the heart of questions about both privacy and publicity for more than a century. Eventually, the disclosure of private facts would distinguish between the degrees to which a person uses the public eye for gain. This is why public officials have little privacy compared to private citizens, and voluntary public figures like celebrities have more protection than public officials but less than private citizens (the original "right to be left alone" did not include such distinctions). One of the reasons why questions relating to status, the boundaries imposed upon access afforded to individuals, and the right to control the commercial promotion of one's image are so prominently debated now is because the core conditions that produced the original seminal arguments about how we consider those boundaries appear to be occurring again. More than a century ago, technology changed the way personal information was disclosed by enabling the lower classes to participate more in the public surveillance process, which in turn expanded the public's appetite for gossip and scandal. Those increases in participation have dramatically increased once again in the twenty-first century because of digital tools and social media platforms. And the resulting turmoil and arguments over the appropriateness of media scandal reportage strongly resemble the nineteenth-century concerns from the events that produced the original rights to privacy and publicity.

## Notes

1. Amy Gajda, *The First Amendment Bubble: How Privacy and Paparazzi Threaten a Free Press*, (Cambridge, MA: Harvard University Press, 2015).
2. Daniel Boorstin, *The Image: A Guide to Pseudo-Events in America*, (New York, NY: Vintage. 1961).
3. Charles William Janson, *The Stranger in America*, (Champaign, IL: University of Illinois Press, 2009).
4. Richard Schickel, *Intimate Strangers: The Culture of Celebrity in America*, (Garden City, NY: Doubleday, 2000).

5. Henry McCloskey, "Privacy and the Right to Privacy," Philosophy 55, no. 211 (1980): 17–38.

6. Alan Westin, *Privacy and Freedom*, (New York, NY: Atheneum, 1967).

7. Michael Schudson, *Discovering the News: A Social History of American Newspapers*, (New York, NY: Basic Books, 1978).

8. *New York Tribune* editor Horace Greeley testified before the British Parliament in 1851 and called the *Herald* a "very bad paper," but also mentioned there were even worse "scandal-rags," quoted in Wingate 1875, 160.

9. Don Carlos Seitz, *The James Gordon Bennetts, Father and Son: Proprietors of the New York Herald*, (Indianapolis, IN: Bobbs-Merrill Company, 1928).

10. Schudson, *Discovering the News: A Social History of American Newspapers*.

11. Richard Hofstadter, *The Age of Reform*, (New York, NY: Alfred A. Knopf, 1955).

12. Schudson, *Discovering the News: A Social History of American Newspapers*.

13. Gunther Barth, *City People: The Rise of Modern City Culture in Nineteenth-Century America*, (New York, NY: Oxford University Press, 1980).

14. Michael Schudson, *The Power of News*, (Cambridge, MA: Harvard University Press, 1995).

15. Robert Cherny, *American Politics in the Gilded Age: 1868–1900*, (Hoboken, NJ: Wiley-Blackwell, 1997).

16. Schudson, *Discovering the News: A Social History of American Newspapers*.

17. Charles Frederick Wingate, *Views and Interviews on Journalism*, (New York, NY: FB Patterson, 1875).

18. Samuel Warren and Louis Brandeis, "The Right to Privacy," *Harvard Law Review*, (1890): 193–220.

19. William L. Prosser, "Privacy: A Legal Analysis," *California Law Review* 48 (1960): 338.

20. James H. Barron, "Warren and Brandeis, the Right to Privacy. 4 Harvard Law. Rev. 193 1890: Demystifying a Landmark Citation," *Suffolk University Law Review* 13, no. 4 (1979): 875.

21. Robert Ellis Smith, "Ben Franklin's Web Site: Privacy and Curiosity from Plymouth Rock to the Internet," *Privacy Journal*, 2000.

22. Gajda, *The First Amendment Bubble: How Privacy and Paparazzi Threaten a Free Press*.

23. Alpheus Thomas Mason, *Brandeis: A Free Man's Life*, (New York, NY: The Viking Press, 1946).

24. Alfred Lief, *Brandeis: The Personal History of an American Idea*, (Mechanicsburg, PA: Stackpole Sons, 1936).

25. Amy Gajda, "*What if Samuel D. Warren hadn't Married a Senator's Daughter: Uncovering the Press Coverage That Led to the Right to Privacy*," *Michigan State Law Review* 35 (2007).

26. "Death's Sad Summons," January 18, 1886.

27. "Death of Mrs. Bayard," February 1, 1886; "Mr. Bayard's Wife Dead," February 1, 1886.

28. "Miss Bayard's Sudden Death," January 18, 1886.

29. "Death's Sad Summons," January 18, 1886, "Mr. Bayard's Wife Dead," February 1, 1886.

30. "Miss Bayard's Funeral," January 20, 1886; "Burial of Miss Bayard," January 20, 1886; "The Late Mrs. Bayard," February 2, 1886.

31. "The Bayard-Clymer Engagement," October 3, 1889.
32. "Mr. Bayard's Marriage," October 27, 1889.
33. "May Preside in House," May 20, 1889.
34. "Wedding Events," November 7, 1889; "Mr. Bayard and Bride," November 8, 1889. For example, the second story reported the setting held "no exterior evidences of festivity," and the dwelling had "not even the usual awning protected the bonnetless ladies from the sun."
35. Warren and Brandeis, "The Right to Privacy."
36. Thomas Cooley, *A Treatise on the Law of Torts 2*, (Chicago, IL: Callaghan & Co., 1888).
37. Warren and Brandeis, "The Right to Privacy."
38. Warren and Brandeis, "The Right to Privacy."
39. Warren and Brandeis, "The Right to Privacy."
40 Brooke Thomas, "The Construction of Privacy In and Around The Bostonians," *American Literature* 4, no. 1 (1992): 719–748.
41. William Prosser, "Privacy: A Legal Analysis."
42. Arthur Vanderbilt II, *Fortune's Children: The Fall of the House of Vanderbilt*, (New York, NY: William Morrow Paperbacks, 1989).
43. Leopold Morris and Alan Schwartz, *Privacy: The Right to be Let Alone*, (New York, NY: Macmillan, 1962).
44. Henry James, *Hawthorne*, (Ithaca, NY: Cornell University Press, 1880).
45. Robert Wilkes, *Scandal! A Scurrilous History of Gossip*, (London: Atlantic Books, 2002).
46. Schickel, *Intimate Strangers: The Culture of Celebrity in America*.
47. For example, see *Bartnicki v. Vopper* 2000, 534; *Scheetz v. Morning Call* 1991, 209; *Machleder v. Diaz* 1986, 52; *Crump v. Beckley Newspapers* 1983, 81; and *Hirsch v. S.C. Johnson & Son* 1979, 132.
48. Neil Richards and Daniel Solove, "Privacy's Other Path: Recovering the Law of Confidentiality," *Georgetown Law Review* 96 (2007): 123.

CHAPTER 3

# Using Political Scandal to Limit Social Justice

## *Neal Allen*

Five days after the conclusion of the historic Selma-to-Montgomery march for voting rights, as the US Congress was beginning consideration of the 1965 Voting Rights Act, Alabama Congressman William Dickinson gave a presentation he called "March on Montgomery: The Untold Story." The newly elected segregationist, attempting to discredit nonviolent activists who had triumphed over state government violence to galvanize public support for integration, offered instead a vision of debauchery and licentiousness by protestors:

> Drunkenness and sex orgies were the order of the day in Selma, on the road to Montgomery, and in Montgomery. There were many—not just a few—instances of sexual intercourse in public between Negro and white.[1]

Congressman Dickinson, who represented residents of Selma and Montgomery in the House of Representatives, was attempting to stop a social movement with a scandal. His charges, which were never directly substantiated and did not keep the Voting Rights Act from a landslide victory in Congress that summer, show how scandal can be deployed against movements for social transformation.

Social movements are inherently composed of people, and the individual characteristics and behaviors of leaders and followers can create points of vulnerability. Congressman Dickinson was attempting to draw attention to the alleged flaws of the marchers, blunting their larger transformative message:

> Has anyone stopped to ask what sort of people can leave home, family and job—if they have one—and live indefinitely in a foreign place demonstrating? This is no religious group of sympathizers trying to help the Negro out of a sense of right

N. Allen (✉)
Political Science, Wichita State University, Wichita, KS, USA

© The Editor(s) (if applicable) and The Author(s) 2016                     29
H. Mandell, G.M. Chen (eds.), *Scandal in a Digital Age*,
DOI 10.1057/978-1-137-59545-4_3

and morality—this is a bunch of godless riffraff out for kicks and self-gratification that have left every campsite between Selma and Montgomery littered with whisky bottles, beer cans, and used contraceptives.[2]

Here scandal is deployed not just for titillation, or to harm the reputation and social standing of particular individuals. Instead, it is used as a nefarious force supporting the continuation of oppressive social structures, and it implies that anyone who questions the status quo by definition stands outside the bounds of morality and proper behavior.

This chapter examines the use of scandal by opponents of social change movements, with a focus on the voting rights march in Selma, Alabama, in 1965. I first lay out my theory of "reactionary scandalization," in which opponents of change attempt to cast change agents as conflicting with societal values and norms. This theory draws on scholarship of voting behavior, particularly the directional voting literature and its "zone of acceptability." I then discuss attempts by the reactionary Federal Bureau of Investigation (FBI) to tar Martin Luther King Jr. as a sexual deviant and communist sympathizer. The next section discusses claims by Alabama Congressman William Dickinson that Selma-to-Montgomery march participants engaged in interracial group sex. Both the criticisms of King and Selma marchers spread to interested citizens, as evident in letters sent to members of Congress in 1965.[3] The failure of these two attempts at "reactionary scandalization" contrasts with the scandalizing power of the contemporary media environment, which amplifies the power of change opponents to monitor and criticize change agents. I conclude by examining an attempt by conservative bloggers and activists to push back against the Black Lives Matter movement, which first emerged in 2012 following the shooting death of Trayvon Martin, an unarmed African-American teen in Florida,[4] by showing that a prominent supporter of the movement was actually white.

Reactionary scandalization connects to this book's larger focus on surveillance because the ability of those with social and political power to acquire and deploy information about change agents threatens the public approval necessary for social change. The contemporary pervasive media landscape has replicated on a societal scale the kind of surveillance only available to government officials like the former Federal Bureau of Investigation Director J. Edgar Hoover in the past. Contemporary social justice advocates must work in a world where everything about them is public, but they have limited control over how they are perceived. They constantly risk that the larger public will turn their back on them and the goals they seek.

In the Civil Rights Movement era, reactionary scandalization operated within a political media environment much more elite-controlled, and much less permeable, than the contemporary political media environment. The lack of social media platforms like Facebook or Twitter (or even the connectivity of the early Internet) limited the reach of social justice critics. Newspaper editors and elected officials still functioned as gatekeepers of knowledge and influence.

I make use, however, of a 1960s communication form (i.e. "snail mail") that parallels contemporary social media, at least in its availability to interested citizens. The letters sent from citizens to legislators demonstrate the reach of scandal-based critiques of social justice movements during the middle of last century, because the narratives of communism and debauchery made their way into the correspondence of everyday Americans. Letters from citizens about Civil Rights, drawn from archival records, demonstrate the possible reach of reactionary scandalization.

## REACTIONARY SCANDALIZATION IN THEORY AND POTENTIAL

The term "political scandal" is most often used to mean a scandal involving an elected official, candidate, or a part of government. This broad understanding includes corruption scandals like Watergate, sex scandals like the infidelities of presidential candidates Gary Hart or John Edwards, or the use of a private email server by then-Secretary of State Hillary Clinton. This chapter focuses on a narrower kind of political scandal, which is deployed by the opponents of social change. This kind of political scandal is directed at preserving existing social and governmental arrangements and uses scandal as a means to delegitimize those working for change. This kind of scandal does focus on the possible foibles of individuals, but is best understood as a limiting force on collective action.

Scandal is fundamentally about societal values and norms. Only by transgressing against common understandings of proper behavior can a given action become a scandal. The phenomenon of scandal is thus implicated in periods of social change, because those very norms and values are under attack. The proponents and beneficiaries of established societal patterns thus have a powerful incentive to "scandalize" their opponents. This "reactionary scandalization" particularly fits the strategic position of change opponents who have been losing battles to change agents. Scandal can be used to shift debate from areas where defenders of the status quo have been unsuccessful to areas where they are possibly stronger.

The politics of Civil Rights in the 1960s fits this pattern. By the time of the Selma marches in early 1965, defenders of segregation had suffered several defeats. *Brown v. Board of Education* ruled segregation in public education as unconstitutional, demonstrating that Southern white political influence was comparatively weak in the Judiciary. The previous four presidents—Harry Truman, Dwight Eisenhower, John F. Kennedy, and Lyndon Johnson—had all been elected while supporting Civil Rights legislation. Johnson had just pushed through a far-reaching Civil Rights Act in 1964, and then beaten legislation opponent Barry Goldwater by the largest margin in modern American history. The change advocates were winning the battle over how to interpret fundamental values like liberty and equality and were on the verge of passing legislation that would bring millions of black voters into the Southern electorate. One response of status quo defenders was to claim that movement leaders like Martin Luther King were communists, and that King and movement supporters were sexual deviants. Scandal here is an attempt to change the subject and shift the debate to ground more favorable to change opponents. Scandal is a process of converting people and ideas from acceptable to unacceptable in the public eye.

Political science scholarship on voting behavior provides the foundation for a model of this type of "reactionary scandalization." Such a focus is useful not just because a central aspect of social change movements is electoral support. The broader goal of mobilizing support from those either opposed or ambivalent is fundamentally about transforming the issue environment. Scholars of formal theory, which seeks to understand human behavior through application of incentive-based theory, have produced models that can be applied to the study of political scandal.

In particular, the work of political scientist George Rabinowitz on "directional voting" helps to build a model of how opponents of change attempt to use scandal against their opponents. He argues that voters will support candidates who they believe will pull public policy toward the voter's ideal position. This theory contrasts with the "proximity voting" theory, which argues that voters will support the candidate or party whose position is closest to theirs. In directional voting, candidates should attempt to clearly articulate a position that is on the same side of the issue space as most voters, and will then attract support from a majority who desires change. This kind of candidate behavior is particularly effective when elections are driven by "symbolic politics," and low-information voters are seeking to push policy in a general direction that fits their basic values.[5]

The theory of directional voting fits the pattern of a social change episode like the Civil Rights Era, in which previously marginalized actors are successful as the majority of the public comes to evaluate the existing social order as inadequate. But Rabinowitz limits the "directional" force of the theory by introducing the "zone of acceptability." He argues that candidates or parties, even when the electorate hopes to move policy in their direction, are constrained from taking extreme positions. Voters will reject a candidate whose personal characteristics or issue positions are very distant from them and will be willing to support a different candidate who clearly wants to move policy in a less favored direction.

Attempts to publicize King's adultery and connection to alleged communists, and to cast Selma-to-Montgomery marchers as sexual deviants, are attempts to push them out of the national zone of acceptability. The hope of Southern segregationists and their allies was to persuade Americans that the supporters of integration were so outside of moral and ethical norms that their proposals should be rejected. If integration was within the zone of acceptability, and most Americans were ready to move public policy in that direction, one response was to change the subject. If Martin Luther King Jr. was a womanizing communist, then possibly integration was not worth supporting. If the Selma-to-Montgomery march was a site of interracial orgies, then possibly their goal of federal voting rights legislation should be rejected. Reactionary scandalization might convert the Civil Rights Movement into a threat to the security and moral fabric of America.

## SCANDALIZING MOVEMENT LEADERSHIP: THE FBI AND MARTIN LUTHER KING JR.

Beginning in 1961, the FBI investigated and surveilled Martin Luther King Jr. in an attempt to find evidence of communist affiliation and sexual misbehavior. Although the FBI had mostly ignored King as a potential subversive in his early work after the Montgomery bus boycott, he attracted the attention of FBI Director J. Edgar Hoover with calls for the hiring of more black agents, and alleging that the Bureau was unwilling to provide protection to black protestors because of its connections to white supremacist southerners.[6,7] Initially focusing on King's associates, agents eventually expanded their surveillance to the Southern Christian Leadership Conference with phone taps and listening devices in hotel rooms.[8] The Bureau captured audio of King having intercourse with a woman who was not his wife in a Los Angeles hotel and mailed a copy to his wife in an attempt at intimidation.[9] Agents also mailed information about King's alleged communist associations and sexual misbehavior to several newspaper editors, including Ralph McGill of the *Atlanta Constitution*. Transcripts of wiretaps and other surveillance were provided to Presidents Kennedy and Johnson and their attorneys general.

None of these media and political elites acted against King as Hoover and the FBI hoped, but the narrative of King as communist and degenerate disseminated widely enough to appear in citizens correspondence to members of Congress.[10] These letters reveal how citizens incorporated criticism of King and the movement into arguments against integration. At the height of the Cold War, the possibility that King and the Civil Rights Movement generally were somehow "communist" was a potentially debilitating accusation. The Cold War political order was organized around the idea that communism was outside of the "zone of acceptability." At a time when the Johnson administration was preparing to escalate the Vietnam War to avoid being tarred as soft on communism, accusations of communist connections were an Achilles heel for change agents. The inherent transformative potential of the Civil Rights Movement threatened those who benefited from segregation and appears in legislative correspondence. One Berkeley, California, resident wrote to his Congressman Jeffrey Cohelan that, "All this Negro Rights agitation is the product of years of work by the Communists. Their program is being carried out to the letter."[11] The planning and strategy of movement leaders were turned into a Soviet conspiracy.

The attempts of the FBI and Hoover to marginalize King did bear some fruit in another letter for Congressman Cohelan. An Oakland resident wrote on April 6, 1965, "Who wishes to follow a 'being' like King: [J.] Edgar Hoover expressed who he is, and who knows better?"[12] The reference to King as a "being" can be read as an attempt to cast him as subhuman, and thus not worthy of respect. Also the writer elevates the authority of Hoover, implicitly expressing allegiance to the established political order.

Legislative correspondence presents an understanding of movement success as tied to King's leadership, and a certainty that marginalizing King will end movement victories. One Dodge City, Kansas, resident wrote to Congressman Bob Dole that, "The trouble in the South can be settled by other means if something can be done with Communistic M.L. King."[13] In an open and (somewhat) democratic society like the USA, this would likely take the form of reactionary scandalization that was suggested by a Cotton Plant, Arkansas, resident in a letter to Senator Fulbright on April 14, 1965:

> I think it's about time someone investigated Martin Luther King and his Civil Rights movements. He has people in his organization who are known communists. Can't this be proven and presented to the public?[14]

This use of guilt by association is a core component of reactionary scandalization. The "public" is presented as a ready and willing audience for information that will marginalize a figure like King and limit the power of the broader movement.

While claims of communist connections (and sexual deviance by leaders like King) did not prevent the passage of the Voting Rights Act, they did contain the seeds of later right-wing reaction to progressive politics that continues into contemporary politics. A McCrory, Arkansas, resident wrote to Senator J. William Fulbright on March 25, 1965, that:

> It is my opinion that it was motivated by communist inspired groups, beatniks, publicity seekers and other people of ill repute, as a sympathetic publicity stunt to [deceive] mild unsuspecting people out of more money for another stepping stone to overthrow our United States Government.[15]

If the Civil Rights Movement was merely a conglomeration of various "people of ill repute," then its message could be pushed to the periphery of American politics.

## Scandalizing the Grass Roots: Selma Marchers as Sexual Deviants

Accusations made in 1965 by Congressman William Dickinson of Alabama have mostly faded from public memory. He never produced the evidence that he claimed would substantiate his claim that "interracial sex orgies" occurred during the march from Selma to Montgomery.[16] The Voting Rights Act passed by the overwhelming margin of 333–85 in the House of Representatives and 77–19 in the Senate. It was expanded in 1970 and reauthorized in 1975, 1982, and 2006. The anti-Civil Rights backlash that Congressman Dickinson was attempting to stimulate did materialize later in the decade, but only after intervening events like race riots and the broader turn against the Great Society welfare state. The accusations made on the House floor by the Alabama Republican are interesting because they demonstrate how scandal can be used as a weapon against those working for change. Where King by 1965 was a Nobel Prize-winning public figure, the marchers were mostly ordinary citizens who had deliberately placed themselves in the public eye with nonviolent direct action. Dickinson seized on the opportunity to defend the segregationist political order in opposition to the public's interest in grass-roots action.

Claiming that the Selma-to-Montgomery marchers were sexual deviants served the electoral interests of Congressman William Dickinson in 1965. He was one of four Alabama Republicans swept into the House by the 1964 landslide for Barry Goldwater in the Deep South. He had beaten a segregationist Democrat only because of the local reaction against the Civil Rights Act and the presidential campaign of Lyndon Johnson. His district, which included Montgomery and surrounding counties in South Alabama, was a stronghold of segregationist Democrats. His status as a Goldwater Republican closed off the possibility of attracting black voters that begin entering the electorate after strong voting rights legislation, and the segregationist was dependent on white voters that had mostly never voted for a Republican in their lives. Demonizing the marchers, which much of his electorate saw as "outside agitators," could cement his position as a defender of traditional Alabama.[17]

After criticism by pro-integration members of Congress, Congressman Dickinson returned to the House floor the next month armed with several affidavits by Alabama residents claiming to have witnessed (or in some cases spoke to others who claimed to witness) acts like "smooching and lovemaking between Negroes and whites," public urination, and public drunkenness.[18] He justified the detailed descriptions, which strained the usual bounds of legislative debate propriety, with reference to a broader desire to affect debate over voting rights:

> I have attacked the conduct of many of the participants for several reasons, one of which is to rip away the façade of righteousness, smugness and respectability erroneously attributed to them, which allowed them to invade my home town and my State like a swarm of rats leaving an overturned hayrick. I can assure you, Mr. Speaker, our modern Canterbury Tales make Chaucer's pilgrims look like veritable paragons of virtue and piety.[19]

The presentation of hearsay evidence that a "beatnik" was compensated for his organizing work with "all the Negro (expletive) he wanted" was justified as part of the defense of the "virtue and piety" of segregation.

While Congressman Dickinson's attempt at "reactionary scandalization" was not successful in blocking voting rights legislation, his message was received by sympathetic citizens, who transmitted it to their elected representatives.

A lengthy passage from a letter sent by an El Dorado, Arkansas, resident to Sen. J. William Fulbright (D-AR) on April 1, 1965, demonstrates how Dickinson's charges could convert the march into a national scandal:

> This article was printed in the *El Dorado Times*, March 31, 1965—describing the ugly, unthinkable conduct of the civil rights marchers and followers. If this charge be true, we urge an investigation and all this brought to the attention of all citizens of these United States and the guilty ones punished. These demonstrations have gained so much popularity that something needs to be done to <u>unglorify</u> them—as they only generate hate and mistrust among white and colored citizens.[20]

The desire to "unglorify" Civil Rights activists is best understood to render them unacceptable in national politics. "Glory" would not adhere to those outside of the national zone of acceptability.

Writers to Senator Fulbright not only called for publicizing Congressman Dickinson's charges, but they also called for specific actions. One Eureka Springs, Arkansas, resident wrote on April 2, 1965, that they trusted the veracity of Dickinson's allegations, and "if found to be true, the President of the United States of America should be impeached."[21] The use of federal troops to protect the second march from Selma to Montgomery was particularly objectionable, as it was "letting our Government spend our tax monies to force debauchery on the people of any Sovereign State." Another Arkansan wrote from Caraway on April 3, 1965, that "it is an outrage that such vile and indecent social behavior be so enacted within our nation and we certainly do not want any part of it in our own State of Arkansas."[22] Federal protection of marchers also drew the ire of a Kansas City, Kansas, resident who wrote to Congressman Bob Dole on April 22, 1965: "Lawlessness and violence that is encouraged, allowed, and supported by the federal government is inexcusable."[23]

It is not surprising that scandalous accusations about Civil Rights activists found purchase among the Southern whites who benefited from segregation. But a writer from Osborne, Kansas, to Dole on March 31, 1965, also found Congressman Dickinson's allegations compelling, as he or she heard them from right-wing radio host Fulton Lewis Jr. "Have been listening to Fulton Lewis Jr. about the Civil Rights March—the speech the Alabama rep. give in the House. Their conduct was a disgrace. The public should be informed."[24] If public support of voting rights was a "disgrace," then their transformational message could be limited.

An exchange between Senator Fulbright and a North Little Rock constituent demonstrates the kind of "reactionary scandalization" that could be deployed against change agents. This lengthy passage from an April 8, 1965, letter from the constituent demonstrates the attempt to push the marchers out of the zone of acceptable behavior, and thus limit their ability to gain support from a sympathetic white majority:

> Dickinson "states that 'drunkeness and sex orgies were the order of the day' during this march." He then goes on to give vivid details which are nauseating

in the extreme. It seems to us at home that this government-protected march rounded up all the scum in both black and white races to intrude on the good people of Alabama.[25]

Marchers are presented as "scum" and "nauseating," placing them clearly outside the bounds of polite society.

Senator J. William Fulbright, who by this point had a consistent anti-Civil Rights voting record, was unmoved by the attempt to blunt the march's message with allegations of group sex and alcohol use. He responds on April 26, 1965:

> I have no way of knowing whether Representative Dickinson is correct in his description of the Selma-to-Montgomery march. So far as I know, he is the only one who has made these allegations, and in any event any illegal activities would fall under State jurisdiction.[26]

Soon after this exchange, the Arkansas senator would vote to end the filibuster of the Voting Rights Act, his first vote in favor of meaningful Civil Rights legislation. While Fulbright had always supported segregation to gain continued election and preserve his influence in Congress, his vote shows the size of the growing consensus behind recognizing the rightness of the claims made by the Selma-to-Montgomery marchers. In 1965, he was in a similar elite position to the editor of the Atlanta newspaper that refused to print FBI allegations about Martin Luther King Jr.'s infidelity and alleged communist ties. Right-wing radio and Southern newspapers could get Congressman Dickinson's message out to a sympathetic slice of the white population, but Southern and national elites were able to resist the influence of "reactionary scandalization."

## REACTIONARY SCANDALIZATION AND CONTEMPORARY SOCIAL MOVEMENTS

The contemporary communication and political environment differ from that of 1965 in two related ways. First, the Internet and the widespread possession of information technology expand the reach of actors like William Dickinson. Second, the power of political and media elites to limit the dissemination of information is diminished. The ability of citizens to easily record audio and video images, and then disseminate them through lightly mediated fora like Twitter, converts all interested parties into a powerful surveillance network that can then reach sympathizers without the need for the mediation of journalistic and political elites. Surveillance can now be enacted by individuals in a manner previously only available to political and media elites.

The significance of these transformations for the role of "reactionary scandalization" can be seen in the following hypothetical. Imagine that during the Selma-to-Montgomery march, two people with different skin colors engaged in romantic physical contact. This is quite possible, since the march attracted people of differing racial groups from across the country. Also then imagine if the majority of white citizens in the area had video cameras in their pockets. A video of a white woman kissing a black man would then likely be disseminated across the country and provide evidence for Dickinson's allegations. People predisposed to see Civil Rights as threatening to national values would have evidence for their predispositions, and a narrative to present to their fellow citizens. Facing competition from Internet "news" sites, mainstream media outlets would be hard-pressed to dismiss the story.

The Black Lives Matter movement that arose in response to the 2012 shooting death of the unarmed African-American teenager Trayvon Martin in Florida, along with several police-involved deaths of African Americans in 2014 and 2015, is a contemporary analog to the voting rights protests of 1965. Social media activists use the hashtag #blacklivesmatter to channel existing grievances with law enforcement into political action, highlighting racial disparities in arrest, incarceration, and subjection to deadly force. The disaggregated movement confronts existing social and political power structures, using nonviolent disruptive tactics to highlight contradictions between American national values and the practices of local and state government. At this point, Black Lives Matter is a decentralized movement and has not yet mounted the kind of grassroots action that can dominate national media like the Selma-to-Montgomery march. The opponents of transformative criminal justice reform, however, have begun the process of reactionary scandalization, but now without the prompting of a political elite figure like a member of the House of Representatives.

Shaun King, a writer, pastor, and activist often associated with the Black Lives Matter movement, came under criticism in August 2015 for presenting himself as white-black biracial, when he is actually white. Conservative blogs and websites uncovered evidence that his birth certificate listed a white man as his father. King said that a different man, an African American, was his biological father. A writer for the conservative website *Breitbart* argued that the detail of a beating suffered by King while in high school in Versailles, Kentucky, which he had portrayed as a hate crime motivated by his biracial identity, was instead motivated by King's being understood as white while dating a female black student. Fox News and other conservative outlets raised questions about whether King had lied about his race—comparing his situation to a related, racial-identity scandal in summer 2015 involving Rachel Dolezal, the former head of a Washington state NAACP (National Association for the Advancement of Colored People) chapter who was born white. These news outlets asked whether King's identity politics helped him gain admission and an Oprah Winfrey-funded scholarship to Moorehouse College, presenting his situation as "a repeat of the Rachel Dolezal scandal?"[27]

The attempt to "out" an activist that most Americans had never heard of as a different race than he claimed is only understandable as an attempt at reactionary scandalization. The Black Lives Matter movement threatens the privileged relationship to law enforcement that whites enjoy in the USA. In order to blunt the moral force of claims to equal treatment, Shaun King is cast as a hypocritical imposter who is masquerading as a member of a discriminated group for personal gain. But what sets the King episode apart from its progenitors in the Civil Rights Movement era is the causal role of individual citizens, who can from their own Internet-enabled device research birth and criminal records. No longer do those frightened of social change have to vainly plea to their member of Congress for "someone" to investigate those that threaten traditional social and political arrangements. Just as Shaun King can use Twitter to highlight the continuing oppression of African Americans, his opponents can use social media to exact a price for speaking truth to power.

## NOTES

1. *Congressional Record—House, v. 111, pt. 5*, p. 6333.
2. *Congressional Record—House, v. 111, pt. 5*, p. 6334.
3. Letters referenced below are from the papers of Rep. Jeffrey Cohelan (D-CA) held by the Carl Albert Congressional Research and Studies Center at the University of Oklahoma, Rep. Robert Dole (R-KS) held at the Robert Dole Center for Politics by the University of Kansas, and Sen. William Fulbright (D-AR) held by University of Arkansas Library Special Collections. I would like to thank the Albert Center and Dole Center for financial support that made this research possible.
4. "About the #BlackLivesMatter Network," BlackLivesMatter.com, http://blacklivesmatter.com/about/.
5. George Rabinowitz and Stuart Elaine Macdonald, "A Directional Theory of Issue Voting," *The American Political Science Review*, Vol. 83, No. 1 (March, 1989), 93–121.
6. David J. Garrow, *The FBI and Martin Luther King, Jr.*, (New York, NY: Penguin Books, New York, 1983), 24.
7. Garrow, *The FBI and Martin Luther King, Jr.*, 54.
8. Garrow, *The FBI and Martin Luther King, Jr.*, 46.
9. Burton Hersch, *Bobby and J. Edgar: The Historic Face-Off Between the Kennedys and J. Edgar Hoover That Transformed America*, (New York, NY: Carroll and Graf, 2007), 375.
10. Newspaper editors, like Ralph McGill of the *Atlanta Constitution*, refused to publish accounts of King's adultery. This reticence was possibly because of the same kind of consensus among media and political elites that kept similar facts involving President Kennedy from being publicized.
11. Jeffery Cohelan Papers, Civil Rights File.
12. Cohelan Papers, Civil Rights File.
13. Robert Dole Papers, Civil Rights 1965 File.
14. J. William Fulbright Papers, Civil Rights File.
15. Fulbright Papers, Civil Rights File.
16. Barone, *Almanac of American Politics 1972*, 6.
17. After the Voting Rights Act, Dickinson would survive several close elections and serve until his retirement in 1992. He was a beneficiary of the district maps that Alabama white Democrats used to split the black vote among several districts, and retained enough white conservative support to overcome the opposition of enfranchised African-American voters.

18. Dickinson also claimed knowledge of photographic evidence showing interracial sex that was in the possession of Alabama law enforcement. He never produced such evidence: Michael Barone, Grant Ujifusa and Donald Matthews, *Almanac of American Politics 1972*, (New York: Gambit Publishing, 1971), 801–802.
19. *Congressional Record—House, v. 111, pt. 5*, p. 8592.
20. Fulbright Papers, Civil Rights File.
21. Fulbright Papers, Civil Rights File.
22. Fulbright Papers, Civil Rights File.
23. Dole Papers, Civil Rights 1965 File.
24. Dole Papers, Civil Rights 1965 File.
25. Here it is significant that while opposition to Civil Rights was still strong in much of the USA, Lyndon Johnson had fully identified himself with nondiscrimination legislation in 1964 and then won a massive landslide victory that Fall.
26. Fulbright Papers, Civil Rights File.
27. Dolezal is a former president of the Spokane chapter of the National Association for the Advancement of Colored People who shifted her affiliation from white to black as a young adult.

# CHAPTER 4

# Chappaquiddick Revisited: Scandal and the Modern-Mediated Apologia

*Grant Cos*

The scandal surrounding Senator Edward M. Kennedy and the events of July 18, 1969, on Chappaquiddick Island reveal a template for our understanding of scandal in contemporary times. Revisiting Kennedy's July 25 televised address to the people of Massachusetts illustrates how he rhetorically responded to scandal in an era in which legacy media, rather than social media, shaped how the public came to know the incident when—after an evening of partying—he drove off a "rickety bridge" and into a pond on Martha's Vineyard.[1] The car accident killed his passenger, Mary Jo Kopechne, 28, who had attended the late-night party. Kennedy left the scene of the accident and did not report his involvement as the car's driver until the next morning. A week later, he pleaded guilty to leaving the scene of the crash.

Kennedy's televised speech to the nation on July 25, 1969, and the Chappaquiddick incident as a whole, combined with the weakening of party politics and a greater emphasis on a politician's character, has been pinpointed as a key moment of change in twentieth-century political scandal.[2] Within the history of scandal and news coverage of these media frenzies, a central part to understanding these events is grasping the politicians' rhetorical response to the mediated accusations hurled at them. Kennedy's speech, which took place one week after the car crash when he pleaded guilty to a charge of leaving the crime scene, serves as a signal moment in which the nascent context for contemporary political-sexual scandal in a media-saturated environment was born. As Kennedy biographer Adam Clymer observed, "Chappaquiddick changed the press … offering a justification for writing about politicians' private lives."[3] Indeed, after Kennedy, the early 1970s brought waves of reports on not only Kennedy, but on many of his colleagues in the House and Senate,

G. Cos (✉)
School of Communication, RIT, Rochester, NY, USA

© The Editor(s) (if applicable) and The Author(s) 2016
H. Mandell, G.M. Chen (eds.), *Scandal in a Digital Age*,
DOI 10.1057/978-1-137-59545-4_4

revealing the failings of Congressman Joe Waggonner, confidante of Richard Nixon, who solicited a cop posed as a prostitute; Congressman Wilbur Mills, the chair of the House Ways and Means Committee, who had an affair with a stripper; and Congressman Wayne Hays, the chair of the House Committee on Administration, who demanded sex from his secretary in order to maintain employment.[4]

In what media scholar and sociologist John B. Thompson identified as the rise of a "politics of trust,"[5] which arose from the changes in American political culture, the public and media placed a premium on elected officials' credibility. The concept of credibility evolves from rhetorical theory, specifically from a construct that Aristotle identified as "ethos."[6] Ethos is the character and competence of a speaker or public person. More specifically, it is an ongoing assessment that the audience has for this person. Ethos is something derived from the audience, so no one person has it in and of his or herself. They attain it through their interaction with an audience.

This chapter argues that a rhetorical assessment of the scandal surrounding the Chappaquiddick incident reveals a harbinger of the contemporary political sex scandal and the diminishment of the public/private divide among public figures. Kennedy took to the media—in a nationally televised address to the "people of Massachusetts"—to explain and defend his actions. His credibility was on the line and his character was called into question. This chapter will review various rhetorical analyses of Kennedy's July 25, 1969, address to investigate how he was able to shore up his credibility in the public sphere. Specifically, it will examine central analyses in the field of "apologia," the act of speaking in defense of oneself, to evaluate the strategies Kennedy used, and to speculate whether these same strategies still exist or could exist within the contemporary context for mediated political sex scandal in America.

The chapter's argument will conduct a condensed textual analysis of Kennedy's speech by way of John B. Thompson's definition of scandal.[7] Thompson points to five elements of symbolic action: scandals involve the breach of norms; scandals involve secrecy or covert activity; people disapprove of scandal's moral breach; people publicly express disapproval with the moral breach; and the "offending" individual risks a damaged reputation. The analysis presented in this chapter will identify all of these elements within Kennedy's speech and contemplate short- and long-term consequences of the speech for audiences that include the people of Massachusetts as well as the broader American public. Let us begin by reviewing the role of apologia in rhetorical theory.

## APOLOGIA AND THE PUBLIC PERSON

Apologia, the rhetorical genre of speaking in defense of oneself when accused of wrongdoing, is an essential frame that helps us understand how Kennedy was able to forestall media surveillance and squelch some of the public accusations hurled at him. Communication scholars B.L. Ware and Wil A. Linkugel defined apologia as a distinct form of public discourse, one in which "an attack upon a person's character, upon his worth as a human being, does seem to demand a direct response."[8] The scandal requires a response from the scandal-tarnished individual since news of the event strikes at the core of the person's moral being, actions, and public reputation. It requires of the accused to address the community with a direct and personal response to incriminating charges. With people in positions of power, "this response is usually a public speech of self-defense, the apology."[9]

According to Ware and Linkugel, there are four strategies available for the apologist: denial, bolstering, differentiation, and transcendence.[10] Denial and bolstering do not change the way the audience thinks about the issue under discussion. Denial moves the speaker away from the issue (*I didn't do it!*), while bolstering allows the speaker to identify with the issue (*I was there but...*). Differentiation and transcendence are transformative because they do attempt to change the way the audience looks at the issue (*I was there but please understand...*). Differentiation strategies have the speaker redefining the situations that create the context, offering a more positive perspective on the issue or event. And transcendence strategies "shift the focus away from the particulars of a situation to the larger, conceptual ideals that the audience views favorably."[11]

Political communication scholar William Benoit[12] offers a contemporary conceptualization of apologia, identifying five major strategies that over-lap with those articulated by Ware and Linkugel: (1) Denial: Simple denial or shifting the blame; (2) Evasion of responsibility: Claiming to be provoked and presenting the situation as an "accident"; (3) Reduction of offensiveness: Bolstering, minimizing the problem, differentiation, transcendence, attacking accuser, and compensation; (4) Corrective action: Offering to repair damages caused by self-action and taking steps to prevent the event from reoccurring; (5) Mortification: Admitting wrongful behavior, expressing contrition, and apologizing to the audience.[13]

## KENNEDY'S SPEECH

In looking at Kennedy's speech, denial and mortification were central strate-gies that he used. In the narrative part of the speech— three paragraphs in— Kennedy, who was married at the time of the incident, makes two strong denials:

> There is no truth, no truth whatever, to the widely circulated suspicions of immoral conduct that have been leveled at my behavior and hers regarding that evening. There has never been a private relationship between us of any kind. I know of nothing in Mary Jo's conduct on that or any other occasion—and the same is true of the other girls at that party—that would lend any substance to such ugly speculation about their character. Nor was I driving under the influence of liquor.[14]

After these two strong denials, the speech moves into a narrative form of the accident:

> Little over one mile away, the car that I was driving on an unlit road went off a narrow bridge which had no guard rails and was built on a left angle to the road. The car overturned in a deep pond and immediately filled with water. I remember thinking as the cold water rushed in around my head that I was for certain drowning. Then water entered my lungs and I actual felt the sensation of drowning. But somehow I struggled to the surface alive.

> I made immediate and repeated efforts to save Mary Jo by diving into the strong and murky current, but succeeded only in increasing my state of utter exhaustion and alarm. My conduct and conversations during the next several hours, to the extent that I can remember them, make no sense to me at all.[15]

Kennedy follows this by letting his audience know the state he was in at the time. In doing this, he emphasizes a stance of mortification:

> Although my doctors informed me that I suffered a cerebral concussion, as well as shock, I do not seek to escape responsibility for my actions by placing the blame either on the physical and emotional trauma brought on by the accident, or on anyone else.[16]

Later in the speech, he places the audience inside the traumatic moment by stating:

> All kinds of scrambled thoughts—all of them confused, some of them irrational, many of them which I cannot recall, and some of which I would not have seriously entertained under normal circumstances—went through my mind during this period. They were reflected in the various inexplicable, inconsistent, and inconclusive things I said and did, including such questions as whether the girl might still be alive somewhere out of that immediate area, whether some awful curse did actually hang over all the Kennedys, whether there was some justifiable reason for me to doubt what had happened and to delay my report, whether somehow the awful weight of this incredible incident might in some way pass from my shoulders.[17]

Communication scholar David Ling found that Kennedy's July 25, 1969, speech helped alleviate immediate problems surrounding his reputation and how the Massachusetts electorate viewed him. But there were larger and long-lasting issues Kennedy would have to contend with post-scandal—such as the black mark that it would strike against his character and even shape his obituary in 2009.[18] Ultimately, the Chappaquiddick scandal would be cemented in the American political consciousness. Ling's analysis went beyond the generic categories of apologia and applied the "dramatistic approach" of rhetorical theorist Kenneth Burke: When someone explains a situation to an audience, five "pentadic" elements (act, scene, agent, agency, purpose) are at work to provide the speaker's view of that situation. In examining the interaction of these parts, one of these elements defines the situation.[19]

Ling found two dominant elements in Kennedy's Chappaquiddick speech. The first was the scene Kennedy drew as he recalled the incidents of that fatal evening. This scene overpowered him as a lone individual, and there was nothing he could possibly do to save a trapped Mary Jo Kopechne. The last part of Kennedy's televised speech was an appeal to his audience, the people of Massachusetts, whether or not they "accepted the whispers and innuendo" of a married senator drinking, partying, and driving under the influence with a younger woman.[20]

Ling argued that Kennedy's speech was set up so that the two parts, working in conjunction with each other, make an argument to transfer guilt onto his audience. The speech attempted to persuade the listener/viewer that

1. Kennedy was a tragic victim of a chaotic scene he could not control. He was a disoriented survivor of a car crash who was fighting his own Kennedy curse.
2. His future depended not on his own decision but whether or not the people of Massachusetts "accepted the whispers and innuendo that constituted the immediate scene."[21]

Therefore, Kennedy presented a rhetorical situation that no ordinary person could transcend and, therefore, entrapped him in that most terrible moment. Kennedy offered his constituents the opportunity to decide his political fate, thereby bestowing on them the burden of a symbolic decision. This placed his listeners in a position of guilt. In order to throw off their collective, symbolic guilt, his listeners would need to reject the "whispers and innuendo" tied to the incident. Kennedy placed his audience in what Burke identifies as a classical rhetorical position, a position grounded in the audience feeling responsible for the speaker's future—a responsibility that is driven by guilt.

Kenneth Burke's conception of guilt is deeply humanistic and informed by language theory. After all, people are language-inventing and language-using beings that conjure up the unique symbolic idea of the "negative" through words such as "no" and "not." The construction of the negative through language enables humans to determine what is good and what is not; what is moral and not moral; ethical and not ethical. It provides us with the capacity to make rightly minded decisions. Therefore, the power of "no" enables us to know when we have made poor moral decisions, and this leads us to experience "guilt." It arises from the imbalance we experience knowing we have transgressed moral rules. It is that sense of disorder we experience, and it motivates us to use language and other symbolic means to right this imbalance.[22] Ling concludes that Kennedy was able to juxtapose the tragic circumstances of the accident with the placement of guilt upon his audience to decide whether or not they should support him.

## Moral Transgression and Secrecy Surrounding Chappaquiddick

It is important to remember that unlike our early twenty-first-century political culture, July 1969 was just one year removed from the tragic events of 1968, which saw the assassinations of Martin Luther King Jr. and Senator Robert F. Kennedy—Ted Kennedy's older brother. Public trust in institutions, politicians and political office in particular, has eroded in the last four decades. The sociologist John B. Thompson asks "why is political scandal more prevalent today?" and explains the phenomenon is "not so much [due] to a decline in the moral standards of politicians, but rather to a change in the moral codes and conventions that are used to assess the behavior of politicians."[23] Seismic shifts in politics and culture were transforming the late 1960s and early 1970s. Many have pointed to Vietnam and Watergate, but Chappaquiddick also plays a pivotal role in the erosion of "ideological politics" and one rooted more in a "politics of trust." Therefore, attacks on the trustworthiness of politicians became more important to modern political scandal.[24]

The Chappaquiddick incident represents a hallmark scandal that clouded the line between one's private and public life. Kennedy's unique position in American culture (as a member of a famous, dynastic political family) enabled him to escape the fate of an ordinary politician—albeit not unscathed—and continue on as a US Senator. The Chappaquiddick incident represents a turning point in the history of political scandal, where the response to Kennedy's situation and his explanation of his actions influenced the approach the press would use with future political scandals.

One product of Kennedy's accident on Chappaquiddick was a number of conspiracy theorists took to dissecting every aspect of that night. In *The Bridge at Chappaquiddick*, the author Jack Olsen quotes an editorial in the Roman Catholic newspaper *The Pilot* (Kennedy himself was Catholic), which calls upon the public to stop its speculation and rumormongering about the events of July 18: "It is time, we think, that this case were closed. It becomes too easily an occasion for rash judgments and self-righteous assertions; it feeds the weakness of those who rejoice in another's misery, who reach for the mote and miss the beam. What had to be said has been said; what answers are available have been given."[25]

For others, the incident embodied the machinations of evil and subterfuge of an extraordinary kind. Zad Rust's book *Teddy Bare*, published just two years after the 1969 accident, posits a cold war, paranoiac vision in which the evil actions of Soviet bloc countries slowly rot out the institutions of the non-Communist West through intermediaries such as Kennedy. Rust notes that it "is of the greatest importance that everyone in the United States and in other countries know and remember forever the true circumstances of the tragedy of the Dyke Bridge, and understand the true character of the man that this Force of Darkness was prepared to introduce into the White House."[26]

Richard and Thomas Tedrow's *Death at Chappaquiddick* strikes an equally adversarial approach, arguing that their journalistic investigation provided "the most complete account of Chappaquiddick" at the time of its publication in 1976. The authors presume Kennedy would run for president in 1976 or 1980 and argue that Kennedy revealed himself to be of weak character and not fit for the presidency, a position that requires of it "a man in complete control of his actions, his mental faculties and his moral direction."[27] The negative focus of these two books illustrates two perspectives of anti-Kennedy advocates in regard to Chappaquiddick. First, that Kennedy's inability to persuasively answer questions about that night resulted in the emergent conspiracy theorists to offer their own take on what happened. Second, when Kennedy shared his construction of the events, his critics assailed him for exhibiting a deficit of character, a weakness befitting moral bankruptcy.

## PUBLIC AND MEDIA REACTION

The immediate public reaction was more difficult to discern. The media landscape was different from what it is today. Communication researchers[28] found that the response to Kennedy's July 25, 1969, television address, which was broadcast nationally, had a negative impact upon his strength as a national political candidate. Kennedy's 1970 Senate race was considered by many political observers to be a "test" case for his viability as a candidate, generally speaking. A study of long-term (16-month) effects of the address found that television played a notable role "in recouping disaffected supporters following a public figure's controversial involvement."[29] Heavy viewers could recall Kennedy's July 25, 1969, address, but had far less knowledge of the issues surrounding the 1970 state election.

Other monitors of journalistic activity saw the press coverage of his televised speech and the Chappaquiddick incident in general as a swarm of attention that outstripped coverage of men landing on the moon. The editors at the *Columbia Journalism Review* noted that there were varying, misrepresentative descriptions and depictions of the accident scene.

How can one tiny island have so many different configurations? How can a road be at once T-shaped, Y-shaped, and even [see *Newsweek* photo] X-shaped? What *does* the Dyke Road junction look like? August 1—two weeks after the accident *Life* printed an eye-level photo looking toward Dyke Road, but not until *Newsweek's* August 11 air view of the site—more than three weeks after the accident—could the reader of national media really visualize it. Where had all the photographers' Piper Cubs, helicopters, and hot-air balloons gone?[30]

In general, the nation's response to the televised address was tepid. According to a Time-Harris poll in August 1969, about 44% of respondents said Kennedy failed "to tell the real truth," 51% said his explanation was inadequate, and 77% said he was wrong not to report the accident immediately. However, 58% of respondents said "he has suffered, been punished and should be given the benefit of the doubt."[31]

## Kennedy's Damaged Reputation

The significance of Kennedy's speech rests—according to rhetorical critic Robert King—in the media and apologist's co-creation of the *tragedy* construct. King argues that Kennedy, with Chappaquiddick, and Nixon, during Watergate,

> drew on a widely accepted, popular sense of tragedy, one that nicely serves the politician who must defend behavior he would prefer to ignore. This meaning shifts the burden from a responsible agent to his suffering; it tends to subsume an unresolved, debatable question into the realm of completed fiction, and, as a result, it falsifies the political reality it pretends to confront.[32]

King identified the "deceptive rhetorical strategies compressed in tragedy,"[33] to detail its misuse by speakers such as Kennedy and the media outlets covering them. With Chappaquiddick, the tragedy was reconstituted through media reportage. Ten years after the incident and as a precursor to his run for the Democratic presidential nomination in 1980, Roger Mudd, the prominent correspondent at CBS News, interviewed Kennedy. King writes that, "Mudd asked about a 'curse' on the Kennedy 'family,' and Kennedy himself, however haltingly, explained Chappaquiddick with familiar diction: 'I have been impacted by a number of tragedies in my life ... This is a circumstance for which I was responsible ... I'm a different person than I was prior to that tragedy.'"[34]

The "tragedy" of Chappaquiddick transforms an older Kennedy into a newer, changed person. The events of Chappaquiddick subsumed him and, therefore, the "transformation from agent to agency to pseudo-agent is ratified by his appearing on an new scene—a news scene—which he can in some measure control and which derives it political value simply by being in the public eye."[35] The co-creation of the tragedy is completed by the act of being physically present—and not by an individual person making a choice. Ultimately, Kennedy's presence at the scene was the calamity. The idea of presence "suggests a quality that projects a media personality"[36] and supplants a truer, actual sense of tragedy based on individual choice and the individual's active role in the event.

## Kennedy's Needs and His Audience's Needs

The writer Susan Wise Bauer (2008) contended that Kennedy had misread his public with his 1969 speech, refusing to offer the public a confession to his involvement in the Chappaquiddick incident. Bauer pointed out that "this was not a confession—Kennedy 'confessed' to concussion (hardly a moral failing). His statement that he 'felt morally obligated to plead guilty' utilizes a phrase commonly applied to situations in which there is no moral fault."[37] Bauer argues that Kennedy did not grasp his public's need for an avowal of wrongdoing and, "more deeply, he had no comprehension of his need to reassure his followers that he had no intention of wielding inappropriate power over them—a need that full public confession could have helped satisfy."[38] Bauer noted an interesting quality in Kennedy's statement and demand for contrition by pointing out that it is possible that he made "an old-fashioned Catholic confession" in private to his priest.[39] But if he did, the public is unaware of it. "Confession of sin was a profoundly private act for the Catholic sinner, an act in which forgiveness of other men and women had almost no part."[40]

Regardless of Kennedy's spoken contrition or explanation, his speech would be difficult to deliver today. Modern apologies are more public because of digital media. People watch the apology within a 24-hour news cycle. They also can immediately respond to and criticize the politician for a lame apology through social media. Take, for instance, media reports on Kennedy handlers assisting him in preparing his speech[41] or the *Columbia Journalism Review*'s editors criticism that journalists (at the time) should have an "ability to clearly convey basic statistics, description, 'housekeeping' data," and yet, it was "more than three weeks after the accident—could the reader of national media really visualize it[?]"[42]

## CONCLUSION

The interpretation one could take away from Kennedy's Chappaquiddick speech, and the media reaction surrounding it, brings us back around to apologia theory. Communication scholars Joy Koesten and Robert C. Rowland added another important concept to this literature by arguing for the strategy of atonement as a rhetorical device to repair one's image and defuse a scandal. "The rhetoric of atonement, as a sub-genre of apologia, offers a political leader the rhetorical tools necessary to let go of the past and heal old wounds."[43] Communication researcher Ryan Shepard extended Koesten and Rowland's ideas, arguing that there is a sub-genre of "simulated atonement" which speakers can utilize in specific rhetorical situations.[44] This strategy "allows wrongdoers to clear the air by acknowledging that misconduct occurred, but permits them to evade accountability by using the trust that they establish with their confession to safely offer reasons for why they are not entirely to blame."[45] Shepard's analysis identifies a rhetorical "transference effect" that allowed Kennedy to take responsibility for the events on the night of July 18, 1969, while simultaneously shifting accountability.

It is almost impossible to imagine that Chappaquiddick would unfold in a similar manner in today's social media–driven world. Today's media environment is vastly different, so a comparison is almost impossible. What is more productive is to reflect on how Kennedy, through much consultation with handlers and speechwriters, utilized an ancient rhetorical form to inoculate himself from political extinction by leveraging the mythic status of his family name and, in the process, eliminating the public/private divide that the press had respected for so long. It would bring short-term, positive effects. After all, he did not resign from political office. Instead, he continued to serve in elected office for decades, becoming "one of the most effective lawmakers in the history of the Senate."[46] However, the long-term consequences would haunt Kennedy's life and our political culture from then on.

## NOTES

1. "Ted Kennedy Car Accident in Chappaquiddick," *Newsweek*, August 3, 1969, http://www.newsweek.com/ted-kennedy-car-accident-chappaquiddick-207070.
2. John B. Thompson, *Political Scandal: Power and Visibility in the Media Age*, (Cambridge: Blackwell Press, 2000), 147.
3. Adam Clymer, *Edward M. Kennedy: A Bibliography*, (New York: William Morrow and Company, 2009), 155.
4. Clymer, *Edward M. Kennedy*, 155–156.
5. Thompson, *Political Scandal*, 111.
6. James Jasinski, *Sourcebook on Rhetoric: Key Concepts in Contemporary Rhetorical Studies*, (Thousand Oaks, CA: Sage, 2001), 229.
7. Thompson, *Political Scandal*, 13.
8. B.L. Ware and Wil A. Linkugel, "They Spoke in Defense of Themselves: On the Generic Criticism of Apologia," *Quarterly Journal of Speech* 59, no. 3 (1973): 273.
9. Ware and Linkugel, "They Spoke in Defense of Themselves: On the Generic Criticism of Apologia."
10. Ware and Linkugel, "They Spoke in Defense of Themselves: On the Generic Criticism of Apologia," 275.
11. Ware and Linkugel, "They Spoke in Defense of Themselves: On the Generic Criticism of Apologia," 280.
12. William Benoit, *Accounts, Excuses, Apologies: A Theory of Image Restoration*, (Albany, NY: State University of New York Press, 1995).
13. Benoit, *Accounts, Excuses, Apologies: A Theory of Image Restoration*.
14. American Rhetoric Top 100 Speeches, "Edward M. Kennedy Address to the People of Massachusetts and Chappaquiddick." http://www.americanrhetoric.com/speeches/tedkennedychappaquiddick.htm.
15. American Rhetoric Top 100 Speeches, "Edward M. Kennedy Address to the People of Massachusetts and Chappaquiddick."
16. American Rhetoric Top 100 Speeches, "Edward M. Kennedy Address to the People of Massachusetts and Chappaquiddick."
17. American Rhetoric Top 100 Speeches, "Edward M. Kennedy Address to the People of Massachusetts and Chappaquiddick."
18. John M. Broder, "Edward M. Kennedy, Senate Stalwart, is Dead at 77," *The New York Times*, August 26, 2009 http://www.nytimes.com/2009/08/27/us/politics/27kennedy.html?_r=0.
19. David A. Ling, "A Pentadic Analysis of Senator Edward Kennedy's Address to the People of Massachusetts," *Central States Speech Journal* 21, no. 2 (1970): 81–86.
20. Ling, "A Pentadic Analysis of Senator Edward Kennedy's Address to the People of Massachusetts," 84.

21. Ling, "A Pentadic Analysis of Senator Edward Kennedy's Address to the People of Massachusetts."

22. Kenneth Burke, *The Rhetoric of Religion: Studies in Logology*, (Berkeley, CA: University of California Press, 1970).

23. Thompson, *Political Scandal*, 107.

24. Thompson, *Political Scandal*, 111–112.

25. Jack Olsen, *The Bridge at Chappaquiddick*. (Boston, MA: Little, Brown and Company, 1970), 241.

26. Zad Rust *Teddy Bare: The Last of the Kennedy Clan*. (Belmont, MA: Western Islands Press, 1971), x.

27. Richard L. Tedrow and Thomas L. Tedrow, *Death at Chappaquiddick* (Ottawa, IL: Green Hill Publishers, 1976), 1.

28. Sidney Kraus, Timothy Meyer, and Maurice Shelby Jr., "16 Months After Chappaquiddick: Effects of the Kennedy Broadcast," *Journalism Quarterly* 51, no. 3 (1971): 432.

29. Kraus, Meyer, and Shelby, "16 Months After Chappaquiddick: Effects of the Kennedy Broadcast."

30. "Chappaquiddick: More Is Not Better," *Columbia Journalism Review* 8, no. 3 (Fall 1969): 2–3.

31. Elliott C. McLaughlin, "Experts: Media Today Would Demand Chappaquiddick Answers," *CNN.com*, August 28, 2009, http://www.cnn.com/2009/POLITICS/08/28/kennedy.chappaquiddick.today/.

32. Robert L. King, "Transforming Scandal into Tragedy: A Rhetoric of Political Apology," *Quarterly Journal of Speech* 71, no. 3 (1985): 290.

33. King, "Transforming Scandal into Tragedy: A Rhetoric of Political Apology."

34. King, "Transforming Scandal into Tragedy: A Rhetoric of Political Apology," 297.

35. King, "Transforming Scandal into Tragedy: A Rhetoric of Political Apology."

36. King, "Transforming Scandal into Tragedy: A Rhetoric of Political Apology," 297.

37. Susan Wise Bauer, *The Art of the Public Grovel: Sexual Sin and Public Confession in America* (Princeton, NJ: Princeton University Press, 2008), 78.

38. Bauer, *The Art of the Public Grovel*, 83.

39. Bauer, *The Art of the Public Grovel*.

40. Bauer, *The Art of the Public Grovel*, 84.

41. Ling, "A Pentadic Analysis of Senator Edward Kennedy's Address to the People of Massachusetts."

42. "Chappaquiddick: More Is Not Better," 2.

43. Joy Koesten and Robert C. Rowland, "The Rhetoric of Atonement," *Communication Studies* 55, no. 1 (2004): 61.

44. Ryan M. Shepard, *The Art of Simulated Atonement: A Case Study of George W. Bush*, master's thesis, University of Kansas, 2007.

45. Shepard, *The Art of Simulated Atonement*, 109.

46. Broder, "Edward M. Kennedy."

# CHAPTER 5

# Televangelism, Audience Fragmentation, and the Changing Coverage of Scandal

*Mark Ward Sr.*

A well-coifed Southern televangelist. A tearful on-air confession of moral failure. Allegations about hush money. For Americans of a certain age, such images are indelibly linked to the televangelism scandals of 1987–1988 when the sins of Jim Bakker and Jimmy Swaggart made international headlines. Now fast-forward to the new millennium. High-profile evangelical preachers who have resigned their ministries in disgrace include Ted Haggard (gay sex and drugs), Mark Driscoll (plagiarism), and Tullian Tchividjian (adultery). The case of Marcus Lamb, however, is the closest twenty-first-century analog to the Bakker and Swaggart affairs. The Dallas-based founder and star personality of the evangelical Daystar Television Network used a live broadcast cohosted by his wife to confess infidelity in 2010 and allege a $7.5 million extortion plot against him.[1] The story had all the "right" ingredients, but few beyond evangelical circles have heard Lamb's name—or those of Haggard, Driscoll, or Tchividjian. By contrast, a sex scandal in 2015 involving Josh Duggar, a then-emerging evangelical leader by dint of his role on television's popular *19 Kids and Counting* reality show, went viral overnight.

Why the media circus over Bakker and Swaggart in the 1980s, yet the media shrug over Lamb, Haggard, Driscoll, and Tchividjian today? And why the feeding frenzy over Duggar when other recent scandals involving far more established evangelical leaders went largely unnoticed? With today's social media and 24/7 news cycle, should not more media equal more coverage and magnify *everything*? And yet the televangelism scandals of the 1980s received far more coverage at a time when technology afforded far fewer media options. And as the Duggar case illustrated, even in today's media universe, some scandals receive outsized attention while others barely register. What accounts for these differences?

M. Ward Sr. (✉)
School of Arts & Sciences, University of Houston-Victoria, Victoria, TX, USA

H. Mandell, G.M. Chen (eds.), *Scandal in a Digital Age*,
DOI 10.1057/978-1-137-59545-4_5

53

An answer begins with *audience fragmentation*. Today's proliferation of media options also cuts the audience pie into smaller slices. In 1986, prime-time Sunday viewing choices for many Americans were limited to three network shows per hour plus a syndicated televangelist on the local independent station. Those who did not fancy another sitcom might well give the preacher and his musical guests a look.[2] Thirty years ago, cable TV reached fewer than half of US households and offered only a handful of channels.[3] Televangelists such as Jerry Falwell, Pat Robertson, Oral Roberts, Rex Humbard, Robert Schuller, and others amassed audiences of up to 7 million weekly viewers[4] and became public figures.

Today, by contrast, Marcus Lamb enjoys a potential reach of 100 million households that was unimaginable a generation ago. His Daystar network is carried via satellite by DirecTV, Dish Network, AT&T U-Verse, and Verizon Fios; via cable by Bright House, Cablevision, Charter, Comcast, Cox, Mediacom, Suddenlink, and Time Warner; and on-demand via streaming apps for iPhone, iPad, Android, Kindle Fire, and Roku.[5] Yet because Lamb competes for audience share with more than 800 cable and satellite channels,[6] he and other televangelists are no longer public figures; they are merely celebrities within their own evangelical subculture. Television has become like radio, a medium originally controlled by a few major networks but in which individual stations now air specialized programming formats. As Webster[7] explains,

> Rather than offering a little something for everyone, channels [today] tend to specialize in a particular type of content … [and] "narrowcast" whatever type of content they believe will attract a desired demographic … [In the past,] every home had a uniform, if limited, universe of programming from which to choose.[8]

Audience fragmentation explains why Lamb's scandal (or those of Haggard, Driscoll, and Tchividjian) aroused scant public interest compared to Duggar, whose *19 Kids and Counting* aired on mainstream television's The Learning Channel. The 3.29 million viewers who tuned into the show's 2014–2015 season premiere made it the third-highest rated program for its time slot in all of television.[9] Two months later, it peaked at 4.41 million viewers to become the number-one Tuesday night program among all female audiences.[10] Given the "persistence of popularity," observed media scholars John G. Webster and Thomas B. Ksiazek,[11] the growing fragmentation of media audiences means "that 'winner-take-all' markets will continue to characterize cultural consumption" while "most niche media will be doomed to obscurity."

Thus the tale of televangelism and its scandals, then and now, points to a key lesson about the relationship between audience fragmentation and media coverage in today's digital media universe. More can actually mean less—as when more media choices fragment audiences into smaller segments and reduce common cultural discourse to what is popular. Make no mistake; the "electronic church" has not gone away.

Evangelical Christians in the United States comprise more than one-fourth of the adult population. Ninety percent of these believers consume evangelical media each month. One in five American adults consumes these media daily ... Far from being superseded by digital technology, the electronic church has proliferated.[12]

But compared to the 1980s, today's electronic church has gone "underground" and is seen on religious channels consumed almost entirely by religious audiences. For that reason, the peccadilloes of Marcus Lamb—and of Ted Haggard, Mark Driscoll, and Tullian Tchividjian—pass with little popular notice.

Any list of top scandals in the 1980s would include those of televangelists Jim Bakker, Jimmy Swaggart, and Oral Roberts—along with the scandals of politicians Gary Hart (adultery) and Oliver North (Iran-Contra), athletes Pete Rose (gambling) and Ben Johnson (steroids), and entertainers Milli Vanilli (lip synching) and Vanessa Williams (nude photos). Thirty years later, scandals about politicians, athletes, and entertainers are still eagerly covered, while those about preachers are not. Nor are scandals about academia, science, literature, the arts, and other fields now relegated to niche media.

## UNDERSTANDING AUDIENCE FRAGMENTATION

Concerns about audience fragmentation have been around since the 1980s. During the decade, the number of cable households tripled from less than one in five to nearly three in five.[13] The number of cable TV networks jumped from 28 to 79.[14] As a result, the audience share of over-the-air broadcast television fell from about 90% of viewers in 1980 to only 77% in 1990. Over the same period, the percentage of households with videocassette recorders (VCRs) rose from 1 to 69%.[15] Remotely controlled TV sets became widespread. Researchers scrambled to explain the increasing displacement of traditional network TV viewing by cable viewing,[16] the use of VCRs,[17] and the practice of "channel-switching" or "zapping" with TV remotes.[18]

This interest in audience viewing patterns occurred during a paradigm shift in theorizing about mass media. A half-century earlier, the new medium of radio was hailed as revolutionary "magic bullet."[19] The propagandist need only broadcast a message into the ether and the masses would be swayed. Mass media created a "total environment," claimed public relations pioneer Edward Bernays,[20] through which governments and corporations might "control and regiment the masses according to our will without their knowing about it." Seen this way, audiences are passive receptors of messages. Yet an alternative to the passive-audience model began to take shape during the 1940s. In a series of panel studies, sociologist Paul Lazarsfeld and his colleagues researched radio from listeners' points of view[21] and showed how audiences discriminated among mass media messages and selectively acted on them—for example, by choosing to see a certain movie or vote for a certain candidate.[22] In the 1950s, media theorist Wilbur Schramm[23] extended Lazarsfeld's model and argued that audiences make media choices by balancing the expected gratification against the required effort in time and concentration. By the 1960s, other theorists linked media gratification to psychologist Abraham Maslow's Hierarchy of Needs or developed their own media-specific hierarchies.[24]

From this research emerged, in the 1970s, the uses and gratifications theory of sociologist Elihu Katz and his colleagues.[25] No longer were audiences portrayed as passive receptors of media messages; instead, audience members were conceived as independent agents who actively discriminated among media and selected those which gratified their needs. Today, numerous studies apply uses and gratifications theory to explain consumer choices in digital media.[26] By the 1990s, audience studies took a new "ethnographic turn."[27] Researchers looked beyond the decisions of individual audience members and discovered they could also bond with other members to form "interpretive communities"[28] united by a shared interpretation of a given media genre. A prominent example is Trekkies, the devoted fans of the *Star Trek* television and movie franchise. Researchers have documented interpretive communities formed around such diverse media genres as crime dramas,[29] advertising campaigns,[30] religious radio,[31] science reporting,[32] and sports broadcasts.[33] "Audiences [that] are specific to definite genres and times constitute a remarkably high degree of solidarity," observed media researcher David Holmes.[34] This solidarity is "channeled totemically and ritually through media [personalities and]. … enable a form of reciprocity [that is] … able to facilitate a sense of belonging, security and community, even if individuals are not directly interacting."

This change in paradigms, from the passive-audience to the active-audience model, provides a context for understanding current debates over the causes and consequences of the audience fragmentation in today's digital media universe. Recently, the Nielsen Company[35] reported that 284 million Americans watched traditional live TV over a three-month period, 160 million watched time-shifted TV using digital video recorders, 153 million watched video disks, 162 million watched videos on the Internet, and 41 million watched videos on mobile phones. Similarly, a survey of more than 1400 adults by the Media Insight Project found that respondents on average used four or five different devices to access the news.[36] The resulting audience fragmentation, caution some scholars, may produce a society divided into media enclaves[37] that degrade civic discourse as the public splits into divergent interpretive communities. Infinite choices, warned Chris Anderson,[38] must inevitably lead to "ultimate fragmentation."[39] Particular concern has been expressed in numerous studies[40] over the fragmentation of news consumption. Not only can audiences choose from among multiple platforms, but also from innumerable specialized or partisan news sources. This, in turn, facilitates "selective exposure" to favored sources and, many believe, fosters audience polarization.[41]

Webster and Ksiazek's[42] survey of the literature on audience fragmentation found that the research falls into "media-centric" and "user-centric" approaches. The media-centric view focuses on media providers and argues that "the most obvious cause of fragmentation is a steady growth in the number of media outlets and products competing for public attention." The user-centric view focuses on "what media users do with all those [media] resources" and holds that audience preferences "reflect user needs, moods, attitudes, or tastes" and that users "are 'rational' in the sense that they serve those psychological dispositions." However, Webster and Ksiazek proposed a third "audience-centric" approach based on the "structuration" theory of sociologist Anthony Giddens.[43] In this view, users ratify the available media choices by the act of using them, while indirectly altering those choices as media providers respond to audience usage patterns with new or revised options.

Yet at bottom, observed Webster and Ksiazek,[44] the "fundamental question about ... fragmentation is how far the process can go. Will future audiences distribute themselves evenly across all media choices or will popular offerings continue to dominate the marketplace?" Their data indicated those media offerings that (1) offer the highest technical or storytelling quality, (2) are useful in social situations (because "everybody's talking about it"), and (3) show up in Internet searches due to their popularity will prosper. Thus, in a fragmented media universe, the scandal surrounding Josh Duggar went viral, while the scandals of Marcus Lamb and other disgraced preachers went nowhere.

## TELEVANGELISM THEN AND NOW

Such a fragmented media universe is a far cry from 30 years ago when the scandals of Bakker and Swaggart burst onto the national news. The electronic church was already an established institution, birthed in the 1920s and 1930s when radio preachers discovered—in the words of one evangelist—that "Unction can be transmitted!"[45] Evangelicals swiftly bought into a utopian "mythos of the electronic church."[46] Eager to save the world through the miracle of technology, they literally transposed the format of the tent crusade to the airwaves.[47] By purchasing Sunday airtime on national radio networks, preachers such as Charles Fuller and his *Old Fashioned Revival Hour* garnered audiences of up to 20 million weekly listeners.[48] When network radio gave way to television in the 1950s, a new generation of broadcast preachers—men such as Oral Roberts, Rex Humbard, and Jerry Falwell—honed their media skills over local stations. Not until the late 1960s, however, did technology allow independent syndicators to affordably make broadcast-quality videotape recordings of their programs. At the same time, Congress mandated that all new TV sets must receive not only the VHF band (very-high frequency channels 2 13) dominated by affiliates of the three major networks, but also the UHF band (ultra-high frequency channels 14–83) inhabited by independent local stations.[49] Roberts, Humbard, and Falwell entered first-run national syndication, each purchasing Sunday airtime on more than 300 stations.[50] During the 1970s, the top ten religious telecasts each attracted more than a million viewers. *Oral Roberts and You,* the highest rated show with 7 million weekly viewers, could draw up to 50 million for prime-time specials featuring celebrities ranging from gospel singer Mahalia Jackson to country comedienne Minnie Pearl.[51] The term "electronic church" was coined[52] and, by the 1980s, warnings were sounded about *The Rising Power of Televangelism*[53] and *Televangelism, Power, and Politics.*[54]

Thus, the 1986–1987 television season premiered with *Oral Roberts and You* as the elder statesman of the televangelism genre, *The Jimmy Swaggart Telecast* as the genre's current ratings leader, and *The Jim and Tammy* [Bakker] *TV Ministry Hour* syndicated on 170 stations and carried by 1300 cable systems.[55] Meanwhile, the prime-time Sunday schedules of the three major networks that season featured *The Disney Sunday Movie* (ABC), *Sixty Minutes* (CBS), and *Our House* (NBC) at 7 p.m., *Murder, She Wrote* (CBS) and *Easy Street* (NBC) at 8 p.m., and the *ABC Sunday Night Movie*, *CBS Sunday Night Movie*, and *NBC Sunday Night Movie* from 9 to 11 p.m.[56] The three Sunday night network movies drew about half of all viewers and left a sizable slice of the ratings pie up for grabs. Competing for this off-network audience were, on average, 16 other channels, which could then be received by the average TV household—though the number was much lower for the 54% of US households that did not subscribe to cable.[57] In such a media universe, televangelism was mainstream fare and televangelists were public figures.

The scandal that, in January 1987, first brought televangelism to popular concern and national media scrutiny involved the venerable Oral Roberts. Seven years earlier, he had seen a vision of a 900-foot-tall Jesus who told Roberts he was destined to find a cure for cancer. Between 1980 and 1986, as fundraising appeals for his new "City of Faith" medical center took increasing amounts of television airtime, Roberts lost nearly two-thirds of his viewing audience. With donations in steep decline, God talked to Roberts again. By his account, the Tulsa-based evangelist physically wrestled with the devil. Then he locked himself in the prayer tower of his Oral Roberts University and claimed God would "take him home" if supporters did not send $8 million by the end of March 1987.[58] The daily drama of "God's hostage" irresistibly drew worldwide media coverage.

Then on March 19, 1987, came the stunning news that Jim Bakker had resigned his TV ministry amid allegations of sexually assaulting a young secretary and paying her $115,000 in hush money. Just as damning were revelations of financial fraud. Since the early 1980s, Bakker's lavish lifestyle had attracted mainstream media scrutiny. Nevertheless, by the end of 1986, PTL Television reported annual revenues of $129 million (equivalent to $281 million in 2015 dollars). That year, PTL's Heritage USA theme park in the Charlotte suburb of Fort Mill, South Carolina, welcomed 6.1 million visitors—a total exceeded only by Disney World and Disneyland. Guests were accommodated in 1100 hotel rooms and campsites, with another 1500 in the planning stages. Five hundred of those new rooms were under construction at the new Heritage Grand Towers, a planned 21-story suite hotel. The 2300-acre PTL complex also featured a resort center, vacation homes, retirement village, condos, timeshares, campground, RV park, water park, shopping mall, restaurants, recreation center, conference center, Upper Room replica, amphitheater, drug rehabilitation center, crisis pregnancy center, prison ministry center, Christian academy, and broadcast training school. Bakker celebrated his 47th birthday on January 2, 1987, by breaking ground on a $100 million replica of London's Crystal Palace that would seat 30,000 worshipers and thus rank as the world's largest church.[59]

When the PTL scandal broke in 1987, the Bakker organization was $70 million in debt (equivalent to $148 million in 2015 dollars) to 1400 creditors. Of that amount, $14 million was owed to contractors working on the unfinished Heritage Grand Towers—even though sufficient funds were raised for its completion. In fact, Bakker had sold 120,000 "Lifetime Partnerships" by promising three nights lodging per year, in perpetuity, for a one-time donation of $1000. In essence, he had sold 360,000 room nights per year for a hotel with only half that capacity. Meanwhile, the press eagerly reported the exorbitant salaries paid to Bakker, his family, and friends. Stories of gold-plated bathroom fixtures and an air-conditioned doghouse at the Bakkers' palatial home symbolized the hubris and excess of the disgraced televangelist. Media coverage of the scandal continued for years: Jerry Falwell's attempt to rescue PTL; Bakker's accusations of a hostile takeover attempt; a 16-month federal grand jury probe; a 1988 indictment for mail and wire fraud; a five-week trial and conviction in 1989; an appeal in 1991; separate investigations by the Internal Revenue Service, Federal Bureau of Investigation, Justice Department, Postal Service, US Congress, and South Carolina Tax Commission; a class-action lawsuit on behalf of 160,000 former Lifetime Partners; Bakker's divorce in 1992; his parole from prison in 1994; and his tell-all book in 1996.

Most Americans gave up on televangelism by February 1988 after Jimmy Swaggart tearfully confessed on his weekly telecast to having immoral liaisons with a Baton Rouge prostitute. "Echoes of the PTL scandal reverberated far and wide. Christian ministries across America saw steep declines in giving ... Public disapproval of televangelists rose to more than 90 percent in numerous surveys."[60] The televangelism genre lost three-quarters of its audience. Yet "none of the major ministries would ever go off the air. Every single ministry ... remained on the air or temporarily left the air only to return later."[61] This was because televangelists forged a new business model adapted to the increasingly fragmented media universe that emerged in the 1990s through the expansion of cable television and introduction of direct-broadcast satellite TV services. By switching their emphasis away from first-run syndication on broadcast television, televangelists forsook the old model of pursuing a broad-based audience and instead aimed their programs at religious viewers attracted to religious cable channels. On-air fundraising and promotion declined as preachers learned that "having their own cable satellite networks [allowed] them to shift their financial appeals to commercial slots outside the programs."[62] Though televangelists since the 1990s have targeted a smaller slice of the pie, the audience fragment they serve is reliably supportive. As noted earlier, 90% of evangelical Christian adults in the USA consume "Christian media" each month, including 1 in 5 who consume it daily.

The advent of digital media has made it easier for televangelists to find a stable audience fragment. Oral Roberts, for example, launched the Golden Eagle Broadcasting channel (now GEB America) carried via DirecTV to a potential reach of 34 million households.[63] *The Jim Bakker Show* is back as a daily talk show carried by half a dozen evangelical channels that potentially reach up to 100 million households.[64] And Jimmy Swaggart's Sonlife Broadcasting Network can be viewed via personal computer, tablet, iPhone app, and the Roku streaming media player—not to mention DirecTV, the Dish Network, local cable systems in 100 markets, over-the-air TV stations in 22 states, and a network of 80 owned and operated radio stations.[65] Compared to three evangelical cable TV networks in the 1980s, today more than a dozen are transmitted via cable and satellite.[66] The reach of Marcus Lamb's Daystar Television Network, the nation's second most-watched evangelical network, has already been described. The most-watched is the Trinity Broadcasting Network; in addition to being the nation's third-largest broadcast group (Trinity owns more TV stations than ABC, CBS, NBC, or FOX), its programming is available to 92% of US households and beamed to every continent through a worldwide network of 78 satellites and 18,000 over-the-air and cable affiliates. On-demand access is provided via mobile app and through the Roku streaming media player.[67]

Meanwhile, nearly 50 independent televangelists—paced by ratings leader Joel Osteen, whose telecast draws 7 million weekly viewers—syndicate their programs on evangelical TV networks.[68] Today's electronic church also encompasses some 3400 radio stations that air religious teaching, talk, or music (of which 1600 stream their programming online), 10 major national evangelical radio networks, and more than 30 independent syndicators that air their programs daily on up to 2000 stations.[69] The leading radio network alone generates 48 million monthly site visits, 12 million monthly mobile visits, 37 million Facebook fans, and 10 million email subscribers simply by aggregating syndicated radio and television programs and streaming them over a single web portal.[70] Thus, broadcasters are hardly irrelevant because "[in] digital media, 'content is king' [and] … who but these experienced content providers are better positioned to not only leverage multiple media platforms, but also drive traffic to them?"[71] Laws passed by Congress in the 1990s deregulated media ownership and led to massive consolidation of the media industry. Religious broadcasting was not immune and is now dominated by evangelical media conglomerates that have the resources to leverage emerging digital media technologies and maximize their audience niches.[72]

Thus, where the old televangelists were public figures whose point of reference was the wider culture wars, the new televangelists are only celebrities within the evangelical audience fragment. Compared to a generation ago, when Jerry Falwell's Moral Majority and Pat Robertson's Christian Coalition sought to change American culture, the rhetoric of evangelicalism and the electronic church has switched from *attacking* to *being attacked*.[73] Evangelicals have retreated into the comfortable subculture of the megachurch where "worship is more a therapeutic means to personal fulfillment than submission to a higher authority."[74] Reflecting and shaping this trend, the electronic church is now shifting "from thrilling success to convenient inspiration … [and to] affirming the individual. Put another way, the Christian faith *itself* may resemble an 'app.'"[75]

When Jim Bakker fell, he took with him an empire built by and for the broad masses of American viewers. But when Marcus Lamb transgressed his only real asset was a TV network, founded by him in 1997 and watched almost entirely by fellow evangelicals. "[My wife] has no blame," he said of his extramarital affair to viewers of his daily *Celebration* telecast on December 2, 2010. "The other person doesn't have any blame. I don't even blame the devil. It's all on me." As for the alleged blackmailers who demanded $7.5 million to keep his affair quiet, Lamb reassured his audience, "Ladies and gentlemen, we're not going to take God's money and pay to keep from being humiliated."[76] Lamb's wife tearfully related how "[God] met me that day" when she learned of the affair, to which her husband repeatedly interjected "Praise the Lord" and then related how God had forgiven his sin. Not mentioned was a lawsuit filed two weeks earlier by three former employees who claimed Daystar funds helped pay for Lamb's trysts in various locations.[77] Yet despite it all, the biggest names in televangelism continued paying Daystar more than $70 million per year to purchase time on the network.[78]

## Popularity and Obscurity

The continuing avidity (to use an industry term) of the evangelical audience fragment for "Christian media" highlights three points. First, the audience for a given media genre can, even without direct interaction, form a community around their shared interpretation of that genre. Second, this phenomenon is not adequately accounted in current theorizing on audience fragmentation. And third, this community perspective is a key to understanding not only how the coverage of scandals has changed, but also how audience fragmentation may impact American public discourse in general.

Grasping the community perspective on media audiences begins by jettisoning the unhelpful distinction between "old" (broadcast) media and "new" (digital) media. These distinctions depend on a *social interaction* view in which different media are seen as simple conduits and evaluated against face-to-face communication. By contrast, the *social integration* view regards each medium as a context for audience members to share rituals and form communities. Fans of radio talker Rush Limbaugh, for example, share in his ritual sarcasm; fans of TV talker Bill O'Reilly share in his ritual skewering of on-air guests; fans of classic TV share in the shows' ritual theme songs; fans of the detective genre share in the ritual "whodunit" conclusion; and fans of televangelism share in its ritual worship. A leading framework for media ethnographers to analyze the meanings audiences give to media content is Thomas R. Lindlof's[79] concept of the "interpretive community." He theorized that the meaning of a media "text" (written or oral) is not a purely idiosyncratic and individual construction since people are situated in communities that share rules of interpretation. An interpretive community first arises through members' shared interpretation of the same media content. Communal interpretation then creates a "text" that gives the reading "historical" validity and thus imparts a stabilizing and directing influence on the community. Next, this validated reading becomes a referent for members' social actions within the interpretive community. Elsewhere I have demonstrated how American evangelicals have, even without direct interaction, been knit into an interpretive community—in fact, a social movement—through their consumption of religious media and its shared media rituals.[80]

This communal perspective is missing from the three paradigms, described earlier, for theorizing about audience fragmentation. To summarize, the "media-centric" paradigm charts the number of media outlets, quantifies their respective audiences, and arranges them from most to least popular. The "user-centric" paradigm portrays consumption patterns (e.g., time-spent-viewing) of the average media user. And the "audience-centric" paradigm measures audience overlap among media outlets, thus gauging how "public attention is dispersed across the media environment"[81] and identifying where that attention is focused. Each paradigm offers a valuable perspective on audience fragmentation, yet each is focused quantitatively on *individual* media use: how many users view a given outlet (media-centric view), in what quantities users consume their media choices (user-centric view), and what outlets are most frequently duplicated by media users (audience-centric view). Missing is a "community-centric" paradigm. Such a view would go beyond the quantitative observation that, for example, evangelicals not only consume religious media but also view mainstream media in proportions similar to their non-evangelical neighbors. Ultimately, a community-centric approach would explore how evangelicals' avidity for religious media is *qualitatively* different than other media they consume, since the genre provides them a basis for an interpretive community with its own codes for social action.

This phenomenon is not new. The evangelical interpretive community has demonstrated remarkable stability since the late nineteenth century, sustained first through mass newsprint and then via broadcast media.[82] What is new in the digital era is the relegation of religion—and of science, academia, literature, the arts, and many other fields—to niche media, so that their discourses no longer overlap with popular media. In the media universe of 30 years ago, the scandals of the televangelists were *American* scandals. Evangelical viewers knew all the salacious details and so did the rest of America. In today's media universe, evangelicals follow scandals such as the Duggar revelations that capture the rest of America, but it no longer works in reverse. The rest of America is no longer aware of scandals involving preachers—or scientists, or academicians, or authors, or artists. For that matter, few younger Americans have ever viewed a sport fishing tournament, a professional bowling match, or a master chess championship—all activities that once received regular network television coverage but now are accessible only via cable's Outdoor Channel and YouTube's BowlTV and Chess Network. The result is not a "massively parallel culture"[83] but a "winner-take-all"[84] media universe in which a cultural mainstream still holds, but the discourses of non-mainstream audience communities are increasingly ghettoized.

A generation ago, audiences had far fewer choices. But because media providers programmed "a little something for everyone," viewers were almost forcibly exposed to a wide range of discourses. Having to hear the sins of Oral Roberts, Jim Bakker, and Jimmy Swaggart was the price viewers paid. Now in a digital world of almost infinite user choice, selective exposure is the rule. Therein lay the paradox: More choices may result in the average media consumer being exposed to fewer discourses. If the scandal over Josh Duggar caters more to popular interest, so be it. Audiences now have in their hands the power to follow the popular scandal *du jour* in innumerable ways. Meanwhile, the transgressions of Marcus Lamb, Ted Haggard, Mark Driscoll, Tullian Tchividjian, and other Bible-quoting preachers can be safely screened out— along with many other inconvenient voices that need no longer concern us.

## NOTES

1. CBN News, "Daystar Founder's Affair: 'Caught Up' in Success?" December, 2010. http://www.cbn.com/cbnnews/us/2010/December/DayStar-Network-Founder-Admits-Extramarital-Affair-/.
2. Tim Brooks and Earle F. Marsh, *The Complete Directory to Prime Time Network and Cable TV Shows, 1946–present,* (New York, NY: Ballantine Books, 2009).
3. Christopher H. Sterling and John M. Kittross, *Stay Tuned: A History of American Broadcasting,* (Mahwah, NJ: Lawrence Erlbaum, 2002).
4. J. Gordon Melton, Phillip Charles Lucas, and Jon R. Stone, eds. *Prime-Time Religion: An Encyclopedia of Religious Broadcasting,* (Phoenix, AZ: Oryx, 1997).
5. Daystar Television Network. *About Daystar Television Network,* 2015. http://www.daystar.com/about.
6. National Cable and Telecommunications Act, "Cable's Story," 2015. https://www.ncta.com/who-we-are/our-story.
7. James G. Webster, "Beneath the Veneer of Fragmentation: Television Audience Polarization in a Multichannel World," *Journal of Communication* 55 (2005), 366–382.
8. James G. Webster, "Beneath the Veneer of Fragmentation: Television Audience Polarization in a Multichannel World."
9. Rick Kissell, "TLC's '19 Kids and Counting' Returns with Series-High Rating," *Variety,* September 4, 2014. http://variety.com/2014/tv/news/tlc-19-kids-and-counting series-high-rating-1201298033.
10. Rick Kissell, "TLC's '19 Kids and Counting' Hits Series High Tuesday with Wedding Episode," *Variety,* October 29, 2014. http://variety.com/2014/tv/Ratings/tlcs-19-kids-counting-hits-series-high-tuesday-with-wedding-episode-1201342715.
11. James G. Webster and Thomas B. Ksiazek, "The Dynamics of Audience Fragmentation: Public Attention in an Age of Digital Media," *Journal of Communication* 62, no. 1 (2012): 39–56.
12. Mark Ward Sr., "Introduction." In *The Electronic Church in the Digital Age: Cultural Impacts of Evangelical Mass Media, Vol. 1.* ed. Mark Ward Sr. (Santa Barbara, CA: Praeger, 2016): 17–27.

13. Sterling and Kittross, *Stay Tuned: A History of American Broadcasting*.
14. National Cable and Telecommunications Association. *Cable's Story*.
15. Sterling and Kittross, *Stay Tuned: A History of American Broadcasting*.
16. Carrie Heeter, "Program Selection with Abundance of Choice," *Human Communication Research* 12 (1985): 126–152; Dean M. Krugman and Roland T. Rust, "The Impact of Cable Penetration on Network Viewing," *Journal of Advertising Research* 27 (1987): 9–13; Dean M. Krugman and Roland T. Rust, "The Impact of Cable and VCR Penetration on Network Viewing: Assessing the Decade," *Journal of Advertising Research* (1993): 66–74; Carolyn A. Lin, "Modeling the Gratification-Seeking Process of Television Viewing," *Human Communication Research* 20 (1993): 224–244; Carolyn A. Lin, "Audience Fragmentation in a Competitive Video Marketplace," *Journal of Advertising Research* 34, no. 6 (1994): 30–39; James G. Webster, "The Impact of Cable and Pay Cable Television on Local Station Audiences," *Journal of Broadcasting and Electronic Media* 27(1983): 119–126; James G. Webster. "Audience Behavior in the New Media Environment," *Journal of Communication* 36(1986): 77–91.
17. Lucy L. Henke and Thomas R. Donohue, "Functional Displacement of Traditional TV Viewing by VCR Owners," *Journal of Advertising Research* 29, no. 2 (1989): 18–23; Lin, "Profile: The Functions of the VCR in the Home Leisure Environment."
18. Carrie Heeter and Bradley S. Greenberg, "Profiling the Zappers," *Journal of Advertising Research*, 25 (1985): 15–19.
19. J. Michael Sproule, "Progressive Propaganda Critics and the Magic Bullet Myth," *Critical Studies in Media Communication* 6 (1989): 225–246.
20. Edward L. Bernays, *Propaganda*, (New York, NY: Liveright, 1928), 47.
21. Elihu Katz. "Communications Research Since Lazarsfeld," *Public Opinion Quarterly*, 51 (1987): S25–S45.
22. Paul F. Lazarsfeld, Bernard Berelson and Hazel Gaudet. *The People's Choice*, (New York, NY: Duell, Sloan, and Pearce, 1944).
23. Wilbur L. Schramm, "How Communication Works," in *The Process and Effects of Mass Communication*, ed. Wilbur L. Schramm (Urbana, IL: University of Illinois Press, 1954): 3–26.
24. Elihu Katz, Jay G. Blumler, and Michael Gurevitch, "Uses and Gratifications Research," *Public Opinion Quarterly* 37 (1973): 509–523.
25. Katz, Blumler, Gurevitch, "Uses and Gratifications Research."
26. Gina Masullo Chen, "Tweet This: A Uses and Gratifications Perspective on How Active Twitter Use Gratifies a Need to Connect with Others," *Computers in Human Behavior* 27 (2011): 755–762; Alton Y. Chua, Dion H. Goh, and Chei S. Lee, "Mobile Content Contribution and Retrieval: An Exploratory Study Using the Uses and Gratifications Paradigm," *Information Processing and Management* 48 (2012): 13–22; Melanie Grellhesl and Narissra M. Punyanunt-Carter, "Using the Uses and Gratifications Theory to Understand Gratifications Sought Through Text Messaging Practices of Male and Female Undergraduate Students," *Computers in Human Behavior* 28 (2012): 2175–2181; Amy Hicks, Stephen Comp, Jeannie Horovitz, Madeline Hovarter, Maya Miki, and Jennifer L. Bevan. "Why People Use Yelp.com: An Exploration of Uses and Gratifications," *Computers in Human Behavior* 28 (2012): 2274–2279; Chian

Sian Lee and Long Ma, "News Sharing in Social Media: The Effect of Gratifications and Prior Experience," *Computers in Human Behavior* 28 (2012): 331–339; Louis Leung, "Generational Differences in Content Generation in Social Media: The Roles of the Gratifications Sought and of Narcissism," *Computers in Human Behavior* 29 (2013): 997–1006; Namsu Park, Kerk F. Kee, and Sebastián Valenzuela, "Being Immersed in Social Networking Environment: Facebook Groups, Uses and Gratifications, and Social Outcomes," *CyberPsychology and Behavior* 12 (2009): 729–733; John Raacke and Jennifer Bonds-Raacke, "MySpace and Facebook: Applying the Uses and Gratifications Theory to Exploring Friend-Networking Sites," *Cyberpsychology and Behavior* 11 (2008): 169–174; Thomas F. Stafford, Marla Royne Stafford, and Lawrence L. Schkade, "Determining Uses and Gratifications for the Internet," *Decision Sciences* 35 (2004): 259–288; Zheng Wang, John M. Tchernev, and Tyler Solloway, "A Dynamic Longitudinal Examination of Social Media Use, Needs, and Gratifications Among College Students," *Computers in Human Behavior* 28 (2012): 1829–1839; Jen-Her Wu, Shu-Ching Wang, and Ho-Huang Tsai, "Falling in Love With Online Games: The Uses and Gratifications Perspective," *Computers in Human Behavior* 26 (2010): 1862–1871.

27. Kim C. Schrøder, "Audience Semiotics, Interpretive Communities, and the 'Ethnographic Turn' in Media Research," *Media, Culture, and Society* 16 (1994): 337–347.

28. Thomas R. Lindlof, "Media Audiences as Interpretive Communities," *Communication Yearbook* 11 (1988): 81–107.

29. Joke Hermes and Cindy Stello, "Cultural Citizenship and Crime Fiction: Politics and the Interpretive Community," *European Journal of Cultural Studies* 3 (2000): 215–232.

30. Steven M. Kates, "Doing Brand and Subcultural Ethnographies: Developing the Interpretive Community Concept in Consumer Research," *Advances in Consumer Research* 29 (2002): 43; Steven M. Kates, "The Dynamics of Brand Legitimacy: An Interpretive Study in the Gay Men's Community," *Journal of Consumer Research* 31 (2004): 455–464.

31. Mark Ward Sr., "Give the Winds a Mighty Voice: Evangelical Culture as Radio Ecology," *Journal of Radio and Audio Media* 21 (2014): 115–133.

32. Anthony Leiserowitz, "Communicating the Risks of Global Warming: American Risk Perceptions, Affective Images, and Interpretive Communities," in *Creating a Climate for Change: Communicating Climate Change and Facilitating Social Change*, ed. Susanne C. Moster and Lisa Dillings (Cambridge, UK: Cambridge University Press, 2007): 44–63.

33. Cristina S. Beck, "You Make the Call: The Co-Creation of Media Text through Interaction in an Interpretive Community of 'Giants' Fans,'" *Electronic Journal of Communication* 1 (1995): n.p.

34. David Holmes, *Communication Theory: Media, Technology and Society*, (Thousand Oaks, CA: Sage, 2005): 147–148.

35. Nielsen Company, "Free to Move Between the Screens: The Cross-Platform Report," 2013. http://www.nielsen.com/content/dam/corporate/us/en/reports-downloads/2013%20Reports/Nielsen-March-2013-Cross-Platform-Report.pdf.

36. "The Personal News Cycle: How Americans Choose to Get Their News," *American Press Institute*, March 17, 2014, http://www.americanpressinstitute. org/publications/reports/survey-research/personal-news-cycle.

37. Cass R. Sunstein, *Republic.Com 2.0*, (Princeton, NJ: Princeton University Press, 2009).

38. Chris Anderson, *The Long Tail: Why the Future of Business is Selling Less of More* (New York, NY: Hyperion, 2006).

39. Anderson, *The Long Tail: Why the Future of Business is Selling Less of More*, 18.

40. Steven H. Chaffee and Miriam J. Metzger. "The End of Mass Communication?" *Mass Communication and Society* 4 (2001): 365–379; Richard Davis, *The Web of Politics: The Internet's Impact on the American Political System*, (New York, NY: Oxford University Press, 1999); John Havick, "The Impact of the Internet on a Television-Based Society," *Technology in Society* 22 (2000): 273–287; Shanto Iyengar and Kyu S. Hahn, "Red Media, Blue Media: Evidence of Ideological Selectivity in Media Use," *Journal of Communication* 59 (2009): 19–39; Paolo Mancini, "Media Fragmentation, Party System, and Democracy," *The International Journal of Press/Politics* 18 (2013): 43–60; Markus Prior, *Post-Broadcast Democracy*, (New York, NY: Cambridge University Press, 2007); David Tewksbury, "What Do Americans Really Want to Know? Tracking the Behavior of News Readers on the Internet," *Journal of Communication* 53 (2003): 694–710; David Tewksbury, "The Seeds of Audience Fragmentation: Specialization in the Use of Online News Sites," *Journal of Broadcasting & Electronic Media* 49 (2005): 332–348.

41. Barry A. Hollander, "Tuning Out or Tuning Elsewhere? Partisanship, Polarization, and Media Migration from 1998 to 2006," *Journalism & Mass Communication Quarterly* 85 (2008): 23–40.

42. Webster and Ksiazek, "The Dynamics of Audience Fragmentation: Public Attention in an Age of Digital Media."

43. Anthony Giddens, *The Constitution of Society: Outline of the Theory of Structuration*, (Oakland, CA: University of California Press, 1984).

44. Webster and Ksiazek, "The Dynamics of Audience Fragmentation: Public Attention in an Age of Digital Media."

45. Mark Ward Sr., *Air of Salvation: The Story of Christian Broadcasting*, (Grand Rapids, MI: Baker Books, 1994): 31.

46. Ward, "Give the Winds a Mighty Voice: Evangelical Culture as Radio Ecology."

47. Ward, "Give the Winds a Mighty Voice: Evangelical Culture as Radio Ecology."

48. Daniel P. Fuller, *Give the Winds a Mighty Voice: The Story of Charles E. Fuller.* (Waco, TX: Word, 1972).

49. Sterling and Kittross, *Stay Tuned: A History of American Broadcasting.*

50. Mark Ward Sr., "In Spirit *or* in Truth? The Great Evangelical Divide, from Analog to Digital," in *The Electronic Church in the Digital Age: Cultural Impacts of Evangelical Mass Media, Vol. 1*. ed. Mark Ward Sr., (Santa Barbara, CA: Praeger, 2016): 193–218.

51. Melton, Lucas and Stone, *Prime-Time Religion: An Encyclopedia of Religious Broadcasting.*

52. William F. Fore, "The Electronic Church," *Ministry*, January (1979): 4–7.

53. Jeffrey K. Hadden and Charles E. Swann. *Prime-Time Preachers: The Rising Power of Televangelism*, (Reading, MA: Addison-Wesley, 1988).
54. Jeffrey K. Hadden and Anson D. Shupe, "Televangelism, Power, and Politics on God's Frontier," (New York, NY: Henry Holt, 1988).
55. Ward, *Air of Salvation: The Story of Christian Broadcasting*.
56. Brooks and Marsh, *The Complete Directory to Prime Time Network and Cable TV Shows, 1946–Present*.
57. Sterling and Kittross, *Stay Tuned: A History of American Broadcasting*.
58. Ward, *Air of Salvation: The Story of Christian Broadcasting*.
59. Melton et al., *Prime-Time Religion: An Encyclopedia of Religious Broadcasting*; Ward, *Air of Salvation: The Story of Christian Broadcasting*.
60. Ward, *Air of Salvation: The Story of Christian Broadcasting*, 175.
61. Stephen Winzenburg, *TV Ministries Use of Air Time, Fall 2004*, 2005. http://faculty.gvc.edu/swinzenburg/tv_ministries_study.pdf.
62. Winzenburg, *TV Ministries Use of Air Time, Fall 2004*.
63. GEB America. *GEB America: Our Story*, 2015. http://www.gebamerica.com/geb-america-our-story.
64. The Jim Bakker Show. *Broadcast Listings*, 2015. http://jimbakkershow.com/watch-us-live/local-tv-station-broadcast-listings.
65. Jimmy Swaggart Ministries. *Sonlife Broadcasting Network*, 2015. http://sonlifetv.com/index.html.
66. Mark Ward Sr., "Major Networks and Personalities," in *The Electronic Church in the Digital Age: Cultural Impacts of Evangelical Mass Media, Vol. 1*. ed. Mark Ward Sr., (Santa Barbara, CA: Praeger, 2016): 255–284.
67. Trinity Broadcasting Network. *TBN Network Overview*, 2011. http://www.tbn.org/about/images/TBN_Networks_info.pdf.
68. Ward, "Major Networks and Personalities."
69. Ron Rodrigues, Jeff Green and Lauren Virshup. *Radio Today: How America Listens to Radio, 2013 Edition*, (Columbia, MD: Arbitron); Ward, "Major Networks and Personalities."
70. Salem Web Network, *Further Your Reach*, 2015. http://www.salemwebnetwork.com.
71. Ward, "Introduction."
72. Mark Ward Sr., "Consolidating the Gospel: The Impact of the 1996 Telecommunications Act on Religious Radio Ownership," *Journal of Media and Religion* 11 (2012): 11–30; Mark Ward Sr., "Dark Preachers: The Impact of Radio Consolidation on Independent Religious Syndicators," *Journal of Media and Religion* 8 (2009): 79–96.
73. Matthew C. Moen, "From Revolution to Evolution: The Changing Nature of the Christian Right," *Sociology of Religion* 55 (1994): 345–357.
74. Molly Worthen, *Apostles of Reason: The Crisis of Authority in American Evangelicalism*, (New York, NY: Oxford University Press, 2013): 256.
75. Jim Y. Trammell, "Jesus? There's an App for That! Tablet Media in the 'New' Electronic Church," in *The Electronic Church in the Digital Age: Cultural Impacts of Evangelical Mass Media*, ed. Mark Ward Sr., (Santa Barbara, CA: Praeger, 2016): 219–237.
76. CBN News, "Daystar Founder's Affair: 'Caught Up' in Success?"

77. "Multi-Millionaire U.S. Evangelist Confesses on His Own TV Network to Cheating on Wife After Being Blackmailed," *Daily Mail*, 2010. http://www.dailymail.co.uk/news/article-1335373/U-S-evangelist-Marcus-Lamb-confesses-cheating-wife-blackmailed.html.
78. CBN News, "Daystar Founder's Affair: 'Caught Up' in Success?"
79. Thomas R. Lindlof, "Interpretive Community: An Approach to Media and Religion," *Journal of Media and Religion* 1 (2002): 61–74.
80. Ward, "Give the Winds a Mighty Voice: Evangelical Culture as Radio Ecology."
81. Webster and Ksiazek, "The Dynamics of Audience Fragmentation: Public Attention in an Age of Digital Media."
82. Ward, "Give the Winds a Mighty Voice: Evangelical Culture as Radio Ecology."
83. Anderson. *The Long Tail: Why the Future of Business is Selling Less of More.*
84. Robert H. Frank and Philip J. Cook, *The Winner-take-all Society: Why the Few at the Top Get so Much More Than the Rest of Us*, (New York, NY: Penguin, 1995).

# CHAPTER 6

# Imagining the Monica Lewinsky Scandal on Social Media

*David Dahl*

Patient Zero, she calls herself.

Monica Lewinsky casts herself as the first victim of the Internet era, a now 43-year-old woman who did not seek celebrity, but whose name nonetheless remains universally recognized two decades after her affair with Bill Clinton nearly brought down his presidency.

"My name is Monica Lewinsky. Though I have often been advised to change it, or asked why on earth I haven't," Lewinsky told Forbes' "30 under 30" summit in Philadelphia in October 2014.[1]

Clinton survived the scandal, and his wife is at this writing running for the presidency of the US. But the mention of Lewinsky's name—imagine her making a dinner reservation—triggers flashbacks to one of the most sordid chapters in US politics.

The affair began in November 1995, by Lewinsky's account. Bill Clinton's presidency was a maddening mix of brilliance, scandals, and missteps that included a failed attempt to enact health care reform. He began flirting with a young intern in his office during a government shutdown. It progressed to a series of sexual encounters, which became public via a complicated series of events and spilled out early on the morning of January 18, 1998, on a gossip website called the Drudge Report.

"At the last minute, at 6 p.m. on Saturday evening, NEWSWEEK magazine killed a story that was destined to shake official Washington to its foundation: A White House intern carried on a sexual affair with the President of the United States!" the Drudge Report said.[2]

Lewinsky later recalled that moment: "Overnight I went from being a completely private figure to a publicly humiliated one," she told an October 2014

D. Dahl (✉)
The Boston Globe, Boston, MA, USA

H. Mandell, G.M. Chen (eds.), *Scandal in a Digital Age*,
DOI 10.1057/978-1-137-59545-4_6

Forbes conference in Philadelphia. "I was Patient Zero, the first person to have their reputation completely destroyed worldwide via the Internet."[3]

The report on the Drudge site opened a floodgate of coverage from the mainstream media, starting with a front-page story in *The Washington Post* on January 21. Normally staid newspapers like *The New York Times* described sex scenes that took place in a small office off the Oval Office. Reporters found themselves both disgusted by the coverage of a matter so private and egged on by the competitive climate and public intrigue. Republicans pushed the story, moving the case to an eventual impeachment in the House and an acquittal in the Senate. It was not about sex, they said. It was about lying under oath.

In truth, it was about both, and more. Courtesy of Independent Prosecutor Kenneth Starr's detailed report, the public learned more about the president's intimate encounters than it ever imagined. Clinton lied to the public, obfuscated in a sworn deposition and, the evidence suggests, obstructed justice.

But beyond sex and lying, the 13-month drama was about power: Republicans, especially those in the House, thought they had the goods to forever cripple their nemesis. But once they realized the public was not with them, it was too late. The Republican Party lost five seats in the House in the 1998 midterm elections, the first time since the Civil War that the president's party picked up seats in the sixth year of his term.[4] In February 1999, the Senate declined to convict Clinton of the impeachment charges.[5]

The media landscape at the time included two relatively new players: talk radio, generally dominated by conservatives united by their hatred of the Clintons, and cable television news, freshly emboldened by its successful round-the-clock coverage of the O.J. Simpson trial.

Enter another actor: the Internet. At the time, Matt Drudge's site was an unattractive collection of links to other websites, plus some individual reporting. His "scoop" disclosing the Clinton-Lewinsky affair was in reality a scoop about a scoop—*Newsweek*'s Michael Isikoff had the story of their affair but was unable to persuade his editors to publish it.

Isikoff and his editors would later say that they felt they did not have enough corroboration, including sufficient confirmation that Democratic powerbroker Vernon Jordan had asked Lewinsky to lie under oath in an ongoing investigation of the matter. Isikoff and his colleagues had listened to secretly recorded tapes of Lewinsky discussing the man she called "the big creep," and a *Newsweek* reporter had confirmed that Attorney General Janet Reno had asked a panel of judges to expand the purview of Kenneth Starr's ongoing investigation to include the Lewinsky affair. But the tapes were vague, the affair implied but not confirmed.

After intense discussions on a Saturday in January 1998, the deadline day for the newsweekly, *Newsweek* editors decided not to publish.

"There are times it's just not worth being first," Isikoff later quoted Washington Bureau Chief Ann McDaniel as saying during their deliberations. "Sometimes, it's just not the right thing to do."[6]

Isikoff notified his sources that the story would not go into print. Drudge disclosed the tale of *Newsweek*'s unpublished scoop hours later.

At that time, there was no Twitter, no Facebook, and no social media. Fax machines were common in offices and used daily, not the dormant artifacts of today. Email was available, but not nearly the overwhelming presence it became. *Newsweek* had no website of its own; it posted its stories on AOL and, in this case, on WashingtonPost.com.[7]

Nonetheless, the story took off, with lurid sex details in the news, and coverage of the Clinton–Lewinsky scandal was ubiquitous, in newspapers, television, and radio. In one famous instance, Lewinsky's lawyer, William H. Ginsburg, appeared on all five Sunday talk shows on a single day. (That feat is now known as a "Full Ginsburg.")

Monica Lewinsky's name appeared in 724 *New York Times* articles in 1998, according to the Chronicle search tool on the *Times*' site. The phrase "oral sex" appeared 162 times, more than any year before or since. "Intern" appeared 857 times that year, again setting a record.[8]

In those words comes evidence that a political sex scandal—a subject that many reporters were reluctant to explore—had been brought into the mainstream.

Some reporters were uncomfortable with covering extramarital affairs—a discomfort Clinton and his allies used as leverage to argue that Starr was out of control and violating the president's privacy—but the truth is it was increasingly common to publish stories about sex and harassment.

In the decade or so before the Clinton–Lewinsky scandal, the media had covered Gary Hart's encounter with a model, dooming his presidential aspirations, and reported on allegations of sexual harassment against Supreme Court nominee Clarence Thomas, disclosures that did not derail his nomination.

But the Clinton–Lewinsky episode was something else entirely. It was explicit—via accounts in Starr's report; it confirmed other earlier reports about Clinton's behavior; it involved lying, under oath, and encouraging others to do so; and the focus was the highest-ranking target of all, the President of the USA.

My own experience reflected the approach of a typical regional reporter in Washington. The day the scandal broke in *The Washington Post*, I was in Richmond, Virginia, to look up a document for a colleague. In the coming months, as the Clinton–Lewinsky scandal played out, I would be torn between covering the dominant story in Washington and my hope to break new ground on other important, but less salacious, stories, including mismanagement and patient deaths at the Department of Veterans Affairs and the misdeeds of a local congresswoman.

But, like most reporters in Washington at that time, I would be drawn back into covering the Clinton–Lewinsky scandal and, ultimately, the impeachment proceedings. The process of impeachment itself—a rarity in US history—was covered at every turn, keeping the details of the scandal before the public to the point of saturation. But non-traditional media continued to broaden the parameters of the story as well.

Larry Flynt, the publisher of *Hustler Magazine*, offered $1 million to anyone who would provide information on politicians' affairs to highlight the hypocrisy of their pursuit of Clinton. One victim was Congressman Bob Livingston, who was in line to replace Newt Gingrich as speaker of the House, but who stepped down because it appeared *Hustler* was about to report he had had an affair.

The involvement of Drudge and *Hustler* foreshadowed many of the dynamics present today. Twitter, digital media, and any number of blogs, websites, and other media outlets increase the competition and speed up the news cycle. They puts pressure on editors to hit the publish button and increase the likelihood of error.

But then, as now, most editors of legitimate publications hew to the same basic scruples—is it true, and not just true, but provably true? Is it fair? Is it relevant?

Indeed, the *Newsweek* editors made a defensible call in holding the Clinton–Lewinsky story back in 1998. They were not sure they had enough confirmation. Sure, it was painful for Isikoff and his colleagues to see others publish first, just days later, but the adage that it is better to be right than first was the controlling approach then and now in newsrooms.

Had the scandal broken in the age of Twitter, there would have been more coverage, but it is doubtful that the outcome would have changed.

In the digital era, one could imagine broader distribution of the parts of the Starr Report, which detailed the Clinton–Lewinsky intimacies and hinted at other liaisons the president may have had. Members of the public, the media, and political operatives no doubt would be tweeting about various passages of the report, creating even more of a firestorm than there already was.

And even if reporters, partisans, and members of the public were tweeting snippets of the liaisons in the Starr Report, we can also imagine Clinton's partisans responding in kind, battling to control the news cycle in the same way they dispatched partisans to fight it out on CNN and regular talk shows in the 1990s.

But more distribution would not have been a different result.

At that time, there was a sizable portion of the public that thought the coverage of the affair was too much, too personal, too political. Republicans faced a considerable backlash. The presence of the story on Twitter and Facebook would have divided the nation further, into pro and anti camps, but would have added to the scandal fatigue. Clinton's political skills—and the Republicans' lack thereof—kept him alive then, and would so in an era of social media.

The public is fundamentally wise and discerning—able to sort out the important and ignore the frivolous. Democracy self-corrects. It thrives on information, but that does not mean every new bit of information is as important as the last. The public was clearly fatigued by the Clinton saga, but it had also made its judgment: This was not a high crime or misdemeanor that merited the president's ouster from the White House.

In the years since, the sex scandals have continued, and the culture has become much more sexually explicit. Many scandals—Anthony Weiner, Gary Hart, Mark Sanford—have had little staying power, or resulted in a very quick outcome, such as Eliot Spitzer's quick departure.

While Lewinsky portrays herself as a victim of the Internet, Isikoff, the *Post*, ABC News, and others were pursuing the story of Starr's investigation into Clinton's affair. Non-traditional media—Drudge and *Hustler* being two examples—may have encouraged the overall scandal stories, but mainstream publications would have broken many of the stories even if Drudge had not posted the first inkling of scandal.

Yet, her argument does hold up in one aspect: the damaging staying power of the Internet. In reviewing the history, I was reminded of how angry and exasperated Clinton left the country, how risky Clinton's behavior was, how much of his potential was unrealized, and how many victims he left behind.

"[T]he reality that Clinton never seemed to deal with was that his risk was not his alone; that his actions had consequences not just for himself and his family and friends but also for millions of people, some who believed in him, some who cared about his policies, some who despised his enemies and did not want them to prevail, some who just wanted to think positively about human nature," Clinton biographer David Maraniss wrote.[9]

One left in his wake was Lewinsky. She has struggled with her career, appeared for a time as a Jenny Craig spokeswoman, created a line of handbags, appeared on a dating show, and more recently resurfaced to turn the spotlight on cyber-bullying.

"The experience of shame and humiliation online is different than offline. There is no way to wrap your mind around where the humiliation ends—there are no borders," she told the Forbes conference.[10]

Other women involved in political sex scandals that came after hers have faded. Yet her name remains recognizable—plummeting in popularity by parents choosing names for their babies after the scandal[11]—and she carries an unwanted celebrity largely because of who her partner was in the scandal and the extraordinary drama that resulted in Congress. But in the years since, the culture has become more explicit, the public less apt to obsess over a politician's sexual life, and more important crises have captured our attention.

## NOTES

1. Clare O'Connor, "Full Transcript: Monica Lewinsky Speaks Out on Ending Online Abuse," *Forbes*, October 20, 2014, http://www.forbes.com/sites/clareoconnor/2014/10/20/full-transcript-monica-lewinsky-speaks-out-on-ending-online-abuse/1/.
2. Matt Drudge, "Blockbuster Report: 23-Year-Old, Former White House Intern, Sex Relationship with President," *The Drudge Report*, January 17, 1998, http://www.drudgereportarchives.com/data/2002/01/17/20020117_175502_ml.htm.

3. O'Connor, "Full Transcript," http://www.forbes.com/sites/clareoconnor/2014/10/20/full-transcript-monica-lewinsky-speaks-out-on-ending-online-abuse/1/.
4. Louis Jacobson, "Do Presidents Always Get 'Shellacked' in Midterm Elections?," *Politifact*, September 7, 2015, http://www.politifact.com/truth-o-meter/statements/2010/sep/07/mary-jordan/do-presidents-always-get-shellacked-midterm-electi/.
5. Drudge, "Blockbuster Report."
6. Michael Isikoff, *Uncovering Clinton: A Reporter's Story*, (New York: Three Rivers Press, 1999), 335.
7. Alicia C. Shepard, "A Scandal Unfolds," *American Journalism Review*, March 1998, http://ajrarchive.org/article.asp?rel=ajrshepard2_mar98.html.
8. *Chronicle: Visualizing Language Usage in New York Times News Coverage Throughout Its History*, http://chronicle.nytlabs.com/.
9. David Maraniss, *The Clinton Enigma: A Four and a Half Minute Speech Reveals This President's Entire Life*, (New York: Simon & Schuster, 1998), 11.
10. Ruth Marcus, "A Call to Action from Patient Zero Monica Lewinsky," *The Washington Post*, October 21, 2014, https://www.washingtonpost.com/opinions/ruth-marcus-patient-zero-monica-lewinsky-goes-public-against-cyberbullying/2014/10/21/593a20fc-5951-11e4-b812-38518ae74c67_story.html.
11. "Monica" was the 81st most popular name for baby girls in 1996 and the 79th most popular in 1997. The name fell to 105 in 1998, the year the scandal broke, and to 151 in 1999, the year of Clinton's impeachment trial, and has fallen in every year since, according to "Popular Baby Names," *Social Security Online*, http://www.ssa.gov/cgi-bin/babyname.cgi.

# PART II

# When Privates Go Public

# CHAPTER 7

# Scandal in the Age of Sexting

*Joshua Gamson*

The first major scandals with "sexting" storylines erupted in 2009, three years before the term made its way into the Merriam-Webster dictionary ("the sending of sexually explicit messages or images by cell phone") and a few years after the term first appeared in print. By then, forms of technologically based sexual encounters—phone sex, erotic photos exchanged by e-mail—had perhaps come to seem clunky-sweet vestigial customs of the late twentieth century.

That sexting lent itself easily to scandal was not too surprising, since phone communication was, and still is, widely understood to be private. Like anything else people do in private, it could be made public, and like almost anything sexual people do, its public revelation would be likely to cause some sort of moral consternation, disapproval, or outrage. It was, and it has.

For the most part, sexting has taken its place in scandals less as a discrete scandalous behavior than as a gotcha mechanism, providing a record—granted, often an especially salacious one, given that sexting encourages loose-fingered fantasy texts and spontaneous exhibitionist genital photography—of an offline sexual relationship. That relationship, extramarital or kinky or non-heterosexual, is the scandalous activity. The story then triggered is an old one: of infidelity and disloyalty, of lying and evading detection, made scandalous by contrast to the role expectations of the person having the affair (for instance, the integrity many expect from public servants), the moral positions they have taken (for instance, advocating for the "traditional family"), or the public image the person has cultivated and profited from (for instance, being a clean-cut boy-next-door).

The 2009 Tiger Woods scandal, for example, began with a *National Enquirer* story claiming Woods was having a relationship with a woman who

J. Gamson (✉)
Sociology, University of San Francisco, San Francisco, CA, USA

H. Mandell, G.M. Chen (eds.), *Scandal in a Digital Age*,
DOI 10.1057/978-1-137-59545-4_7

was not his wife, after which several other women claimed to have had sexual encounters with him.[1] When some of these women later released explicit text messages allegedly between them and Woods, they were scandalous, for sure—spanking, and threesomes and golden showers, oh my!—but mainly side shows to the central cheating scandal. They included not just fantasy sex but practical planning for get-togethers; they were proof of ongoing sexual infidelity.[2] Similarly, in early 2010, *In Touch* magazine reported that actress Sandra Bullock's husband Jesse James was having an "affair with a model" ("The Ultimate Betrayal!") and offered their "steamy texts" as evidence.[3] In these sorts of sex scandals, sexting is the electronic lipstick on the collar, and penis pictures, as some commentators like to say, are the new "smoking gun."

In a couple of high-profile cases, however—that of quarterback Brett Favre and New York Congressman Anthony Weiner, the focal points of my discussion here[4]—sexting itself generated a scandal. No face-to-face meetings were alleged, no exchange of bodily fluids, no lipstick-stained collars (or semen-stained dresses) to be cleaned, no hiding of credit card receipts. In both cases, pictures of penises were sent by male public figures to women they had never met, and both involved text messaging, hard-core in one case and soft-core in the other. Both led to extensive media and public coverage, much of it jokey or shaming or both, and had serious career and personal consequences for the participants. They were real scandals about virtual sex.

As such, they appear to be a new kind of sex scandal. These early sexting scandals offer an opportunity to investigate what has and has not changed as sex scandals have entered an era in which surveillance is increasingly pervasive, virtual sex has become technologically accessible, and the revelation of "private" life has become a commonplace form of entertainment, such that "a desire to be watched and to watch others being watched pervades almost everything we do."[5] If scandal is understood as "the publicization of a transgression of a social norm,"[6] and the exposure of private life is increasingly normative, precisely what social norms do sexting scandals broadcast? If scandals can "reveal much about historically distinctive constructions of the public/private divide," what altered constructions might they uncover? These cases, I will argue, offer a snapshot of sex scandals in transition.

As I recount and analyze these scandals, I will suggest that one of their most significant characteristics is actually their familiarity. Despite its technological novelty and its elimination of the face-to-face aspect of sexual encounters, sexting was quite easily absorbed into existing sex scandal narratives. The structures that generate and sustain sex scandals have remained largely unchanged, and so does their storytelling. At the same time, though, new themes poke through: of the changes wrought by new media on the publicizing of private lives, and of the "new rules" of sexual life in the "Internet age." These sexting scandals serve to publicize both emerging sexual norms—and the disgrace visited upon those who have not learned them—and the increasingly troubled zone of "the private" in a world of sophisticated surveillance technologies.

## Brett Favre: "Grandfathers Shouldn't Sext"

The alleged behavior that landed quarterback Brett Favre in a sex scandal was quite mild by past sex scandal standards and, by the time it came to light, two years in the past. In August 2010, Deadspin, a tabloid-style sports website owned by Gawker Media, broke the story that in 2008, football star Favre allegedly sent text messages and penis pictures to a young, unmarried woman named Jenn Sterger, at the time a 24-year-old model, TV host, and "Gameday Host" for the New York Jets, the team Favre had recently joined. Favre was about 15 years older than Sterger, married, and by the time the story broke, a grandfather. According to Deadspin, Sterger had been the recipient of quite a few "athlete dong photos," and one person in particular "who was very into cell phone-donging her was none other than Brett Favre."[7]

The two had never met, although Favre had asked, through an intermediary, for her phone number. Sterger declined, but then received "strange, friendly messages" on her voicemail that appeared to be from Favre—the man never identified himself, but gave clues such as "new to the team" and "gray hair"—which she ignored. One night, the story went, she got "a picture on her phone which was so shocking that she just tossed it across the room. It was his dick. Brett Favre's dick." Multiple other photos followed. In one, Sterger reportedly told Deadspin, Favre—if indeed it was Favre—was masturbating while wearing a pair of Crocs.[8]

A few months after posting this rumor, Deadspin purchased the pictures, texts, and voicemails from a third party,[9] and the story was quickly picked up by tabloid papers like the *New York Post* and *Daily News.* Within a day, the NFL announced it was launching an investigation into possible "personal conduct violations" and sexual harassment, although Sterger herself was not filing any charges;[10] with the league's official investigation as a legitimate news peg, the story spread widely to non-tabloid media such as *The Washington Post*, ESPN, and *USA Today.* A few days later, a masseuse who had been hired by the Jets came forward, claiming that, also in 2008, Favre had sent a "seamy stream of phone calls, e-mails, and texts" about his "bad intentions."[11] Favre said very little publicly, aside from that he hated "if this has been a distraction" and just wanted to "keep focus on the game." Reports circulated, however, that in private, Favre had offered his teammates a "teary apology"[12]—a "sappy mea culpa," the *New York Post* called it[13]—for the distraction. "I need you guys to carry me tonight," Favre told them, according to an ESPN interview with kicker Ryan Longwell.[14]

Even as the NFL issued serious statements about its "workplace conduct training program" and the goal of making sure that everyone associated with the league "understand their responsibility and conduct themselves in a responsible fashion,"[15] and sports writers wondered how the scandal might affect his play,[16] Favre was the source of much public tittering. A few weeks into the scandal "Saturday Night Live" produced a spoof ad for Wrangler, one of several companies for which Favre had served as a highly paid endorser—among them, Remington rifles and Snapper lawn mowers—deploying his "prowess on the field, coupled with good ol' boy charm and grizzled stubble."[17] The "SNL" skit featured Jason Sudeikis as Favre, tossing a football with his buddies and touting the "all new Open Fly Jeans from Wrangler," pausing only to snap pictures of his manhood. "Why let zippers or buttons slow you down?" he asks, pixels hiding his crotch. "With Open Fly jeans, it's always out and camera ready.... Look, I put my pants on just like anyone else, one leg at a time. Then, I pull my penis out and sometimes I take a picture of it." He had become, the *Minneapolis Star Tribune* suggested, literally "laughable."[18]

Two weeks into the scandal, Sterger had hired a lawyer, who had complained that "her life's been turned upside down by this" but, despite losing nine pounds, was "doing her best to stay focused on work and being a 26-year-old woman."[19] Sterger eventually provided materials for the NFL's investigation, which reviewed substantial documents, heard hours of testimony, and used "high-tech forensic work to trace the electronic pathways and transmission of any photos or messages that might have been sent during communication between them."[20] In December, the league announced that "the forensic analysis could not establish that Favre sent the objectionable photographs to Sterger," and that the review had found no evidence that Favre and Sterger had ever met in person or that Sterger had engaged in any "inappropriate conduct." However, since Commissioner Roger Goodell had determined that "Favre was not candid in several respects during the investigation, resulting in a longer review and additional negative public attention for Favre, Sterger and the NFL," fined Favre $50,000 for "failure to cooperate."[21] ESPN noted that Favre, even while sitting out the next game due to post-concussion symptoms, earned that money back "over about three minutes of action."[22]

Favre, who had already retired once before and then returned to work, filed retirement papers a month after the investigation concluded. For her part, several months after the scandal subsided Sterger—who had been discovered as a college student in the stands at a Florida State football game, had posed for *Playboy* and *Maxim* and written for *Sports Illustrated*, and had gigs at ABC and Spike—took a job hosting kickboxing specials for Fuel TV. She appeared on *Good Morning America*, telling George Stephanopoulos she wanted "people to know me and to know that I'm not a gold digger and I'm not a home wrecker."[23] She then moved to "a quiet part" of Los Angeles where, *The New York Times* reported, she "landed a few small roles in movies" and a "steady boyfriend."[24]

The brouhaha may seem outsized in relation to the alleged sexual transgression, but that is not an unusual feature of sex scandals. What is perhaps more surprising is how, despite the novelty and virtuality of sexting, the Favre scandal narrative played out through quite old-fashioned, conventional scripts. Indeed, the basic elements of the case seemed to lend themselves quite easily to several stock storylines.

Occasionally, Favre was faulted for being "unfaithful" to his wife, Deanna, and commentators sometimes expressed sympathy for her presumed humiliation, but that was rare, perhaps because everyone involved agreed that Favre and Sterger had never met in person. Instead, many commentators, especially in the tabloid press, presented the scandal as the story of a dirty old man, an athlete past his prime, trying to win the ego-reinforcing attention of a young bimbo-who-might-also-be-a-gold-digger. Favre was the "gray-haired grid great" throwing "a Hail Mary pass to a comely young sideline reporter."[25] The "gridiron granddaddy"[26] sent "an embarrassing slew of steamy propositions and lewd photos;"[27] the man no longer "spry enough to play pro football"[28] fired "cringe-inducing," "pleading" messages and "snapshots of a penis" in a "ham-fisted bid to charm the brunette beauty."[29] In a sense, his fall from grace—and his fall from masculinity—had already taken place, and the scandal simply confirmed the decline.

In this version of the telling, Sterger was the "former Playboy pinup" and "almost-too-hot-for-TV hostess,"[30] a young Deanna Favre look-a-like whose "fake breasts" were her "only qualification to land a job with the Jets,"[31] a "sideline siren"[32] a "walking photo-op" who was "hell-bent on cashing in on her 15 seconds" of fame.[33] She was, as the female figure has been in many an earlier scandal,[34] the woman who took down a powerful man with her sexuality. Although she later fought back against the bimbo, fame-whore, and gold-digger images, Sterger also inadvertently played into this storyline. In an e-mail to Deadspin writer A.J. Daulerio, apparently printed against her objections, she wrote, "I don't roll that way. That way meaning old ... or married. Some big boobed hoes have morals and souls believe it or not." She referred to Favre, although she had not met him, as a "creepy douche."[35]

Sexting, which was rarely discussed in any detail in these stories, fit quite easily into this familiar narrative. The apparently unsolicited penis picture became the pathetic, creepy-douchey act of a flasher (dirty). Sexting, as a symbol of youth technoculture, became in Favre's apparently bumbling hands a marker of his distance from youth (old). As one British commentator sniffed, "Grandfathers shouldn't 'sext.'"[36]

Sex scandal stories begin as stories about individual sexual transgression, and then typically become stories of individual failings including hypocrisy, dishonesty, disloyalty, and risk-taking. As I have noted elsewhere, though, over time they also tend to "morph into institutional morality tales"[37] with lessons about the routine workings of institutions, including their routine pathologies that give rise to the scandalous behavior. The Favre case followed this blueprint, too. The story, even as it was also being told as a dirty-old-man tale, quickly became one about the NFL's handling of gender relations in the workplace, and about the gendered culture of sports more broadly; indeed, this is what justified the coverage of the scandal by more serious-minded news outlets. As one *Washington Post* columnist put it,[38] "If it boils down to the dalliances of a famous man, it's none of my business. But if it's more than that, if there's sexual harassment in the workplace, then the matter takes on an entirely different tone."

This frame did not in fact require engagement with the question of whether sexting constitutes a "dalliance" or whether cell phone communications between adults are the business of others. The genital pictures, voicemails, and text messages were relevant not as shocking sexual behaviors but as possible violations of workplace sexual norms, akin to in-person unsolicited advances or the creation of a hostile environment. For instance, a *USA Today* writer argued that the NFL had been given "the unwanted yet educational opportunity to remind its players ... that the locker room, playing field and team headquarters are a workplace. And that when women are there, either with a credential or a contract, they are there to work, and to be treated as such."[39] The NFL, in its public statements, essentially agreed, steering clear of questions of sexual morality altogether. They were "working hard" on their workplace training, Commissioner Roger Goodell said, which they expected to roll out "by the end of the season."[40] When the NFL's investigation concluded, Goodell announced that the $50,000 fine he had imposed on Favre, in fact, would help fund that training program.

Told this way, the story became one of the "boys' club" cultures of the NFL. Behaviors like those of which Favre was accused were more typical than not, protected by the other men in the club, and the notion that female workers are treated as respected equals required educational reminders and trainings. Sexting was notable not for its novelty, but for its similarity to other forms of boys-will-be-boys behavior, from cat-calling to locker-room towel snaps to the bros-before-hos code, that were endemic features of the male-dominated sports world. Indeed, when the NFL announced its findings and "slap on the wrist" fine,[41] it was this institutional culture, more than Favre's sexting, which came under fire. Sterger's lawyer, Joseph Conway, called the NFL's decision "an affront to all females" that showed "once again that, despite tough talk, the NFL remains the good old boys' league."[42] Sterger's father echoed: "Their decision is a complete travesty to women," he said, "and they are just treating him this way because he is the NFL's golden boy."[43]

Jenn Sterger appeared neither enraged nor surprised. Although she found Favre's electronic pursuit of her intimidating, she told *Good Morning America*, she never considered herself a victim and never wanted anything from Favre, not even an apology. "I knew what I was getting myself into working in sports, you know?" she said. "It's the boys' club."[44]

If the stories of the horny, ham-handed grandpa and the typical boys' club member had very little new in them, the Favre scandal coverage also included, if somewhat more quietly, a telling new theme: how new technology was changing the sports world. The distinctive element of the scandal, the sexting, in these stories symbolized a "new era" in sports characterized by entertainment criteria and the exposure of private behavior rather than athletic performance—of a new relationship, that is, between public and private selves.

This frame in part simply lamented changes in sports media characteristic of media industries more generally. For instance, a *USA Today* columnist, noting how quickly NFL-partnered television networks had "jumped on" the Favre story, argued that gone are "the days of sports media ignoring stories about the alleged personal scandals of athletes they cover";[45] a *Christian Science Monitor* writer added that "the story remains a testament to how sports is becoming as much 'Access Hollywood' as 'NFL Films.'"[46] *The Washington Post*'s Howard Kurtz[47] argued that sports figures' "private behavior has increasingly come under the media microscope," and that "in this TMZ era" tabloids run the show; "those of us in the so-called respectable press," he said, "had better get used to it." New technology has contributed to this shift, the argument went, by making it easier to catch and circulate private behavior for commercial entertainment purposes.

Favre, in these stories, was shown to embody these institutional changes—the media-driven erosion of public-private boundaries—perhaps because the mechanism of his fall was so new, so technological, and so literally about the exposure of private parts. Favre, a *USA Today* writer said, was "the perfect metaphor for the modern athlete": "Here's a quarterback who has weathered 289 consecutive starts, yet he gets undone by a cellphone? He's gone from problems with picks to woes with pictures."[48] A *Globe and Mail* writer argued similarly. Favre, he asserted, had been "celebrated as an everyman/superman," but then was undone by a path "more distinctly of the moment": by his cell phone pursuit of Sterger, herself "a creation of the Internet age," and by the Deadspin website, "a perfect example of how twenty-first-century culture feeds upon itself."[49] He had gone, a *National Post* columnist argued less charitably, from "the epitome of what we were told quarterbacks were supposed to be" to "a selfish, drama-loving diva," adept at "giving us something to laugh at," delivering entertainment suited to "an America now riveted by mindless manu-factured drama."[50,51]

Favre was caught, this narrative suggested, between the old media rules and the new media ones. A *USA Today* columnist captured this interpretation:

> Fifteen years ago in a world with no Deadspin and no TMZ, with no text messages and no cellphone cameras, [athletes'] personal transgressions—real and alleged—would have gone unnoticed, except perhaps for a few supermarket tabloid headlines.... [Tiger] Woods and Favre would have been like dozens, perhaps hundreds, of well-known professional athletes before them, living one life in public, another in private, and pulling it off with hardly anyone knowing, often for the entire length of their careers. Of course, men like Woods and Favre don't come from that world. They live in, and in fact have come to symbolize, another era. Someday, it will likely be viewed as the Internet era in sports, a time when athletes found out their extravagant salaries came with a price: their privacy. Only because they were so entitled did some not realize this until it was too late.... While Favre's reputation and future twist in the wind, we can imagine how he must be wishing, as Woods likely did, for a time when athletes got away with almost everything. It must sound downright sublime to live without the Internet, without cellphones, without anyone to catch you doing anything wrong.[52]

Favre's awkwardness with new communications technologies underlined his ties to an earlier, pre-Internet, pre-sexting era, and his slowness to discover the erosion of privacy for sports stars until it was too late.

On his HBO show *Real Time with Bill Maher*, comedian Bill Maher brought this "new rules" theme into momentary bloom, hinting at what would become a more flourishing public conversation in the soon-to-unfold Anthony Weiner scandal. "New Rule," he began. "If a woman rejects your first dozen advances, don't up the ante by sending her a picture of your penis." In a provocative rant, Maher tied the Favre scandal to the decline of white male political power, arguing that the Favre scandal "isn't about sports or sex or how necessary caller ID is—it's about how pathetic and clueless white American males have become." Central to his argument was the charge that some people, in particular men in power, are unaware that the rules of publicity and privacy, from which they used to benefit, have changed. The revelation of their inept sexting is the evidence. "Let's just dwell for one more moment on how stupid it is to forget that in 2010 when you text someone a picture of your genitals, you're not just sending it to that person, but to every person she has in her contacts, and then everyone on the planet who has access to the Internet," said Maher.

Maher noted that in one alleged texted picture, Favre was "pleasuring himself" on a bed while wearing pair of Crocs. "Is there any better metaphor for the sad state of America today," Maher asked, "than an over-the-hill white guy lazily masturbating in plastic shoes?"[53]

## ANTHONY WEINER: "TWITTER MAKES US STUPIDER"

Although Brett Favre got there first, Anthony Weiner was by far the most prominent pioneer in the still mostly uncharted territory of sexting-while-a-public-figure. If Favre's story was easily integrated into existing narratives, the Weiner scandal even more faithfully followed the well-trodden scandal script of "accusation or revelation, broadcast, denial and/or confession—and frequently, a comeback or attempted comeback."[54]

Weiner's sexual transgression was first alleged in late May 2011, when conservative blogger Andrew Breitbart published claims that Weiner sent a picture of his "underwear-clad erection"[55] to a 21-year-old "pretty Seattle coed"[56] via his Twitter account. Weiner denied that the crotch in question was his own, claiming his Twitter account had been hacked. "Tivo shot. FB hacked. Is my blender going to attack me next?" Weiner tweeted.[57] He threatened criminal action, then a few days later said he could not "say with certitude" if the picture was of him, and then disappeared for a few days.

When tabloids published explicit text conversations, allegedly between Weiner and several women he had met online, and Breitbart announced plans to publish more incriminating pictures, Weiner called a press conference. There, two weeks into the scandal, he confessed and apologized. "I made terrible mistakes," he said. The picture was of him, he said, and he had "exchanged messages and photos of an explicit nature with about six women over the past three years." He broke down. "I am deeply sorry for the pain this has caused my wife Huma, and my family, and my constituents, my friends, supporters, and staff.... I have done things that I deeply regret ... I am deeply sorry ... I am deeply ashamed."[58]

Despite pressure from the Democratic Party to resign, Weiner said he would instead take a leave of absence and get professional treatment. However, the scandal continued unabated, with new half-naked photos that he took at the Congressional gym surfacing. Also new Facebook chats with a Vegas blackjack dealer published on Radar Online and in *The New York Post* ("your pussy still tight and wet for me baby?" and "I want to feel you cum with my fat cock in you," etc.);[59] new evidence of other "risqué online chats" and an image of "a man's erect penis" sent to another woman allegedly from a Weiner account;[60] and new wiener jokes emerging daily on late-night television and in headlines ("Weiner Roast," "Weiner's Pickle," "Hide the Weiner"). Finally, less than three weeks after the story broke, Weiner resigned.

And so, there it was, the familiar sex scandal arc.

A year later, Weiner entered the next common, if optional, scandal phases of reinvention and comeback. In July of 2012, *People* magazine ran a story about Weiner and his wife, Huma Abedin, accompanied by a photo of them and their 6-month-old baby. "Anthony Weiner: 'I Feel Like a Different Person,'" said the headline. He was now a "happy househusband," shampooing his kid's hair over the sink, doing the laundry while his wife, an aide to Secretary of State Hillary Clinton, continued her career with his support. It had been a painful time, Abedin said, but Weiner "has spent every day since then trying to be the best dad and husband he could be." It took a lot of work, she said, "but I want people to know we're a normal family."[61] The implication, of course, was that there were no more texts to strangers about tight pussy and fat cock and no more dick pictures.

The next April, *The New York Times Magazine* offered a lengthy profile of the couple as they "painstakingly pieced their private life together," moved through to the other side of the scandal and prepared to re-enter public life.[62] Weiner was rehabilitated. Six weeks later, he announced that he would be running for mayor of New York City. *The New York Times* noted his "surprising rebound from scandal" as he "vaulted to the front of the race for mayor."[63]

Weiner did not, as we know, become mayor of New York. Instead, the scandal cycle simply repeated itself. A gossip site called The Dirty revealed that Weiner, using the pseudonym Carlos Danger, had exchanged X-rated texts with a woman, and also sent her a photo of his penis—*after* his resignation from Congress and the birth of his child, while he was supposedly becoming a "different person" and working hard to repent for the actions for which he had professed to be deeply sorry, deeply ashamed, and deeply regretful. The woman, Sydney Leathers, also charged that Weiner had contacted her to ask her to delete the chats and pictures. Wiener/Weiner jokes were dusted off. Other mayoral candidates, and the New York chapter of the National Organization for Women, called for him to drop out of the campaign. *The New York Times* and *People* magazines turned against him.

He apologized again, with his wife at his side at a July 2013 news conference, and asked voters for a second chance. "Generally speaking, though," former Clinton official Chris Lehane told *The Washington Post*,[64] "you only get one bite at the apology apple." Indeed, Weiner's political career finally came to its end. (Fulfilling another common sex scandal plotline,[65] Ms. Leathers soon had breast augmentation surgery and filmed "a full-out porn flick" with "a Weiner look-alike."[66])

Revelation, cover-up, confession, salacious sexual details, late-night jokery, long-suffering wife standing uncomfortably by her man, resignation and fall, comeback, and fall again: The Weiner scandal story practically told itself.

The Weiner scandal was also a conventional sex scandal in its institutional storytelling. From the very first revelations, reporters and commentators, especially those in the non-tabloid press, treated the scandal as one of political gamesmanship—that is, as a story not just of individual immorality or stupidity, but one that revealed the normal operations of political institutions that give rise to and are affected by scandals.

*The New York Times*, for instance, suggested that the budding scandal was "an example of how easy it is for political rivals to harm each other's reputations."[67] Weiner's opening claim that he had been hacked fed directly into this narrative, as did the suspicions of the initial Twitter picture recipient, Genette Nicole Cordova, who told *The Washington Post* that she assumed it was an attempt at "defaming the Congressman and harassing his supporters."[68] The *Times* and others briefly focused on the partisan activities of Breitbart and the #bornfreecrew, "a small group of determined, self-described conservatives" who had been tracking Weiner online and warning young women about him.[69] This sort of storytelling suggested that the scandal revealed—was perhaps even generated by—the motivation to inflict damage on rivals endemic in political institutions.

Indeed, as the scandal unfolded, the routine machinations of politics, more than Weiner's sexual proclivities, quickly moved to center stage. House Democratic leaders, reports said, were in a "panic" over the "spectacle" and "circuslike story," which "exploded at a time when [Democrats] believed they had the Republican Party on the defensive over an unpopular Medicare proposal."[70] They launched an "orchestrated effort" to force his resignation,[71] were "exasperated" in their attempts to "persuade him he is damaging himself, his family and his party by remaining a member of the House."[72] They took the moral high road, calling his behavior "offensive,"[73] "indefensible,"[74] "bizarre and unacceptable."[75] They suggested that Weiner, as Rep. Nancy Pelosi magnanimously put it, needed professional help "without the pressures of being a member of Congress."[76]

In this narrative, Weiner's problem was not the cock shots but his political vulnerability. Because his "aggressive media presence and penchant for partisan bombast," a *Time* writer asserted,[77] "had ruffled feathers in the New York delegation and beyond, [Weiner] was left with few if any allies." Surviving a scandal, *The Washington Post* asserted, takes "a combination of personal resolve, crisis-management skills and the right political circumstances."[78] These sorts of stories suggested that had he managed to collect the loyal allies required for political survival, Weiner's sexting might have been embarrassing but not ruining.[79]

The normal routines of politics revealed by scandal were overtly, if unsurprisingly, central in the comeback phase as well. The high-profile *New York Times Magazine* piece, which was the centerpiece of Weiner's reemergence two years after he resigned from Congress but before he lost in the mayoral election, told the story as one of political strategies—of, as the article's title puts it, Weiner's "post-scandal playbook." Weiner and Abedin were the ultimate political couple; they met at a Democratic National Committee retreat, and both their personal lives and political fortunes were closely linked to the Clintons.[80] Weiner, with backup from Abedin, was engaged in strategic storytelling, the normal business of politics. The *People* magazine shoot from the year before, Jonathan Van Meter reported, had been calculated to beat the paparazzi at their own game, and the *Times Magazine* piece was itself a way to "give voters what they want—and gauge public reaction."[81]

When, not long after the publication of the *Times* magazine cover story the second Weiner sexting story emerged, very little coverage was devoted to sexual morality; there were plenty of eye-rolling jokes about the corny, racially charged Carlos Danger pseudonym, but the sexting itself was a stale joke. Instead, the focus was mainly on Weiner's failure as a politician. The revelation, *The New York Times* reported, "collides with the narrative Mr. Weiner has offered throughout his campaign, in which he has repeatedly suggested he has spent his time since leaving Congress rehabilitating himself and repairing his family relationships."[82] *People* ran a "Then and Now" comparison of Weiner's claims from the year before to the current situation, transforming its own earlier Mr. Mom profile into a politician's pack of lies.[83] "The latest revelations have, at a minimum," a *Washington Post* writer suggested, "damaged the remorse-and-redemption theme that fueled Weiner's mayoral bid."[84]

Thus, as in earlier scandals, the Weiner story became a reminder of the ordinary, if problematic, rituals and tactics characteristic of its institutional location. Weiner's sin was not just being a "pervy pol" or "lusty lawmaker," as the *Daily News* liked to call him.[85,86] His sexual transgressions served to emphasize his political conformity: There he was, performing "standard" contrition rituals, enlisting his wife in well-trodden damage control strategies, enacting plays from a political playbook, courting and testing voters, offering strategic narratives, and so on. Weiner might be lusty and pervy, but he fell, the story went, because of how bad he was at political performance.

Conventional as it turned out to be, it would be a mistake to conclude that the Weiner scandal was simply a repeat of earlier political sex scandal narratives. Running across and through these familiar elements was a new theme, muted in the Favre scandal coverage but now given fuller voice: that of a public figure felled by a technology whose power and workings he has not yet fully understood. Like Favre's, Weiner's story was, to a degree, a scandal *about* new media and the anxieties surrounding them. Hoisted on his own petard, Weiner became a symbol of the changing lines between real and virtual and public and private.

As with Favre, this theme was inflected by its institutional location. Social media were sometimes presented as particularly troubling to politicians, who were struggling to harness them for political gain. One danger, visible at the beginning of the scandal, was that social media could give political adversaries more potential ammunition with which to work. "As Democrats and Republicans embrace Twitter and other social media tools as a way to interact with their constituents and woo voters, many have discovered a downside to online communication: cyberstalkers who track and criticize their every move," wrote a *New York Times* columnist.[87] This was reasserted after the scandal, as well, when Weiner's attempts to lay low were thwarted, since in an "age when anyone with a smartphone can press a button and play gossip columnist, Mr. Weiner's movements have been tracked as if he were Lindsay Lohan or Paris Hilton."[88]

More commonly, however, the trouble reporters and commentators pointed to was that new media make it easier for politicians—and everyone else—to do stupid, risky things. The scandal, they suggested, revealed what one *Washington Post* writer called the New Idiocy. "New Idiocy," the writer[89] asserted, "is much easier and more mortifying than Old Idiocy. Before, sex scandals required leaving your chair. Now? All you have to do is surround yourself with cats and caption a photo unwisely, and a few weeks later all heck breaks loose." Weiner was not drunk or high, she continued, nor even "drunk with power," but was acting like a *typical* Twitter user. "Twitter makes us stupider than usual. 'I've placed personal information unwisely on the Internet' is another way of stating 'I am a human in the twenty-first century.'" Another *Washington Post* editorial writer argued similarly. "Tweeting is new-ish," she began, "and dangerous as a loaded pistol at a brawl." What happened to Weiner, she suggested, could have happened to "anyone who snaps, tweets, or texts, especially to young people who have grown up in this share-all world of Facebook, for whom 'friend' is a verb and relationships are often anonymous and virtual."[90] That is, Weiner was not deviant but normal, one of us, a somewhat desperate foreigner in the new media land of "young people," inadvertently revealing a culture he had not mastered.

Weiner thus symbolized not just new ways to be "stupid," but also a new set of rules in a media environment in which surveillance should be assumed, and pretty much every communication should be considered public. He was routinely portrayed, for instance, as an avid social media user with a novice's understanding of the new rules. Many reporters noted that Weiner was "an adept user of new media"[91] and a "technophile" who "has clearly considered the role of Twitter in honing his public image," making fun of Sarah Palin, Michelle Bachman, and others in a "strikingly punchy and personal" style.[92] Yet, as *The New York Times* put it, "Twitter trouble found Mr. Weiner in an unexpected way." *Washington Post* columnist Eugene Robinson[93] captured the new-rules argument:

> For all his dazzling smarts, for all his New York savvy, Weiner was both ignorant and naïve about the Internet. There are certain things about the cyberworld, and about human nature, that anyone tempted to make a hobby of "sexting" really

ought to know. First is the fact that the Internet is not, repeat not, a private space. It is essentially a public realm in which it is difficult, if not impossible, to be active yet remain unobserved ... Weiner also was apparently unaware that the Internet never forgets... Weiner ignored the fact that a person known only as a "friend" on Facebook, or someone to "follow" on Twitter, is still basically a stranger.

Noting that Weiner's "transgression involved sexual fantasy, not sexual fact," Robinson—like most others making this argument—condemned it nonetheless as an imposition akin to being "a flasher in a raincoat," and "seriously, irredeemably creepy." (Nowhere in the Weiner scandal coverage can you find the suggestion that sexting might be considered pleasurable, safe, and consensual sex play.) The larger point, though, was that Weiner's mistake was not so much sexting as sexting *naïvely*, mistaking the cyberworld for a private one.

Weiner's story, this line of reasoning went, revealed something uncommonly "creepy" about Weiner, but more than that, it revealed a confusion about boundaries that was not at all uncommon. As another commentator put it, "We are dealing with the gray space where fidelity meets Facebook and with the boundary between our 'real' lives and our online lives, which is constantly being pushed, and never where you expect it." The confusion, she suggested, "comes when we mistake people for the shorthand, social-networked versions of themselves," when we mistake a Facebook friend for an actual one, a "politically charged hashtag" for activism, and sexting for sex.[94]

Weiner's case, then, came to publicize these confusions. As journalist Joann Wypijewski[95] insightfully wrote at the time, the media were of course "using sex to sell papers and ads" but also "to channel the anxieties of the age" about the "cesspool" of politics and even more about life in the "private-public Wild West." The fact that the sex involved "no contact, no fluids, no baby, no payment, no strings," the fact it was "America's first full-out political techno-sex scandal," is exactly what made the Weiner scandal so compelling as scandal. It gave form to the anxiety that, "for all the grown-ups' professed sophistication," they could neither confidently discern nor successfully follow the new rules of the virtual world.

## Conclusion

In many ways, the Favre and Weiner scandals—the first major American sexting scandals—serve as powerful reminders of the strength of media storytelling genres. Despite the newness of the alleged moral transgression each involved, the narratives proceeded largely according to existing scripts. The men were treated quite similarly to the long line of male scandal figures who came before them, as violators of informal norms surrounding sexual "decency" and formal codes of conduct, and as national jokes: They were publicly judged, tried, and punished. The women, too, were central-casting familiar: long-suffering, humiliated wives standing by their men, innocent victims of powerful men or fame- and wealth-seeking manipulators—or both.

The newness of this particular sexual behavior, especially the absence of any sexual contact, was quite easily subsumed into these familiar storylines. The institutional stories, too, developed as scandals have typically done, as the same act was mobilized to illustrate the pathologies of institutional settings that gave rise to it—the masculinist boys' club of professional sports, the calculated gamesmanship of professional politics.

In these ways, it seems the more things change the more they stay the same. This is a useful reminder not to overestimate how much technological change and the rise of surveillance culture has transformed media storytelling. That should not be surprising. After all, sex scandals do not bubble up from below but are created by institutional actors in interaction with media organizations. Sex scandals take the narrative form they do, wedging the twenty-first-century phenomenon of sexting into twentieth-century scandal narrative molds, because they are shaped by the relatively stable interests of institutional actors. The media terrain has certainly shifted as journalism has undergone "tabloidization,"[96] such that the stuff of scandal (personal lives, rumor, spectacle) has become more widely publicized; but the structures of the institutions in which scandals emerge—of sports and political industries, for instance—and the interests of the actors within them have changed very little.

Still, as we saw, the media narratives through which the Favre and Weiner sex scandals unfolded—shaped, of course, by their different institutional environments—also gave rise to some new media frames.[97] The Favre media coverage, for instance, began to register changes in the media environment itself. After all, the scandal was told as a story of how sports journalists had become supplicants to—rather than prestigious superiors of—tabloid journalism. The Favre scandal became an illustration of sports in the "Internet age," and Favre a symbol of the clueless man unaware of the "new rules" of privacy and publicity and of sexual interaction. The Weiner coverage, within its conventional scandal arc, also brought the theme of new rules into even greater focus: Weiner, by mistakenly imagining that online communications were private and unwatched, was said to reveal the confusing, shifting boundaries between private and public and the routine surveillance of personal life to which we are all now subject.

## Notes

1. Barbara Liston, "Tiger Woods Admits 'Transgressions,' Apologizes," *Reuters*, December 2, 2009. http://www.reuters.com/article/2009/12/02/golf-woods-idUSGEE5B11VL20091202.
2. See also Orin Starn, *The Passion of Tiger Woods*, (Durham, NC: University of North Carolina Press, 2012). For a complex analysis of the Woods' scandal and the "cultural anxieties about race and sexuality in America" circulating within its narration, see Paul Apostolidis, "Sex Scandals, Racial Domination, and the System Correlation of Power-Modalities in Foucault," *Journal of Political Power* 42, no. 2 (2011): 179–198.

3. Tammy Todd, "Jesse James' Alleged Mistress Michelle 'Bombshell' McGee Alleged Second Twitter Page," *Examiner.com*, March 18, 2010. http://www. examiner.com/article/jesse-james-alleged-mistress-on-twitter-backlash-for-michelle-bombshell-mcgee.

4. This essay is based on a comprehensive review and analysis of media coverage of the two scandals, which I collected through database searches with the assistance of Allison Deck-Shipley, to whom I offer great thanks.

5. Hal Niedzviecki, *The Peep Diaries: How We're Learning to Love Watching Ourselves and Our Neighbors*, (San Francisco, CA: City Lights Books, 2009).

6. Paul Apostolidis and Juliet A. Williams. *Public Affairs: Politics in the Age of Sex Scandals*, (Durham, NC: Duke University Press, 2004).

7. A.J. Daulerio, "Brett Favre Once Sent Me Cock Shots: Not A Love Story," *Deadspin*. August 4, 2010. http://deadspin.com/5603701/brett-favre-once-sent-me-cock-shots-not-a-love-story.

8. Daulerio, "Brett Favre Once Sent Me Cock Shots: Not A Love Story."

9. A.J. Daulerio, "Brett Favre's Cellphone Seduction of Jenn Sterger," *Deadspin*. October 7, 2010. http://deadspin.com/brett-favres-cellphone-seduction-of-jenn-sterger-upda-5658206.

10. Jarrett Bell, "Goodell Seeks Facts About Favre's Conduct," *USA Today*, October 13. 2010, 7C.

11. Dan Mangan and Anne Karni, "Pass Interference—Brett Hit on Me, Too: Masseuse," *The New York Post*, October 10, 2010, 3.

12. Bart Hubbuch, "Holding the Phone; Three-TD Favre Mum on Scandal," *The New York Post*, October 12, 2010, 66.

13. Dan Mangan "Sad-Sack Brett 'Sorry' to Team," *The New York Post*, October 12, 2010, 5.

14. Kevin Seifert, "Brett Favre Cried During Apology to Team—NFL Nation—ESPN," *ESPN.com*, October 11, 2010. http://espn.go.com/blog/nflnation/post/_/id/29568/brett-favre-cried-during-apology-to-team.

15. Bell, "Goodell Seeks Facts About Favre's Conduct."

16. Gary Myers. "NFL in Rush for Favre Facts," *New York Daily News*, October 11, 2010, 54.

17. Rupert Cornwell, "Favre's Fall Latest Blow to Image of All-American Hero," *The Independent*, October 19, 2010, 50.

18. Cheryl Johnson, "Will Wrangler (and Deanna) Stick with Brett?" *Minneapolis Star Tribune*, October 26, 2010. http://www.startribune.com/will-wrangler-and-deanna-stick-with-brett/105731658/.

19. Christian Red, "Hostess in Distress," *New York Daily News*, October 26, 2010, 49.

20. Adam Schefter, "NFL's Brett Favre-Jenn Sterger Probe Goes High Tech, Source Says," *ESPN.com*, November 21, 2010. http://sports.espn.go.com/nfl/news/story?id=5834856.

21. Jeremy Fowler, "NFL Fines Favre $50,000 For Not Cooperating in Probe," *St. Paul Pioneer Press*, December 28, 2010.

22. The Associated Press, "Brett Favre Fined for Not Cooperating in Sexting Probe," *ESPN.com*, December 30, 2010. http://sports.espn.go.com/nfl/news/story?id=5965863.

23. *Good Morning America*, ABC News, April 12, 2011.

24. James McKinley, "Deceived By Her Looks," *The New York Times*, January 20, 2013, ST9.

25. Brian Costello and Don Kaplan, "Brett Got Sexty With Gal: Report," *The New York Post*, October 8, 2010, 3.

26. Mangan and Karni. "Pass Interference—Brett Hit on Me, Too: Masseuse."

27. Costello and Kaplan, "Brett Got Sexty with Gal: Report."

28. Jim Souhan, "In a Fitting Conclusion, Favre at Center of Storm," *Minneapolis Star Tribune*, October 12, 2010, 1C.

29. Mangan, "Sad-Sack Brett 'Sorry' to Team."

30. Costello and Kaplan, "Brett Got Sexty with Gal: Report."

31. C.K. Korhonen, "Brett Favre and Jenn Sterger: A Rational View," *Bleacher Report*, October, 11, 2010. http://bleacherreport.com/articles/487345-brett-favre-and-jenn-sterger-a-rational-view.

32. Dan Mangan, "Bombshell NFL Probe," *The New York Post*, October 9, 2010, 5.

33. Mary Ann Reitano, "Brett Favre/Jennifer Sterger Scandal: Where are the Facts? – Part I of III," *Bleacher Report*, October 16, 2010. http://bleacherreport.com/articles/492671-the-brett-favrejennifer-sterger-scandal-where-are-the-facts-ndash-part-i-of-iii.

34. Joshua Gamson, "Jessica Hahn, Media Whore: Sex Scandals and Female Publicity," *Critical Studies in Media Communication* 18, no. 2 (2001): 157–173.

35. Daulerio, "Brett Favre Once Sent Me Cock Shots: Not A Love Story."

36. Cornwell, "Favre's Fall Latest Blow to Image of All-American Hero."

37. Joshua Gamson, "Normal Sins: Sex Scandal Narratives as Institutional Morality Tales," *Social Problems* 48, no. 2 (2001): 185–205.

38. Michael Wilbon, "For Favre, Scandal Could be a Career-Ending Injury," *The Washington Post*, October 13, 2010, D1.

39. Christine Brennan, "Favre Case: Technology vs. Privacy," *USA Today*, October 14, 2010, 3C.

40. Nathaniel Vinton, "Sterger, NFL May Meet Next Week About Favre," *New York Daily News*, October 23, 2010, 52.

41. Toddy Venezia and Dan, Manganm "Sneaky Favre is Just 'Fine,'" *The New York Post*, December 30, 2010, 9.

42. Fowler, "NFL Fines Favre $50,000 For Not Cooperating in Probe."

43. Nathaniel Vinton, "Sterger's Dad 'Absolutely Furious,'" *New York Daily News*, December 31, 2010, 70.

44. *Good Morning America*, ABC News, April 12, 2011.

45. Michael McCarthy, "Networks Zoom in on Favre Flap," *USA Today*, October 11, 2010, 3C.

46. Mark Sappenfield, "Brett Favre Scandal Headlines Bad-Boy Edition of Monday Night Football," *The Christian Science Monitor*, October 11, 2010.

47. Howard Kurtz, "Bloggers Are Scooping Sleaze Into the Mainstream News World," *The Washington Post*, October 18, 2010, C1.

48. Reid Cherner and Tom Weir, "Will Favre Be Sacked By Cellphone?," *USA Today*, October 13, 2010, 3C.

49. Stephen Brunt, "Sports Heroes Undressed," *The Globe and Mail*, October 13, 2010, S1.

50. Bruce Arthur, "After Years of Playing with Fans' Emotions, Brett Favre Finally Gives Everyone Something to Laugh A," *National Post*, October 13, 2010, S1.

51. This notion that in becoming a figure of entertainment, Favre went from revered masculine prototype to disdained feminine stereotype (a diva) draws on a long historical construction of emotionally based leisure as "feminine" and less worthy than the "rational, detached and public territory of 'masculine' culture." See Su Holmes, "A Term Rather Too General to be Helpful: Struggling with Genre in Reality TV," in *The Shifting Definitions of Genre: Essays on Labeling Films, Television Shows and Media*, eds. Lincoln Geraghty and Mark Jancovich, (Jefferson, NC: McFarland, 2008): 21–39.

52. Brennan, "Favre Case: Technology vs. Privacy."

53. Bill Maher, "New Rule: If a Woman Rejects Your First Dozen Advances, Don't Send Her a Picture of Your Penis," *The Huffington Post*, October 15, 2010. http://www.huffingtonpost.com/bill-maher/new-rule-if-a woman-rejec_b_764893.html.

54. Gamson, "Normal Sins: Sex Scandal Narratives as Institutional Morality Tales."

55. Max Read, "Did Anthony Weiner Tweet a Picture of His Weiner?," *Gawker*, May 28, 2011. http://gawker.com/5806545/did-anthony weiner-tweet-picture-of-his-weiner=.

56. S.A. Miller, "Weiner Goes to Great Lengths, Under Siege, But Gal Blames Stalker," *The New York Post*, May 30, 2011, 5.

57. Maria Newman, "Congressman Says Hacker Sent Lewd Photo Using his Name," *The New York Times*, May 30, 2011, A16.

58. Jijo Jacob, "Full Text: Anthony Weiner's Sexting Apology," *International Business Times*, June 7, 2011. http://www.ibtimes.com/full-text-anthony-weiners-sexting-apology-288929.

59. Jen Ortiz, "20 Sexts Sent By Anthony Weiner To A Las Vegas Blackjack Dealer," *Business Insider*, June 7, 2011. http://www.businessinsider.com/anthony-weiner-lisa-weiss-facebook-radar-2011-6.

60. Chris Cuomo and Chris Vlasto, "Rep. Anthony Weiner: 'The Picture Was of Me and I Sent It,'" *ABC News*, June 6, 2011. http://abcnews.go.com/Politics/rep-anthony-weiner-picture/story?id=13774605.

61. Sandra Westfall, "Anthony Weiner: 'I Feel Like a Different Person,'" *People*, July 30, 2013, 58–60.

62. Jonathan Van Meter, "Anthony Weiner and Huma Abedin's Post-Scandal Playbook," *The New York Times Magazine*, April 10, 2013, MM24.

63. Raymond Hernandez and Michael Barbaro, "Weiner Agrees to Get Treatment as Calls for Resignation Intensify," New York Times, A1., June 12, 2011.

64. Karen Tumulty, "Weiner Admits to More Lewd Messages," *Washington Post*, A1., July 24 2013.

65. Gamson, *Jessica Hahn, Media Whore: Sex Scandals and Female Publicity.*

66. Marshall Sella, "The Year of Living Carlos Dangerously," *GQ*, November 2013.

67. Newman, "Congressman Says Hacker Sent Lewd Photo Using His Name."

68. Felicia Sonmez, "Weiner Calls Lewd Photo on Twitter a 'Distraction,'" *Washington Post*, A4., June 1, 2011.

69. Jennifer Preston, "A Twitter Group Warned About Weiner," *New York Times*, A21., June 8, 2011.
70. Raymond Hernandez, "Democrats Push Weiner to Step Down," *New York Times*, A25., June 9, 2011.
71. Hernandez, "Democrats Push Weiner to Step Down."
72. Hernandez and Barbaro, "Weiner Agrees to Get Treatment as Calls for Resignation Intensify."
73. Hernandez, "Democrats Push Weiner to Step Down."
74. Alison Gendar, Matthew Lysiak, and Jonathan Lemire, "Weiner Goes in for Sex 'Tweet'-Ment!," New York Daily News, 5., June 12, 2011.
75. Dan Bilefsky, "More Photos and More Calls for Weiner to Resign," *New York Times*, June 13, 2011, http://www.nytimes.com/2011/06/13/nyregion/more-photos-and-more-calls-for-weiner-to-resign.html
76. Gendar, Lysiak, and Lemire, "Weiner Goes in for Sex 'Tweet'-Ment!"
77. Adam Sorensen, "Contrite and Not Quite Defiant, Can Anthony Weiner Survive Scandal?" *Time*, June 6, 2011, http://swampland.time.com/2011/06/06/contrite-and-not-quite-defiant-can-anthony-weiner-survive-scandal/.
78. Karen Tumulty and Paul Kane, "Weiner's Political Survival is in Doubt," *Washington Post*, June 8, p.A1., 2011.
79. The discussion of Huma Abedin, too, often focused on her role in "the standard contrition ritual," nearly always considering her in relation to how her boss and presumed political role model, Hilary Clinton, handled the Monica Lewinsky scandal.
80. Van Meter, "Anthony Weiner and Huma Abedin's Post-Scandal Playbook."
81. Van Meter, "Anthony Weiner and Huma Abedin's Post-Scandal Playbook."
82. David Chen and Javier Hernandez, "Weiner Admits Explicit Texting After House Exit," *The New York Times*, July 24, 2013, A1.
83. Westfall, "Anthony Weiner: 'I Feel Like a Different Person.'"
84. Tumulty, "Weiner Admits to More Lewd Messages."
85. Gendar, Lysiak, and Lemire, "Weiner Goes in for Sex 'Tweet'-Ment!"
86. Alison Gendar and Corky Siemaszko, "Anthony's Parts Not So Private as Pix Hit Web," *New York Daily News*, June 9, 2011, 3.
87. Preston, "A Twitter Group Warned About Weiner."
88. Laura Holson, "Hiding in Plain Site," *The New York Times*, November 6, 2011, ST1.
89. Alexandra Petri, "Twitter Makes Fools of Us All," *The Washington Post*, June 7, 2011, A17.
90. Kathleen Parker, "Briefly, Don't Hit That Button," *The Washington Post*, June 5, 2011, A17.
91. Karen Tumulty and Felicia Sonmez, "Fueling a Photo Furor," *The Washington Post*, June 2, 2011, A4.
92. Ashley Parker, "Congressman, Sharp Voice on Twitter, Finds it Can cut 2 Ways," *The New York Times*, May 31, 2011, A17.
93. Eugene Robinson, "Why Weiner Had to Go," *The Washington Post*, June 17, 2011, A25.
94. Monica Hesse, "Tangled Web of Weiner's Affairs," *The Washington Post*, June 8, 2011, C1.
95. Joan Wypijewski, "Weiner in a Box," *The Nation*, July 4, 2011, 7–8.
96. Barbie Zelizer, *The Changing Faces of Journalism*, (London: Routledge, 2009).

97. It is beyond the scope of this chapter, but a casual comparison to another institutional arena, education, underscores these dynamics of continuity and change. Some teachers have been busted for sexting (see Anne E. Marimow, "Fromer [sic] D.C. Teacher John Solano Sentenced to Five Years in Child Porn Case," *The Washington Post*, October 7, 2013. https://www.washingtonpost.com/local/crime/fromer-dc-teacher-john-solano-sentenced-to-five-years-in-child-porn-case/2013/10/07/af69acbc-2f82-11e3-9ccc-2252bdb14df5_story.html), generating brief, mostly local coverage that treats them more as crime stories than as sex scandals. But this is not really where the main sexting-scandal action has taken place in schools. Instead, multiple scandals have emerged that are not about the transgressions, hypocrisy, and fall of powerful figures but about the behaviors of groups of teenagers. Since 2009, male students in Virginia, Michigan, Illinois, North Carolina, Pennsylvania, Missouri, and elsewhere have been charged with child pornography possession when nude images sent to them by girls were found on their cell phones (Ellen Biltz, "'Sexting' Charges Face By 2 Teens," *The Free Lance-Star*, March 11, 2009; Hanna Rosin, "Why Kids Sext," *The Atlantic*, November 2014; Darcy Spencer and Tonya LaFleur, "Sexting Scandal at Two Bethesda Schools," *NBC Washington*, 2010), or posted online (Liz Fields, "Police Bust Virginia Sexting Ring Involving More Than 100 Teens," *ABC News*, April 5, 2014. http://abcnews.go.com/US/police-bust-virginia-sexting-ring-involving-100-teens/story?id=23208357); sensational local and national news coverage has then focused largely on the prevalence, even the normalcy, of sexting among youth, and struggling to explain "why kids sext" (Rosin, "Why Kids Sext.") to presumably non-kid audiences. These cases arguably comprise a more unadulterated sort of sex scandal, especially viewed against the Favre and Weiner scandals, taking the anxiety about new, technologically generated rules of publicity and surveillance move it from periphery to center. Further, in school sexting scandals (as in the leaking of hacked photos of celebrities [M. Isaac, "Nude Photos of Jennifer Lawrence are Latest Front in Online Privacy Debate," *The New York Times*, September 2, 2014, A1]), the center of gravity may have begun to shift. What scandalizes is not just that people sext, but even more so the stealing of those images and texts, the hacking and making-public of something intended to be private, the deliberate crashing of the public-private border. Of course, like nearly all sex scandals to date (Hinda Mandell, "Scandal-less," *Bitch* 64 (2014): 51–54), these are still scandals that stem from and focus attention on heterosexual male power. The images that circulate, like money or trading cards, are almost exclusively of young women's bodies, not men's genitals. The new frontier of sex scandals may thus publicize not the fall of powerful, creepy men but their reassertion.

# CHAPTER 8

# Anthony Weiner: A Meditation on the Politics of Prurient Need

## Steve Almond

In June of 2011, Anthony Weiner, the brash congressman from New York City, resigned, after it was revealed he tweeted suggestive photos of himself and sent sexually yearning text messages to several women.

Weiner did not step down because he broke any laws, or because his desires made him behave in stupid and dishonorable ways, or even because his constituents turned against him. He stepped down because the media was going to flog the story until he did.

The entire episode, from rumor to resignation, lasted two weeks. The producers of the "news cycle"—the term of art for what is, in fact, the clever recycling of a few shiny items, cosseted in relentless punditry—could speak of almost nothing but Weiner.

And thus we were transported back to the Land of the Starr Report, that sad province where the Fourth Estate, in its desperation to enthrall and thereby profit, abdicates what the antique moralists among us might call a conscience.

For that feverish fortnight, actual grown-up Americans rose from their beds and put on their grown-up clothes and drove their grown-up cars to their grown-up offices and pretended, collectively, that the most important event occurring on earth was not the possibility that the USA would default on its debt, or the mounting evidence that our planetary thermostat had gone kablooey, or even any of the three and a half wars in which we were, as a nation, then mired.

No, the big news was that a horny guy did some dumb shit.

\*

*This chapter is based off the article "To Gaze Upon a Weiner," which the author published in The Rumpus, an online magazine, in 2011.*

S. Almond (✉)
Author and cultural critic, Boston, MA, USA

H. Mandell, G.M. Chen (eds.), *Scandal in a Digital Age*,
DOI 10.1057/978-1-137-59545-4_8

"Horny Guy Does Some Dumb Shit." That's your *Onion* headline.

\*

Long ago, in a past life, I left my job as an investigative reporter for a newspaper in Miami. I had lost my faith in journalism, but I still spent a lot of time with journalists because nobody else liked me. One night, a former colleague dropped by my apartment. She was an intense young woman who had spent some years in Central America, reporting on the atrocities visited upon those small and vulnerable countries. Now she worked for a major news magazine.

We talked for a while about the demands of her new job. She seemed agitated. I might have served her wine. Eventually, she confessed that she was working on the Monica Lewinsky story. In fact, she said, she was one of the only people on earth who had, in her possession, at that very moment, copies of the secret tapes made by Linda Tripp, in which Lewinsky described her trysts with President Clinton.

"They're right out in the car," she said. "I could get them."

She stared at me for a moment, with her beautiful dark blue eyes, and there was something awful in them: a desperation to include me in her sin.

I am not someone much burdened by self-control. But I did not want to hear those tapes. And I wanted that woman out of my house.

\*

A friendly reminder: Thomas Jefferson took one of his slaves as a lover. Grover Cleveland had a child out of wedlock while in office. JFK fucked everything in sight.

The White House correspondents knew all about JFK's tomcatting. But they did not regard it as a story. It was a private weakness, or a private need, one that never rose to the level of a public interest. They were busy reporting on boring stuff like the Cuban Missile Crisis and Civil Rights.

\*

Think about that: if JFK had been president in 2011, there is a good chance he would have been hounded from office for his "moral failings."

\*

It is worth asking why Anthony Weiner's indiscretions were so newsworthy, as compared to those of his contemporaries. Weiner, after all, did not frequent prostitutes for kinky sex, as did David Vitter, the Louisiana senator. Nor did he sleep with a member of his staff, then attempt to pay that staffer and her family tens of thousands of dollars in hush money, as did John Ensign, the former Nevada senator. Nor did he win high office by trumpeting his moral superiority in the realm of family values, as did both Vitter and Ensign.

But there were a number of factors that made Weiner such a desirable target. First, he lived and worked in New York City, where every misdeed is magnified. Second, Weiner exuded an attitude of overweening ambition that many in the media took to be arrogance. And third, he made the fatal mistake of denying any wrongdoing with a righteous vagary that acted upon the reporters then circling him as chum does on a pack of famished sharks.

Still, Weiner's most dire mistake was more basic: He took a picture.

\*

We live in a visual era. For a story to stick in the current media environment, there must be, as the TV people so charmingly put it, *footage*. Much of the reason our media provided so little coverage of the wars in Iraq and Afghanistan is because there was very little good footage of Americans dying or Americans killing. At least, there was no good footage they were willing to air.

As with so much else in the modern condition, this speaks ultimately to a failure of the imagination. Stories are not enough. If we cannot see it, it is not happening.

\*

With Weiner, we could see it. There it was. The scrawny chest, poignantly waxed and flexed. The pair of gray underwear bulging with no-longer-private needs. The secret dispatches tapped out to women he had never met, whom he did not really know, the words almost touching in their raw and hollow need, drawn straight from the pornographic idiom every man harbors in his lizard brain.

\*

Not only did Weiner supply us images and a script, he transmitted these via the new technologies, with which the old media are entirely obsessed.

These technologies have nothing to do with the traditional virtues of journalism: the dogged pursuit of money and power, the ability to explain complex chicanery in simple terms, an abiding concern for the public good. On the contrary, they have accelerated our most pathological compulsions: to consume data passively, to graze the Internet for stimulating distractions, and to forego the rigors of moral reasoning. Watching our Fourth Estate treat some brandidate's latest electronic fart as "news" is like watching an insecure chaperone attempt to moonwalk at a high-school dance. It's what all the kids are doing, right?

\*

The technologies by which Weiner sought to display his manhood and find a human connection—he was doing both—are the same technologies by which we are all voluntarily eroding our own zones of privacy.

A century from now, when historians take stock of the early years of the millennium, they will note a vast and mostly unheralded irony: Even as our citizens were objecting to widespread government surveillance, we were becoming deeply committed to forms of self-surveillance.

Of course, we do not think of Facebook or Twitter or any of the social media networks in this manner. We see ourselves as engaged in a communal experience. But the price of connection in these spaces is unilateral disclosure. We are essentially trading discretion for attention. Think of all those photos we post, the opinions we broadcast, and the confessions we make. Think of the public record we leave behind through our purchases, every credit card we swipe, every Internet site we visit, every ATM we use, and every survey we fill out. It is all quietly being converted into data, into profiles, fed into hungry algorithms.

What happens when a culture so quickly conflates intimacy and public disclosure?

\*

The fake moralists who staff the Opinion Industry—having fueled the obsessive coverage of guys such as Weiner, generally for partisan reasons—love to then retreat from their handiwork and draw lofty conclusions about what it all means. They trot out aphorisms like, *Power corrupts* and *It's the cover up that kills you.*

But the Weiner saga resonated, fundamentally, because it was about loneliness and sexual desperation and the way in which our private anxieties can be conveniently relocated in a public scandal. Not a lot of us can afford to pay high-priced hookers or pay tens of thousands of dollars in hush money. But we have all surrendered to more homely forms of temptation.

I wonder how many of the reporters who took part in Weiner's downfall have ever sent a sexually yearning text message? Or taken a photo of themselves in a state of arousal?

I know I have. Have you?

We all leave evidence of our need. It is what humans do. When this evidence threatens to surface, we lie.

\*

What a complicated and Christian pleasure it is for us to watch someone else punished for our sins.

\*

We are forever telling the world the same two stories about ourselves. One is about the person we want to believe we are: wise, compassionate, and upstanding. The other is about the person we know ourselves to be: petty, cruel, and sexually destructive. The best of our literary art arises from the collision of these two stories.

But journalists do not like to admit to such literary inclinations, so they have to pretend that something else is going on, that they are engaged in the dissemination of actual news. *It's a tough job, ma'am, but someone's got to do it. Can you imagine what would happen if you didn't know that Congressman Anthony Weiner was a dumb guy who did horny shit? How would we ever keep our children safe?*

\*

Once Weiner had resigned and the morality play had come to a satisfactory conclusion, it was time to talk about *fallout.* What will the *fallout* be? It is one of those dependably disassociating "news" words. Now that we have trashed this guy's life, let us step back, as if we are just innocent and thoughtful bystanders, and assess the damage.

The immediate impact, politically, was pretty clear. Weiner was one of the few legislators who stood up to the corporate kleptomaniacs who still dominate the policy discourse of this country. He spoke in blunt terms about the ways in which the rich seek to impose their will upon the rest of us. His resignation made it that much easier for the powerful interests aligned against common decency to practice their black arts. Our political culture was further sapped of its capacity to solve our common crises of state.

*

It bears mentioning that Anthony Weiner did attempt a political comeback.

In 2013, he decided to run for mayor of New York City. By this time, Weiner and his wife had a young son. He presented voters a 20-page plan called, "Keys to the City: 64 Ideas to Keep New York City the Capital of the Middle Class," that proposed reforms in the city's approach to education, hunger, transportation, health care, housing, job creation, and taxation.

But none of his actual policy ideas mattered. Because Anthony Weiner was no longer a politician, per se. He had been reduced to a caricature, a walking scandal, a genital pun.

Knowing this, and in the hopes of rehabilitating his image, Weiner agreed to bare his soul for a long profile in the *New York Times Magazine*. He used the piece to ask voters for a second chance and, more subtlety, to shift the blame for his actions to the prevailing technology.

"And if it wasn't 2011 and [Twitter] didn't exist, it's not like I would have gone out cruising bars or something like that," he insisted. "It was just something that technology made possible, and it became possible for me to do stupid things. I mean, the thing I did, and the damage that I did, not only hadn't it been done before, but it wasn't possible to do it before."[1]

*

Alas, the problem is never the tool, but the user.

Shortly after the profile appeared, allegations arose—which is to say, reporters saw fit to raise allegations—that Weiner had continued to send explicit text messages to at least three women in 2012, after his resignation from Congress. He used the alias "Carlos Danger."

Danger described himself as "an argumentative, perpetually horny middle-aged man." (Full disclosure: I myself am an argumentative, perpetually horny middle-aged man.)

In the face of another media onslaught, Weiner held a press conference. With his wife at his side, he announced that he would continue his run. He wound up with less than 5% of the vote.

*

The essential crisis revealed by the Anthony Weiner affair has nothing to do with Weiner himself. It has to do with our confusion over what really matters to us as a people and whether we can put aside the childish forms of titillation and dishonesty that hold us back from genuine moral progress.

Joan Didion, in writing about the Lewinsky scandal, noted that most Americans did not want that story told. They understood that the President had done some untoward things in the private realm. But they were more concerned about the things he did in the public realm, which affected them.

It was the media who rolled out the Lewinsky scandal, and who kept pumping time and money and fake emotions into it, as if it were a new product we desperately needed in our lives.

*

But we did not need it—not then, and not now. What we need is mature and ethical governance.

*

Weiner himself is gone from politics. He will be locked forever in a kind of tabloid pillory. Given his neediness for acclaim, he is likely to return to us at some point, in the pinstriped cloak of a pundit, the bruised grin of an ironic cameo.

For the rest of us, the question remains: What can we do? How can we put an end to this kind of crap? The answer is pretty simple.

Stop gazing at the Weiner.

This is how it works in America right now: You vote with your attention and your money. You do it every day, whether or not you mean to. Every single time you give in to your worst impulses and click on a link that involves gazing at a Weiner or listening to a phony candidate tell lies (or even getting teased for telling lies), every time you choose to indulge in a "story" that you know has no real moral impact on our governance, you are taking part in the degradation of this country.

*

When I say *you*, of course, I mean *I*.

*

The goal of the media in late-model capitalism could not be more transparent. They are an industry. Their agenda is profit. All they want is your ears and eyeballs, on behalf of the sponsors. If you click on sexual hi-jinx and hairstyles and corporate propaganda, that is what they will keep serving up. They will do so to the exclusion of those stories that might illuminate the growing perils of our species, and their potential remedy.

*

I think now (for whatever reason) of my grandfather Irving Rosenthal, who believed that all men and women should share equally in the bounty of our planet. He recognized the unlikelihood of this ever happening, given the prevailing greed of his homeland. Still, he remained convinced that a daily investigation of *The New York Times* might yield some elusive cause for hope.

As a consumer of news, he was interested in the policy portion of politics. What were our elected officials doing to provide opportunity to all men, to keep the buses running on time, to help the disenfranchised? What were journalists doing to keep those officials honest?

Real investigative journalism is hard work. It takes a personal and institutional commitment—of time, money, and talent. That is how actual public corruption is rooted out. That is how Watergate happens. But it does not happen unless there is an audience to support that endeavor.

*

It does not take much work to post a dirty photo, or to sit around a refrigerated television studio bloviating about a dirty photo, or to camp out on the doorstep of the politician in that dirty photo. That is not journalism; it is voyeurism.

When we consume such dispatches, when we succumb to our own prurience, we are pushing real journalism to the sidelines. The chief beneficiaries of this arrangement are the country's moneyed interests, who continue to exert an ever-larger influence on our public discourse.

Consider the fate of the campaign finance reform laws that arose from Watergate. They have been stripped away over the years. According to the Supreme Court, money now qualifies as a form of political speech. Forget one man, one vote. The richer you are, the more votes you get. It should come as no surprise that the gap between rich and poor continues to grow. Or that Washington has become trough for influence peddlers, or that politicians think more about corporate profits than the public good.

In the world of punditry, it has become a lucrative strategy to vilify the foxes in Washington. But it turns out we are the foxes. That is us, panting over salacious photos and texts, over gossip and polls numbers, then crying foul because our innocent little henhouse has been plundered.

*

History will look back upon the Weiner affair with mirth and great sadness. It will be viewed as yet another parable about our sexually neurotic and lonely population, unwilling to face up to its adult challenges.

But we write our own history. We need not service our devils. It is possible that Americans can and will grow up, that we will demand of our Fourth Estate an honest accounting of our condition.

They are not going to get any better until we do.

## Note

1. Jonathan Van Meter, "Anthony Weiner and Huma Abedin's Post-Scandal Playbook," The New York Times Magazine, April 10, 2013, MM24.

CHAPTER 9

# The Topless Professor in the Digital Age

*Diana York Blaine*

Who, feeling a funny desire stirring inside her (to sing, to write, to dare to speak, in short, to bring out something new), hasn't thought she was sick? Well, her shameful sickness is that she resists death, that she makes trouble.—Hélène Cixous, *The Laugh of the Medusa*[1]

The national scandal that erupted on my campus after semi-nude photographs of mine were broadcast on TV has its roots in something more complicated than the "topless professor" headlines could possibly transmit. In a world that too often seeks to simplify our complicated lives, this story actually reflects how I came of age as a feminist in a society that simply does not tolerate women who contest the ideologies that constrict us. This chapter details how I walked through this experience while continuing to teach students, provide care to my dying father, and stay true to my core beliefs about a woman's right to live unshackled by the patriarchal system.

In the spring of 2006, my father was dying. After a number of years managing his care, the time had come to let go, and, having learned hard lessons handling my mother's death a decade before, I knew we would need professional help taking care of him. I paid a visit to the physician who had been seeing him since his diagnosis of congestive heart failure in 2000. She had helped get dad stabilized, and he had six years of good quality life thanks in part to her ministrations.

"Why don't we consider hospice?" she asked me after I had described dad's failing condition. Relief flooded my body. The situation was resolving exactly as I hoped it would with no manipulation on my part. Hospice care, paid for by insurance, guaranteed I could keep my promise to my father that I would help him remain in his home, safe, and comfortable, for as long as possible. Dad,

D.Y. Blaine (✉)
The Writing Program, University of Southern California, Los Angeles, CA, USA

© The Editor(s) (if applicable) and The Author(s) 2016
H. Mandell, G.M. Chen (eds.), *Scandal in a Digital Age*,
DOI 10.1057/978-1-137-59545-4_9

a stoic 82-year-old World War II veteran, loathed being dependent. With the assistance of trained professionals, he would be able to die where he should, and, I believed, *as* he should, at home and—as much as possible—with his dignity intact.

I had not always been so concerned with my father's dignity. We had had our power struggles as I fought my mother's battles for her, getting caught up from a young age in the middle of a relationship that was not my own. I had also exercised my rights as an entitled child of middle-class parents in flush mid-to-late-twentieth-century America. Thanks to these two separate but parallel dynamics, respect for authority, particularly that of my father, had never been my inclination, and I had battled with him long into adulthood. It had taken my mother's diagnosis of multiple myeloma in 1995 to force me to quit struggling with her husband. After conceding that I was going to lose the battle I had been fighting for as long as I could remember, waving the flag of surrender felt like its own form of victory. As my mother's life began to ebb, mine started to flower.

Not knowing our history, the doctor was surprised that I embraced her suggestion of hospice. She said families usually reacted defensively to the suggestion that their loved one was dying. While the sunlight poured in through the window of her office that beautiful spring day, I recounted to this sympathetic physician why I was able to let dad go with a clear conscience, that I had finally come to accept him for exactly who he was and, crucially, for who he was not. The cancer that had ultimately killed my mother had also fundamentally changed me, and during that awful experience, I realized it was time to let old wounds heal, to let her disappointments with her marriage be hers and not mine. This insight, that I was not my family's judge and jury, had set me free to love my father and live my own life. There had actually been much good in our family history, despite mom and dad's unresolved issues. They had both done their best for their children, no questions asked, including supporting me all the way through a long education, culminating in a PhD in literature from University of California, Los Angeles.

As dad was dying, I was teaching gender studies and writing at a prestigious private university in southern California, a fact that brought my father much pride and pleasure every time we discussed my schedule. Over the six years I had been working there, I had the opportunity to become a hero to students on campus. Young people were receptive to the message of civil rights relayed by the authors we read in my Feminist Theory course. They also appreciated my willingness to participate in their student events, a willingness which brought me into contact with undergraduates I had not encountered in classes.

The previous spring, in 2005, I was told that one of these young women, a freshman who had attended a workshop I had given on loving your body, had been sexually assaulted by an athlete. The news made me physically ill. As the case was catapulted into the headlines, I felt the institutional power structures at my university were again failing to act sufficiently to protect young people from getting ground-up by the machinations of historically privileged groups on campus, namely the Greek system and our football program. Coincidentally, during these disturbing few weeks, the main speaker at our Take Back the Night rally said that while he was pleased a large assemblage of females was in attendance, it was really men who needed to band together to end rape. Women did not have the collective power to stop men from attacking them, the speaker observed, but males did, and they needed to hold each other accountable even if, perhaps especially if, these actions betrayed their conventional loyalty to each other.

The timing of the latest sexual assault and this speaker's stark observation catalyzed something for me. I knew I needed to speak up. The subsequent editorial that I wrote for the school paper castigated the most powerful men on campus for failing to join us that night in our march against rape. This opinion piece caused its own firestorm. I suggested that the responsibility for ending sexual assault be placed in the hands of males at our male-dominated university and that made me the object of robust vitriol. One colleague who was reading the football websites, noting that some rabid fans were making death threats, even recommended that I get a bodyguard. To an extremely vocal faction I—rather than rape—had become the horror.

A year later in 2006, in the doctor's office, I told her the ability to treat my dad with the respect he deserved had also freed me to own my decisions and to respect myself as a mature adult. I recounted to her the outpouring of disdain that I had experienced from infuriated, anonymous Internet trolls reacting to my editorial because I took an unpopular stand against sexual assault. I also told her I was unmoved by these vociferous accusations of my unworthiness, that I knew who I was and what I stood for. That mine was not an unexamined life.

"You're ready to stand naked before the world," she replied.

We finished up our business, arranging medical care for my father so that he could die at home and not in some clinical setting. She prescribed me *Paradise Lost*, actually wrote the title of Milton's masterpiece on a prescription pad, and then we hugged one another and parted ways.

Later that same day I was standing in my kitchen where I received a phone call from one of my oldest and dearest friends.

"Hey what's up, Kelli?"

Her response was not what I anticipated. "Rayleen's sister says there's naked pictures of you on the 5 o'clock news."

Needless to say my mind reeled. Condense every nightmare you have ever had of appearing in public without your clothing into a single instance, while knowing that you are not asleep and you are not just in public but in the electronic media for the whole world to see. For a split second, I was not sure I could handle what was happening. However, next I experienced a moment of ferocious clarity. It was as if my soul had sounded its depths and found firm ground instead of quicksand. I knew which three photos were being broadcast in Los Angeles that evening. I also knew why and by whom they had been exposed. And I also knew what my response was and was going to be. The certainty that I had no reason to abandon myself never wavered, which was fortunate since I was about to embark upon an international scandal starring yours truly as the unlikely femme fatale.

But first, a word or two about my breasts. I am not sure when they initially caught my attention but I do recall when they began to catch the attention of others. The first time was after a disastrous game of touch football at the local park when a bigger kid on the other team had violently knocked me to the ground, outraged that this ten-year-old girl with a golden arm was throwing touchdown passes over his head. When my brothers brought their sobbing injured little sister home, my mother took one look at me and announced that my career as quarterback was over:

"You are never playing football again and we are going to Sears to get you a bra."

At least that is how I remember the conversation going, the simultaneous prohibition of masculine achievements conflated with the entrance into female bondage. And I remember that bra, awful tight nightmarish thing. I was never one of those girls who fantasized about the trappings of femininity, wedding, family, children, even as I knew they were on some inevitable hazy horizon. As a girl, I had looked forward to driving, having a career, maybe being the president some day. As far as I could tell, wearing a bra was not a prerequisite for any of these.

A few years later, sitting with a group of older teens I had met at a community theater, I waited with baited breath as the boys went around the circle making pronouncements about each girl's breasts. While I had not aspired to be Barbie (President Barbie? I did not think so), by then I knew that women needed to please men, visually at least, and probably in other ways that I had yet to learn. Where would I rate? What power would I be able to wield by virtue of my body? Finally, it was my turn. The alpha male's face arranged into a sympathetic smirk. "Well," he said, "more than a mouthful's a waste." I recall a dim sense of relief. Somehow there was a bar and I had vaulted it, perhaps not spectacularly, but enough. It felt like permission to move on to other things that I found truly interesting, none of which revolved around what my tits looked like.

Sadly, as women, while our bodies may be ours, we simply do not own them, or at least our ownership of them is not simple. Other subsequent power struggles ensued for me ("her breasts are all right if you like big nipples," spat one spurned suitor to his chum), as they have for tens of millions of other women in the USA, and by the time I was in my early 20s, I felt deep shame about my body, not just my breasts, but my stomach, my arms, my thighs (the meteorological epithet "thunderous" had been hurled at them, by Jove!)— even my fingers, which were large like my giant Eastern European dad's. I had grown to fear the arrival of a Prince Charming who would try to shove a ring on those chubby digits, only to drop it and run screaming back into the forest in search of a sylph.

Even as my external confidence was remarked upon by many, these inner fears began to constrain my life in palpable ways. For example, in my early twenties, I attended a bachelorette party in Palm Springs, California. We had rented a private house where, one afternoon, fueled by vodka and moxie, the gals all lined up topless in the pool for a photo. This was the mid-1980s, long before today's de riguer sexting of selfies, and even though there was no possibility of publishing these pictures on a non-existent Internet, it still felt quite transgressive and naughty. The gathered women shared a sense of joy as they dared to expose themselves to the camera. All of them, that is, but me. I refused, self-righteously arguing that I would be a professional one day and could not risk tawdry photos floating around. (Insert ironic laughter.) But really I was just embarrassed about my body, not comfortable revealing it even in this relatively safe environment with 12 or so other women who were willing to reveal themselves to each other and to the anonymous lens of the camera.

If my body had become a problem, and it had, then a solution was warranted. I found one in Feminist Theory. Mine had not been a particularly political upbringing. Mom had largely hidden her liberal leanings from dad, a conservative, in order to keep peace in the home. In spite of her own brilliance, including matriculation into the Medill School of Journalism at Northwestern University in the 1940s when that field was still reserved for and dominated by men, she had been socialized to believe that women needed male approval, and she had passed that belief onto me—or at least tried her best to do so. Feminism, which made women unpalatable to men, hairy legs and all, was not a part of our mother/daughter bonding. I recall wondering as a child why this accomplished, articulate mother of mine would come home and put dinner on the table for her family every night while my father sat and watched television. Hadn't she worked all day too? What gave him the right to be waited on?

When I was offered women's literature classes to teach while finishing up my dissertation, these nascent questions were finally answered. It was while preparing the syllabi that I first encountered so many voices that resonated with my own, women who spoke of wanting freedom, having selves, rejecting dominant ideologies. I experienced many epiphanies during that period of my life, finally realizing that since I was female, there was no way for me to go along with the social order as it was currently constructed *and* to have an authentic life. I also had a new perspective on my mom's attempts to change me. Her fears that I would be unpalatable to men, too big, too strong, too smart, too independent were not based on her personal predilections, or on some fundamental inadequacy of mine. They were reflections of the patriarchal power dynamic that relegated women to a secondary and servile role. Each time she attempted to undermine my abilities, to silence my voice, to make me smaller, she was doing it out of an urgent loving need to equip me to be supported by men, the same socialization she had received.

So like many other intelligent women in our country, I had grown up with a healthy sense of my own powers, but only if they publically mirrored male ones and were dedicated to the perpetuation of male culture. I could excel in school as long as I was not trying to revolutionize the classroom or the canon, and as long as I was willing to suspend my female embodiment, viewing women through the gaze of males who alternatively worshipped and reviled them. Thankfully, in a paradoxical dynamic born of this same sexism, no one was available to teach the "chick lit" courses at two local universities. Administrators were looking for an adjunct with ovaries to teach these classes that no permanent faculty would stoop to, and, due to the female name on my query letter, I guess I fit the bill.

What I did not know, nor did these administrators know, was that I was finally going to be exposed to, and expose subsequent generations of students to, ideas so incendiary that in ways they undermine the very structure of the institutions and society that so patronizingly permitted their dissemination. At one of the small conservative colleges where I was working, the dean of faculty actually stopped me in the hallway to ask accusingly "what is this queer theory I am hearing about?" This question was not in the spirit of intellectual inquiry. He was making it clear, the content of my course was threatening some unspoken sense of propriety. While he took no further action besides taking pains to corner and shame me that day, it was apparent from his tone they had gotten more than they bargained for when they hired *me* to teach their "By and About Women" class. I had the feeling I was supposed to be wearing white gloves and serving tea while quoting Emily Dickinson.

During this time, I realized the problems in my personal life were not caused by my insufficient femininity, but by the artificial expectations of femininity that had been placed on me and my millions of sisters. I was not failing to live up to the definition of woman in my culture; the definition of woman was failing *me*. With this knowledge, I was finally truly free to write my own ticket, the one I had been wanting to write all along, to look in the mirror and see a woman, exactly perfectly ideally wonderfully woman, rather than to see where my body did not comply with some artificial—and dangerous and damaging and toxic and soul-destroying—fiction. If this sounds like heady stuff, it was. I realized I could begin to integrate the two aspects of myself: the rational mind (read male) and the flesh manifestation (read female). The two were not at odds. One did not need to be sublimated to the other nor did I need to rewrite my identity to comply with the rules. The rules needed to be rewritten. I was going to be able to survive the mind/body split. Take that, Descartes!

What had begun as part-time work to supplement my final years of graduate school blossomed into a way of life both personally and professionally. Upon finishing the PhD, I was hired as a tenure-track professor of American literature at a school in Texas, but not before I checked to make sure they had a Women's Studies program and that I would be teaching Feminist Theory as well as fiction. After four wonderful years there, inspiring students who had never even heard of feminists unless the word was hurled as an insult, I chose to relocate to Southern California so that my partner could take a tenure-track job in his field. I knew quitting an assistant professorship meant that I was unlikely to procure another one, and that putting my own career aspirations on the back-burner for the benefit of my male romantic partner mirrored sexist dynamics I had learned to resist. But I weighed myriad factors, and made the decision with an open heart. I had discovered in the traumatic loss of my mother a new sense of purpose, one that I found infinitely more satisfying than conventional definitions of success. I knew in an inchoate way that I was being led somewhere and I was willing to go, temporarily unemployed though I may be.

So in 2000, we moved home to California, I found my dad dying of congestive heart failure, I was offered a full-time position teaching composition at a private school in the region, and the clock began ticking inexorably toward "the scandal." The job came as a surprise, and I certainly had not imagined taking a step backwards into composition instruction, but shortly after starting this decent full-time position in the Writing Program, I was asked if I could teach the Intro to Feminist Theory course for the Gender Studies program as well because no tenure-track faculty were available to do it. *The more things change*. I asked my chair if I could be released to another program and he permitted it. Needless to say, I was joyous at the opportunity to return to my true love. Teaching writing has been, and is, filled with its own satisfactions, yet this required skills course is not the place to exercise the full arsenal of my powers as a feminist thinker. But a Gender Studies class? Oh yes.

That one-off gig became a staple of my teaching schedule, and by the time 2005 rolled around I was firmly established as an advocate for the marginalized on our campus. Feminism had also continued to inform my personal life, and, appropriately, the two were often hard to separate. Students had been asking me what I thought of issues outside of the classroom, ranging from current political events to popular media narratives to what their boyfriends said to them at a party the previous weekend. They would joke about "What Would Blaine Do?" They told me fantasized about a Dr. Blaine pop-up doll they could wear on their shoulders that would spout off to the sexists these young women encountered in class, at home, and on the streets.

Around this time, social media was beginning to pick up speed, and I considered starting a blog. If students wanted to hear what I had to say beyond the time we spent in class, then a web presence would be the logical place to do this. So I asked one of my former students if I could hire her to make one for me. She loved the idea, as did her partner, a graduate student in interactive media who is credited with being the world's very first blogger, and together they signed up for the project. "But," she said, "it will have to wait until we get back from Burning Man."

Burning Man. It rang a foggy bell. I remembered years earlier seeing an article about this bohemian arts festival in the desert, filled with wild people high on drugs. I was not an artist, nor did I even drink anymore, let alone take narcotics. Burning Man was the last place I would consider going. Or so I thought. Imagine my surprise when my intuition said, "you are also going to Burning Man." And I realized, to my surprise, that at 43 years old, I was going to Burning Man.

As Fate would have it, I had taken an unpaid leave of absence that semester to join my husband in England where he was teaching. Since our dogs had not been able to get passports, I had decided to forego the trip and was planning to cancel my leave, no longer justified by the semester abroad. A wise older mentor told me to take the time for myself instead even though I was not going to travel. In spite of my financial fears, I appreciated her counsel. Life would end at some point; my journey did not need to include obedience to a robotic sense of duty. Thus, when the opening to attend Burning Man arose, even though the event was 75 miles north of Reno, Nevada, and smack in the middle of the second week of classes, I was free as a bird. So I flew.

During my sojourn in the desert, some 20 years after that bachelorette party in Palm Springs, I finally permitted that topless photo of myself to be taken. In fact, I asked someone in my camp to take it. This moment in August of 2005 signifies my freedom from self-loathing, culturally imposed but expertly internalized by me over decades of socialization. It is hardly an erotic pose. In the picture, my arms are outstretched in joy, my face a study in bliss. If I am free to walk about the planet, including without clothing, what fetters can truly be said to bind me beyond those of gross mortality? Who would not consider this moment a photo opportunity? I certainly did.

A few months later, I traveled to London to visit my husband, who was staying in a tiny flat in Bayswater that belonged to one of his professors from graduate school. When I say tiny, I mean tiny, and so instead of disrobing in the closet-sized bedroom, we did so in the relatively larger living space whose walls were adorned with nudes painted by the faculty member's wife. One night as I removed my clothes, I caught site of an odalisque reflected in the mirror behind me. In our dishabille, she and I were, well, mirror images of each other, and I was highly amused by the visual. "Hey," I called to my spouse. "Look." He too chuckled at the similarity between art and life in that spontaneous moment and took a few snaps. Then it was done. I took lots of other pictures on that trip, none of which featured me or anyone else in pin-up mode.

Meanwhile, my website was completed and went online in September 2005. The student who had engineered it chose to name it "The Adventures of Dr. Diana." When I asked her why, she explained that she saw me as a female Indiana Jones figure. This was not at all how I defined myself, yet this was how *she* saw me, a woman of courage who faced obstacles and vanquished them, and I decided to let it stand. Life may be serious business sometimes, but it is not my business to take myself so seriously that I could not enjoy this re-inscription of the male archetype as a female academic butt-kicker instead.

She also instructed me to open an account on the new photo-sharing website, Flickr. It was not even a year old at that point, and I certainly had never heard of it, but I began habitually uploading photos to the account, even though I could not imagine why. I was pretty sure no one would care to see my dogs and vacation snaps of Yosemite, but she explained that the most recent photos would be displayed along the top of my blog, adding visual interest. So I obeyed, marveling at the notion of publicly posting pictures of our boring lives. I was not surprised that while my website began gaining readers, only a tiny handful of people bothered to click on those photos at the top of the page that took them to the separate Flickr account where the majority of photos were stored. I had grown up on *New Yorker* cartoons joking about the torture of being forced to endure someone else's travel slides and thus was positive that this over-sharing of images was a fad. But 2005 was long before today's explosion of selfies, snapchats, instagrams, and so on, and I had no idea how image obsessed we would become as a culture.

So during the Fall of 2005, I had uploaded the Burning Man shot, my personal declaration of independence from the need to have a different set of breasts than those I had inherited from evolution and ancestry, and the two pictures of me from London, which I viewed as wry commentary on women's bodies as aesthetic objects in western civilization. I had no reason to omit them from the other hundreds of other slices of life depicted on Flickr, and while I was not seeking attention or trying to shock by including them in my album, I also did not believe that the unclothed human body ought to be taboo. So there they sat, along with pictures of Halloween in Minneapolis, birthday parties, and the giant redwoods. Nobody was perturbed that digital images of my mammary glands were available for public view. And their mere presence did not make them scandalous.

All of that changed in Spring 2006. My website, dianablaine.com, had caught the attention of a conservative student who had never stopped dogging me since the editorial the previous year. Once he found my blog, he redoubled his attacks on his pseudonymously named Cardinal Martini website ("Look Muffy, a Blog for Us!"), featuring anti-Diana Blaine articles every single day. In over 30 lengthy posts during the course of a few weeks, he called me "a malignant narcissist," "delusional," "deranged," "illiterate," "man-hating," "angry," and "insane." I realized this obsessed anti-suitor would discover those three photos as he trawled for material. I say "discover" because they had never appeared on my dianablaine.com website. You had to go to Flickr and find my profile and root through several hundred pictures to view them. (In fact, during the scandal, I received calls from frustrated media-types who could not even *find* the images and demanded, I direct them to the photo site. I found this rather ironic, that the offending nudes offended by existing and yet were so obscure they could not be unearthed.) Therefore, I had a decision to make. Do I delete those pictures to protect myself? Or would that constitute complicity with the very dynamic that I was fighting personally and professionally to resist? I went with the latter, refusing to stand down in the face of male disapproval. And so, sure enough, this person went to the Flickr site, saw the pictures, and started screaming.

Sadly, there had been yet another rape on campus committed by a high-status male, this time, the quarterback of the football team, and it was this latest sexual assault that had the local news searching for information about him on the web. Their quest led them to the Cardinal Martini website, where they found an angle even more provocative than a pattern of violence against undergraduate women: naked pictures—and of a *teacher*'s body at that! Sex sells, as we have heard *ad nauseam*, and Channel 4 jumped to capitalize on this fact. They sent a reporter to my university, placed him in front of the entrance sign, and began to construct a scandal where none existed. "Topless Professor," screamed the headline. *Viola*, I was famous.

In another amazing coincidence of fate, I was just finishing a class I had created on the topic of scandal. I had not taught this subject before and the idea had actually come to me in meditation the previous year when searching for a theme for a new literature class. As I had taught my students, scandals require two basic necessary components: an act, and media coverage of that act. So I knew that while the pictures themselves were not a scandal, the presence of television reporters breathlessly informing their viewers that a controversy was taking place over my pictures made them into one. These images, the journalist asserted, were "causing concern" in my workplace. Actually, they were not causing anything until Channel 4 brought them to the attention of the school. I was relieved that the television coverage included the administration's official response: that personal websites were not the business of the university or under its purview, they were protected under free speech, and that the school supported academic freedom. What a relief! I knew that once they had said these things that I, an untenured faculty member, was not going to be fired.

Since I was personally comfortable with my choices, and I was professionally safe as far as I could tell, I was free to sit back and enjoy the ride. It was fun watching the broadcasts as I did what I am trained to do as a gender and literature scholar, interpret media representations. In this case, *I* was the subject, but I could view the reports objectively because they were so formulaic, revealing our mainstream ideologies and the ways in which we use rhetoric to construct them. After those first days in May 2006, the scandal continued to grow, bringing ideas I had hoped to share with a wider audience to, well, a wider audience. That same Flickr site that had maybe 25 views over the months now had over 1 million; the Adventures of Dr. Diana blog went from enjoying a small loyal readership to exploding into a tornado of lively debate; I received calls from media outlets like *Inside Edition*; was featured in a *Village Voice* column, debated a conservative on MSNBC's *Rita Cosby Live and Direct*; got my own interview on Channel 4 to respond to their initial salacious report; received over 5000 emails, queries from porn producers, a literary agent in New York, and even a few fan letters from a prisoner in Singapore.

Viewing this event as a teaching moment, I blogged about what was happening, naming one of the first posts "Boring Lecture from the Naked Lady." In this post I explained the dynamics of scandal, the politics of the body and gender in the USA, and why a few mild pictures could therefore garner such hysteria:

> Scandal requires two things: a precipitating event and media interpretation of that event. So in this case, for example, the precipitating event would be the appearance of those photos of mine on my Flickr site. Now in and of themselves they are not scandalous, for they have been there for months and nobody cared. All of my friends and family know of them, colleagues and yes some students have as well, and while I have had good conversations with these folks about the meaning of the female body in our culture, none of these discussions caused "scandal" because no one had any vested interest in controlling me by trying to spin their appearance as inappropriate.[2]

My scandal students, equipped with the knowledge to understand exactly what was happening, took great satisfaction in parsing this situation right along with me. I was gratified to have taught them how to understand why our culture reacted so severely when women like Erica Jong and men like Walt Whitman dared to exert their sexuality in print, and surprised but not ashamed to have ended up providing them with a contemporary example during finals week.

A few weeks later, it was my father's imminent death, not the scandal, which was on my mind as I walked into my building to teach the first day of summer school. My chairman waylaid me as I headed for my office. "Well," he said, "as you might imagine we need to talk." "No," I replied honestly, "I didn't think we would." Since the school had released that initial statement, there had been no other official communication, and I had chosen to take them at their word, that this photo firestorm was my own business and freethinking college professors were not to be persecuted. Therefore, I really did not think a calling on the carpet was imminent, but I was wrong. "First," he said to me once we had found a private room in which to talk, "I am hearing about this from the very highest levels in the administration." (*So that means the president*, I thought to myself.) "And I want to make it clear, it's not about the pictures." (*Of course it is, or why else am I sitting here when I have Xeroxing to do?*) "It's that the administration feels that your response has been too self-aggrandizing." (*Huh? I know what all those words mean, but what do they mean in this context?*) I actually felt sorry for him having to perform this unappetizing task, but I was far beyond conceding to anyone at this point. "I regret you have had to deal with this," I said, "but If I have to choose between this job and my status as a public intellectual, then I will resign." "Oh no, no, no, god no, that's not at all what's happening, don't think that, there's no problem." He was adamant. "Well then," I said, "there's nothing else to say, is there? I need to go prep." And so I did.

When I got home that day I asked my husband what he thought the "self-aggrandizing" comment meant. He said, "It means you are a woman and you are not apologizing." Well that is right. If I am supposed to apologize for not doing anything wrong except being a woman who is self-determining, then once again the rules need to change, not me. The apology owed is from patriarchal culture, the one that would have amputated my will if it could have. By patriarchal culture of course I do not mean men, per se, although many sexists are male. I experienced plenty of criticisms from women during this period also. When I appeared on *Rita Cosby Live and Direct*, I was pitted against Martha Zoller, a conservative woman who objected to my exposing flesh as a breach of "decorum." (I cheekily asked in response if I should be wearing a burka.) Another conservative female blogged that "photos like this are fine if they are in a husband's wallet." *In a husband's wallet.* Could there be a clearer expression of the traditional relationship between women and men in American society? Men own women, and women's sexuality is for male pleasure, only to be exchanged for financial support. Through it all, I continued to hold firm that self-fashioning did not constitute an aberration of morality. Sexism did. When Rita Cosby asked me during our interview if I understood why people think the images are "way too much." I replied:

> You know, I live in a culture that surrounds me with Playboy bunnies and air brushed women all day long, extremely artificial images, and it seems to me a stink arose when a woman decided to put her own pictures out there for noncommercial purposes and so it's confusing to me why I pass so many sexist, exploitative images of women all day long and nobody cares about that.[3]

Since the attempts to control me reflected larger sexist dynamics, I was not surprised to find conservative people and institutions castigating me, but I was surprised by the mixed reaction on "WMST-L." This listserv, founded in 1991, provides an international electronic forum for academics who specialize in Gender Studies to exchange information related to pedagogy. I have been a member of the WMST-L listserv since 1996, and when my new website fell under attack because I had published the anti-rape editorial a year earlier, academics on the listserv were supportive of my case since it related directly to our right to speak freely as professors dedicated to the eradication of sexism. Many of these contributors again came to my defense a few weeks later when news broke of the scandal. For example, one member said, "My only criticism for Professor Blaine is that she tried to justify the existence of the photographs in the first place. There is no reason for her to be ashamed."[4] A lively and informed conversation went on for several weeks, as different approaches to feminism fueled different takes on the scandal, including the relationship between the personal and the professional. An anti-porn educator was simply unable to validate my posting images of breasts even as she expressed sympathy for my belief that I was resisting, rather than complying with, convention:

> images today carry a certain authenticity, a statement about us as important and real, even though they are unreal and inauthentic in their capturing of reality. These are some of the reasons I think posting images of ourselves are more complicated that Diana suggests and they have the potential to feed into the hegemonic visual culture, not undermine it.[5]

Her thoughtful response falls in line with that person's politics. Another asked, "What is gained when you have hurt yourself or your reputation by putting such a picture on the web? I don't say you shouldn't; I just throw out the doubt and problem."[6]

As earnest as many of these responders were, there still seemed to be some basic (primal?) desire on the part of a very few to scapegoat me, to make me responsible for errant wielding of female sexuality, and that was the surprising aspect. The most aggressive objector said "i [sic] have trouble following why you want to present yourself in an 'eroticized' way to your students, the university community, and anyone who finds your website."[7] I explained my case to her and the list, but this "trouble" that she had was not assuaged by my responses. She refused to believe I was both defiant about the pictures and yet surprised they had attracted attention. Her argument implied that unless I posted them to start a revolution I could not defend their presence from a political perspective. And if I *did* post them to start a revolution, then I must be lying when I said I never expected anyone to see them or care that they were there. What I experienced as paradox, a series of actions building upon one another across the course of time leading to an unanticipated outcome, she and a few others insisted was disingenuousness on my part. This shaming from peers was perhaps the only real disappointment I felt when the world's eyes were upon me.

But ultimately the cacophony of voices on the list and off, some vilifying, others grateful for my courage, many intrigued by exposure (no pun intended) to ideas they had never encountered and inspired by the intellectual foment, underscored my initial belief: that the quest for meaning in life comes ultimately from one's relationship with self. French philosopher Michel Foucault[8] suggests in modern democracies we are regulated by what he refers to as internalized disciplinary power as much or more than external means. Adding gender to the mix complicates our personal quest—the female bildungsroman cannot avoid fundamental engagement with the heroine's sexuality. And so in a culture where the journey is most frequently coded in masculine terms, I was happy to provide a glimpse of what it looks like through the eyes of a woman. I left that Flickr site up long after I had moved on from blogging so that people could see how women are viewed ("national geographic breasts" spat one voyeur in disgust), and to see a woman who embraced herself anyway, unmutilated middle-aged mammaries and all.

In spite of my confidence, I did consider all of the possible objections with care. My hope is to contribute to the good of the world, not to detract from it, and I was sensitive to the concern about someone being both in a sexed body and a teacher of young adults. *Breasts? But you have students. What were you thinking?* Here is a typical example from a new reader named Adam:

> I appreciate your stance, but ... well ... aren't you the least bit concerned that by putting your naked pictures where students could see them, you may have unwittingly caused a distraction in the learning environment? Do you feel that these pictures may undermine your ability to teach to certain students effectively? Not attacking, just wondering if you've thought about the other side of the issue at all.[9]

Yes, Adam, I have thought about "the other side of the issue," and I would like to think the very thoughtfulness that I have shown throughout this lifetime makes me a valuable instructor. First of all, male professors are often viewed uncritically as objects of romantic fantasy, yet no one argues that this detracts from their ability to teach. As to the existence of my explicit images, I am happy to report all these years later that no one seems to have been driven mad by the sight of my breasts, been unable to concentrate in school, had to drop out, or reacted with an excess of moral turpitude after taking a class from a professor with three topless photos lurking somewhere online. My students continue to find an iconoclast a welcome contributor to their personal and intellectual development. (Is that too self-aggrandizing to say?) And my university values me as well, as demonstrated by my 2015 promotion to Professor of Writing and Gender Studies as well my receipt of a Mellon Mentoring award. Finally, I have faith in students, a faith my detractors do not always seem to share. I believe this email I received from a former student sums up the capacity of young people to withstand the vicissitudes of life, something as educators we are tasked with helping them learn to do. I would like to close the chapter with it:

> Hello! I just received a call from my mom after she saw NBC's preview of "a USC professor posing topless on a website." I asked, "Is it Diana Blaine?" and then went to check your website to find that, yes indeed, it was you! Why did I think of you? I guess it could've been because you're one of the few professors I know with a website, but also perhaps because of your powerful and free stance as a feminist! Well, I was proud to call my mom back to say that it *was* you and you were my professor!!! Hope all is well.—Jessica[10]

All *is* well, Jessica. And I hope all is well with all of you, body, and soul.

## NOTES

1. Hélène Cixous, "The Laugh of the Medusa," trans. Keith Cohen and Paula Cohen, *Signs* 1, No. 4 (Summer, 1976), 877. The author would like to thank the journal *Signs* for generous permission to publish the epigraph here.
2. Diana Blaine, "Boring Lecture from a Naked Lady," dianablaine.com, May 9, 2006.
3. Diana Blaine quoted as a guest on "Rita Cosby 'Live & Direct,'" MSNBC, aired June 29, 2006, http://www.nbcnews.com/id/13632345/ns/msnbc-rita_cosby_specials/t/rita-cosby-live-direct-june/#.VdeDoflVhBc.It.
4. Comment on WMST-L, "Re: Feminist Professor's Website Attacked," May 11, 2006.
5. Comment on WMST-L, "Re: Feminist Professor's Website Attacked," May 10, 2006.
6. Comment on WMST-L, "Re: Feminist Professor's Website Attacked," May 9, 2006.
7. Comment on WMST-L, "Re: Feminist Professor's Website Attacked," May 10, 2006.
8. Michel Foucault, *Discipline and Punish: The Birth of a Prison*, New York, NY: Random House, 1995.
9. Adam, email correspondence to dianablaine.com, May 9, 2006.
10. Jessica, email correspondence to dianablaine.com, May 8, 2006.

# CHAPTER 10

# An 'Office Sex Romp' and the Economic Motivations of Mediated Voyeurism

## Kathleen M. Kuehn

On January 30, 2015, about 50 patrons at a local pub in Christchurch, New Zealand, witnessed, recorded, and distributed photos and videos of two office co-workers having sex inside an adjacent insurance building after business hours. The videos/photos quickly went viral after posts on Facebook, YouTube, and Reddit were picked up by mainstream news organizations and blogs and viewed by millions of people worldwide. Branded by the media as the "Christchurch office sex romp," the event went from story to scandal within days. Details revealed that the individuals involved were a married, senior-level manager in his 50s with teenage children and his 25-year-old secretary, who had just recently broken off an engagement. Both the man's wife and the woman's ex-fiancé reportedly learned of the affair on Facebook, just like everybody else.

The story would occupy the top news of New Zealand's major media outlets in the days that followed. For example, three different versions of the same story occupied the "top articles" on *The Press* website (Christchurch's daily newspaper) for several days after it broke. (A large fire would eventually bump the headlines to the second, third, and fourth most-read story for the latter half of the week.)[1] Much of the coverage focused predominantly on legal aspects of the case, although eyewitness reports would certainly color the event with celebratory statements about what amused bar patrons had seen, or commentary about the live band's decision to stop playing once it realized the audience had been lost to the adjacent sideshow.[2]

The Christchurch sex romp occurred less than six months after NSA-whistleblower Edward Snowden appeared at a pre-election event in Auckland, New Zealand, to proclaim: "If you live in New Zealand, you are being watched." Although Snowden's statement referred to mass surveillance by the state, it under-

K.M. Kuehn (✉)
Media Studies, Victoria University of Wellington, Wellington, New Zealand

119
H. Mandell, G.M. Chen (eds.), *Scandal in a Digital Age*,
DOI 10.1057/978-1-137-59545-4_10

scores the wider cultural debates surrounding privacy and surveillance taking place at the time. A poll carried out by Amnesty International in early February 2015, the *same week* the Christchurch scandal went internationally viral, found that 63% of New Zealanders opposed the mass surveillance of citizens' personal communications by the state.[3] Specifically, the survey questions spoke to *personal* interactions—that is, private—as opposed to those occurring in a public space. State surveillance is distinct from peer-to-peer surveillance because of differences in structure and power. However, even peer-to-peer surveillance can be indiscriminate and detrimental to those who are watched. The wider discourse around surveillance certainly seems worth noting, however, if only to highlight its absence from how media framed the sex romp scandal.

Of the 30 news articles analyzed about the story, not a single one actually featured the term "surveillance." Instead, a majority of the media discourse surrounding the sexual affair centered on whether or not the two employees could be fired from their jobs, their retribution rights against those who recorded and circulated the sexual encounter, and debates about "privacy in public." Discussions about surveillance or other social, cultural, and even ethical factors were comparatively absent from the discourse.

A symptomatic reading of the discourses produced around this scandal by media organizations focuses on what was not said—rather than what was said.[4] This chapter argues that the "Christchurch office sex romp" can be understood within the context of the contemporary surveillance society, defined as one based on post-panoptic, lateral monitoring practices that make up an increasingly central part of contemporary cultural practice. It examines the production, circulation, and "democratization" of scandal (or at least the democratization of those caught in a scandal) as symptomatic of a society that is neither critical nor reflexive about the economic value that motivates surveillance at the expense of other social, cultural, or ethical concerns. As this case study illustrates, the productive value of surveillance as entertainment—what the journalism scholar Clay Calvert calls "mediated voyeurism"—is particularly instrumental to the process of normalizing surveillance in societies of control.[5]

## THE SURVEILLANCE SOCIETY

For the sociologist and surveillance scholar David Lyon, "All societies that are dependent on communication and information technologies for administrative and control processes are surveillance societies."[6] Despite its seemingly sinister connotations, "surveillance societies" describe those in which surveillance is a key feature of modern life. The surveillance society is not merely a product of state or government power but a society based on the capture, analysis, and application of information to everyday lives. It is now readily acknowledged that private companies and everyday people also engage in these surveillance processes. Surveillance societies are, therefore, societies in which social relations are organized by a ubiquitous gaze; that gaze functions along a spectrum of "care to control" for purposes that might range from security and protection to leisure and entertainment. In other words, surveillance now exceeds the goal of totalitarian state control to encapsulate a much more expansive set of routine activities carried out by a wide range of "watchers."

Until recently, the dominant framework most surveillance scholars have used to theorize the role and function of surveillance is through the French philosopher Michel Foucault's conceptualization of the "panopticon."[7] The panopticon describes the architectural design of a circular prison in which the guard sat in a central tower ringed by the inmate's cells. As part of this design, well-lit prison cells clearly illuminated the inmate's figure so guards could quickly notice and punish prisoners' missteps. At the same time, the backlighting made it impossible for the prisoner to tell if the guard was watching or not. The purpose of the design assumed total and constant surveillance through the prisoners' *unverified* visibility. Because the prisoners never knew when they were being monitored, they would *self-regulate* their behavior as if always under watch.

Foucault saw the panopticon as a metaphor to explain how modern institutions exert power for the purposes of social control. He observed that *discipline*, as opposed to force or punishment, marked the best and most efficient mode of governance. A self-disciplinary model of power meant that individuals would interiorize the figurative "all-seeing" gaze of the guard and automatically regulate their behavior in accordance with social norms and expectations. While Foucault acknowledged panoptic power could function as a negative form of coercion, he also importantly noted the capacity for surveillance to induce *productivity*, particularly on behalf of capital.

Panoptic power hinges on the *knowledge* of one's potential visibility to others. According to Foucault, "visibility is a trap."[8] Closed-circuit television, for example, functions on a panoptic logic; to assist in crime prevention, potential criminals must know a camera is present and that authorities may be potentially monitoring the feed (or will review it later). It is the very knowledge of the *potential* to be seen that causes the potential criminal to modify his or her behavior accordingly. Reducing theft in this way not only maintains social order, but has economic benefits, as well.

Increasingly, post-modern approaches to surveillance technologies, practices, and cultures aim to account for the ways in which various cultural practices are captured for purposes that include—but also exceed—discipline, governance, and social control.[9] Foucault's conceptualization is perhaps losing some purchase in the era of "ubiquitous surveillance," which media scholar Mark Andrejevic defines as "the prospect of a world in which it becomes increasingly difficult to escape the proliferating technologies for data collection, storage and sorting."[10] This ubiquity means that the recording and capturing of everyday activities and interactions are increasingly *invisible*; therefore, the self-disciplinary aspect of disciplinary technologies is irrelevant to many contemporary surveillance contexts. In today's society, much surveillance occurs without our knowledge, so there is no incentive to self-regulate behavior if there is no expectation of being seen. For example, it is not always obvious how the information collected by biometric identification systems (e.g., fingerprint or retina scanners), facial recognition technology, supermarket loyalty cards, or videos taken by a stranger's mobile phone will be used, circulated, or valorized. In the same way, it is not clear how the sale of these data to third parties will be used either, or if consumers are aware of this resale at all.

For this reason, social theorist Gilles Deleuze coined "control society" to describe a departure from the way eighteenth- to twentieth-century disciplinary regimes enclosed or trapped individuals in order to control them.[11] Traditional disciplinary institutions like the family, factory, military, or prison no longer function as effective sites of control in the way they once did for Foucault; rather, as Deleuze argues, "the operation of markets is now the instrument of social control" as the power once held by these traditional sites give way to private corporations.[12] The implied notion of visibility is also missing from societies of control unlike disciplinary societies, which governed by restricting mobility to normalize behavior through surveillance. Visibility is thus not a requisite to power in control societies, because the measures, practices and resources utilized to govern are increasingly automated, ruled by markets, capital, and code.

## Surveillance and Scandal

As communication scholars James Lull and Stephen Hinerman note, "Indeed, everywhere we look, sordid stories of how personal desire triumphs over conventional morality are told for profit."[13] The notion of "scandal," which they define as "a breach in moral conduct and authority," suggests attention to a story or issue that violates moral norms.[14] The *spectacle* of scandal, moreover, has always been tied to surveillance and visibility. As sociologist John B. Thompson argues, scandal is:

> symptomatic of this broader transformation in the nature and extent of visibility which has characterized the development of modern societies ... [Scandal is] rooted in the characteristics of a world where visibility has been transformed by the media and where power and reputation go hand in hand. Scandal matters because, in modern mediated worlds, it touches on real sources of power.[15]

While Thompson refers primarily to political scandals, his point is transferrable to the contemporary cultural moment as well. It is one in which surveillance practices and their outcomes are normalized by an economic logic of social, reputational, and financial capital that similarly undergirds much of the current media and pop culture landscape.

Certainly, extramarital office affairs and acts of voyeurism are neither new nor surprising in contemporary culture, but what differentiates the current case study is the subjects involved. Globally circulated sex scandals traditionally feature celebrities, politicians, or other powerful figures rather than two unknowns from a small New Zealand city. More "traditional" scandal fare involves cultural and political power brokers whose "leaked" celebrity sex tapes, extramarital affairs, and hacked nude celebrity photos are regularly featured in the tabloids and mainstream press. Yet digitally networked, mobile technologies have been long credited for "democratizing" all kinds of social, cultural, and political practices, including the production of celebrity,[16] information, and news and culture.[17] The democratization of surveillance is another social practice enabled by networked technologies, as demonstrated by how social media allow people to monitor others without them knowing and offers the capacity to record and circulate public or private moments in real-time.[18] Digital platforms—with the assistance of the mainstream media—enable our intense monitoring and judging of those caught in internationally circulated scandal, particularly as the habitual recording of everyday activities becomes increasingly common and invasive.[19]

These so-called democratizing practices are not, however, merely determined by technological developments but shifting social practices as well. The growing dependency on digitally automated technologies for the purpose of convenience and efficiency undergirds many routine activities like banking, shopping, or communicating with friends, for instance, further normalizing the idea of being watched. As Calvert writes, "The more accepting we are of having our own behavior visually monitored and recorded, the more our comfort level with watching others' activities increases."[20] The Christchurch sex romp can be read as symptomatic of broader political, economic, social, and cultural changes that intersect with longstanding curiosities and critiques, including moral and ethical codes of conduct.

The democratization of scandal can be understood as a product of what Calvert calls mediated voyeurism: "the consumption of revealing images of and information about others' apparently real and unguarded lives, often yet not always for purposes of entertainment but frequently at the expense of privacy and disclosure, through the means of mass media and Internet."[21] Importantly, mediated voyeurism captures moments or events not intended for public consumption, but are commercially distributed for their perceived economic value. In a culture of mediated voyeurism, Calvert argues, "the proclivity and affinity for mediated voyeurism rises to the forefront of our media consumption."[22] Among other qualities, mediated voyeurism sacrifices personal privacy for others' enjoyment.

Significant political and economic changes in the late twentieth century intensified the culture of mediated voyeurism.[23] Fears about rising crime and workplace inefficiencies contributed to the widespread rollout of video surveillance technology in both public and private places. These technologies served both safety and economic purposes, not just in terms of crime prevention and financial loss but to boost worker productivity and efficiencies as well. Meanwhile, changing economic realities in newsrooms sought new cost-cutting measures that increasingly relied upon infotainment, tabloid-style news, user submissions, and other inexpensive content. Coupled with the deregulation and marketization of media firms in many capitalist countries, the dependency on free or inexpensive content also saw the rise of surveillance footage as entertainment.

Within this context, Calvert discusses the normalization of society's voyeuristic tendencies as conditioned through a pop culture landscape of surveillance-based entertainment, including early reality TV (e.g., *Jerry Springer*, *Cops*, *The Real World*) and "news" magazine shows (e.g., *Dateline*, *20/20*). Other scholars like Rachel Dubrofsky and Mark Andrejevic have similarly noted the alignment between reality TV and social media.[24] They demonstrate how both media forms signal the extent to which lateral surveillance makes up an increasingly significant part of the media market. Andrejevic, a media scholar, argued in 2002 that the participatory aesthetics of reality-based programming served as "training grounds" for the online interactive economy, which at the time referred mainly to the growing proliferation of Internet webcams, life-blogging, and burgeoning social network sites. Dubrofsky, a cultural critic, later extended this argument about the popularity of reality TV's influence on the way users readily acclimated to the practices of self-display and surveillance on social network sites like Facebook. Of particular significance is the way reality television "habituates audiences and participants to the use of surveillance technologies for entertainment purposes."[25] Lyon—the surveillance scholar—explains that the visibility inherent to entertainment-based surveillance is no longer a trap but part of the "trip"—and one that many people quite enjoy.[26]

## METHODS AND FINDINGS

A symptomatic reading of the discourses surrounding the Christchurch sex romp illuminates what this particular story says about the contemporary cultural moment.[27] As discourses encompass both language and practice, the symptomatic reading in this case looks at both the event itself (the recording and distribution of a sex act) and its reporting. While a "close" reading attempts to understand what the authors intended to convey, symptomatic readings approach a text or discourse to explain the larger cultural codes or context that inform the meaning ascribed to it. Approaching a text this way allows the interpreter to comment on the discourses constituting it, and the way these elements are situated within a broader set of social or cultural arrangements, hierarchies, or conditions. As the literary critic Fredric Jameson noted, symptomatic readings attempt to get beyond surface-level observations to locate latent or hidden meanings. Such an approach is based on the idea that meaning lies not just in what is said, but largely in what is unsaid. Although Jameson refers to literary works, his point that texts should be understood in relation to their political moment nevertheless informs the analysis here. The text itself is also understood as symptomatic of a current cultural moment. In other words, symptomatic texts serve as "symptoms" of a larger culture problematic and their analysis can therefore provide clues about its inner workings.[28]

A Lexis-Nexis search of newspaper articles about the "Christchurch sex romp" revealed a sample of 30 stories from a range of international publications after eliminating duplicate and irrelevant findings. The sample had a global distribution that included publications from New Zealand, the USA, Ireland, the

UK, and Australia, with articles referencing the viral story's expanse to other countries as well. The news discourse surrounding the story focused primarily on three interrelated themes of privacy, reputation, and employment, all of which were overwhelmingly discussed from a legal framework. These themes will be discussed before turning to those that are notably absent.

Much of the discourse surrounded terms and questions of privacy, but particularly the right to "privacy in public." Of particular focus is the issue of whether or not the couple had "a reasonable expectation of privacy," which serves as the definitional basis for any privacy defense. Interviews with lawyers, law professors, and other legal analysts primarily discussed this "reasonable expectation" in terms of location and building aesthetics (e.g., lighting, window visibility; lack of drapes; window glazing) as well as the nature of the activity itself.[29]

Discussions about the man's and woman's employability marked the second-most common discussion in the stories. Namely, these conversations focused on whether or not the couple could, would, or should be fired for breach of contract and/or creating embarrassing (and, therefore, negative) publicity for their employer. The terms and conditions of these issues were all discussed from a legal framework.

The related discussion of victim's rights marks a tertiary theme in the legal discourse, which primarily asked what privacy rights the subjects of the viral video/photographs could claim against those who took them. Discussions centered on personal damage claims or what rights they might face to legally remove the footage from the web. Elements of victim-blaming were also present, as noted in statements such as "they should have turned the lights out"[30] and "it's all their fault."[31] Equally, few stories criticized the on-looking revelers as "bad neighbors" or engaging in "shameful" behavior.

As mentioned, symptomatic readings are just as concerned with what is present as with what is absent. Given the centrality of surveillance to everyday life and its place in the wider political discourse about state surveillance at the time, it seems surprising that not a single article uses the word, or discusses the event, in terms of surveillance. Less than a handful of stories ($n = 4$) refer to the sex romp recording or images as "voyeurism." This is the case even despite quotes from patrons stating, "The whole pub knew about it and was watching, while they were totally oblivious to it"[32] or "[onlookers] aren't guilty of voyeurism or being perverts. They just didn't think it through."[33] Only one article discussed the legal implications for "those with voyeuristic inclinations"[34] but did not unpack or problematize the issue as voyeurism in any specific way.

In addition to the lack of discussion about surveillance and mediated voyeurism, wider social and cultural implications are equally absent. For example, while the news stories contribute to producing the scandal's spectacle, there are no comments about how or why this became a global news story, or what the global distribution says about contemporary notions of a surveillance-based economy. Only one commentator—comedian Michele A'Court—offers an indictment of the scandal but blames technological advances alone for leaving moral considerations aside. She writes, "For many, television has been mistaken for real life. And now for many, real life is taken for television."[35] (Never mind that the event differs from reality TV, of course, in that reality TV participants have knowledge of their visibility and provide their informed consent of its recording and distribution.) Yet there is no mention of what inclines people to tape and circulate a private act, nor is *serious* consideration given to the impact of doing so on the couple's reputation, even as the media dug for more details about their lives.[36]

This lack of reflexivity seems strange—if not problematic—in a surveillance society that readily acknowledges the value of reputation, which draws the rhetorical question underlying this particular case: Is the lack of critical reflexivity about surveillance society symptomatic of its normalization?

## SEX ROMP AS SURVEILLANCE

It is easy to frame the "problem" with the Christchurch scandal in terms of a panoptic morality play or public shaming. But in the current case, there is no indication that on-looking revelers recorded the sexual encounter under a disciplinary premise (e.g., behavioral sanctioning, normalization, or compliance). There is also no indication that onlookers knew of the tryst's adulterous nature, either. The power dynamics between those involved simply do not match up to a Foucauldian disciplinary mode of governance (save perhaps the wider message that sex acts ought to be conducted with the lights off). Eyewitnesses reportedly described the event in terms of its entertainment value: a "good sideshow" or, as one pub-goer put it, "We all had a good laugh. It was the highlight of the night." Rather than a mechanism for social control, the decision to record and circulate the images appears to have primarily functioned for the purposes of entertainment. But entertainment for whom and for what purposes? What explains the compulsion to record and distribute?

A symptomatic reading of this event suggests that the bridge between the different sites of production involved (i.e., witnesses, social media, mainstream media) is the value that mediated voyeurism has for capital. This assertion takes reasoning beyond the dominant discourse around legality, privacy, and morality to account for the unspoken economic motivations. Importantly, economics are not configured as distinctly financial or material. Yet following the logic of mediated voyeurism, surveillance as entertainment is made productive for capital in a number of ways. There is the potential to build social capital via accolades from witnesses' friends and online followers, which cues one to the satisfaction of having entertained others. The business model of social networking sites like Facebook and Twitter already depend on the habituated uploading of surveillance-based entertainment, while mainstream media organizations—operating under the economic constraints of profit returns—are just as incentivized by sensational, cheap, and free content. Many media companies now mine social media platforms for content to broadcast. In this case, media outlets helped construct the spectacle in exploiting a cheaply produced story that had already sold itself. Even porn site operators saw the economic value of the recording, which news media reported were looking to obtain copies.[37]

Surveillance as entertainment is productive for capital in control societies regulated by market imperatives. For most people, this value may not even be explicitly recognized, given the way mediated voyeurism has been habituated in a socio-cultural context where surveillance is already ubiquitous. The entertainment value of surveillance is therefore motivated by its productivity for capital. Valorizing surveillance as entertainment, then, further incentivizes the impulse to record and distribute. The potential subjects of mediated voyeurism, and thus scandal, have been effectively democratized. It is now the case—as sociologists Kevin Haggerty and Richard Ericson argue—that no individual or group can escape the monitorial gaze.[38]

The idea that surveillance as entertainment is productive coincides with wider discourses about safety, efficiency, and economics that legitimized the expansion of surveillance over the past several decades. Yet the often unspoken paradox of surveillance technologies is that they are productive for some individuals or institutions at the expense of others. This is notable in the way media discourse illuminates how mediated voyeurism can have an inverse effect on productivity when it undermines reputational capital. The challenge surveillance poses to reputation is significant within a post-industrial, political economic context that values reputation as a "brand." Over the past several decades, there has been an intensified focus on quantifying and managing reputation as an "intangible asset" based on not only the sum of the images people hold about an individual or organization but their behaviors as well. Its value is immaterial but can be traded for material benefits or other forms of capital.

Digital technologies, including social media, are often blamed for undermining the ability for people, organizations, and institutions to control things like reputation.[39] So although media discourses focused primarily on the legal ramifications of the videotape, these discussions were primarily motivated by the latent concern of reputational damage—an embarrassing social situation for two people discursively constructed as a legal one centered on the reputational "disrepute" brought to their employer's brand. Reputational concern is further exemplified by official statements publicized by the employer and nearby businesses featured in the videotape looking to distance themselves from the story. Many news articles, for example, quoted a spokeswoman from a nearby business whose sign is visible in the videotape as a means of distancing her company from the scandal. The insurance firm where the couple actually worked also immediately issued statements reassuring clients the matter would be addressed. Even the ex-fiancé of the woman involved made a public statement to a local radio station as a means of clarifying that their relationship had already terminated when the affair took place, which could be read as its own form of reputational management.

Therefore, while media discourse focused primarily on the legal ramifications of the case, what undergird these discourses are actually latent economic concerns. In this case, the threat surveillance poses to (reputational) capital in the process of being valorized as entertainment. A symptomatic reading interprets the dominant focus on legal issues as indicative of capital's centrality—rather than morality, ethics, humanity—to everyday life. We ultimately see that the threat to capital posed by an act of surveillance provides the basis for framing the discourse around legal issues at the expense of broader social and cultural implications.

## CONCLUSION

The Christchurch sex romp matters because the notable absence of surveillance discourse points to the growing invisibility of surveillance practices in other areas of social life. Behind the distraction of spectacle lies a burgeoning contemporary ethos that renders surveillance largely inconsequential, pedestrian, and amoral. For instance, the constant surveillance and circulation of the self is encouraged by contemporary media's interactive promise, which has become a "habitual, mundane, a seamless part of one's daily practices."[40] The recording and circulation of mobile videos capturing a late-night office romance can, therefore, be read not so much as a moral corrective but as an unintended consequence of mediated voyeurism partly motivated by the habitual practice of constant input and circulation of data about the self. Arguably, the desire to gain likes, comments, shares, or retweets boosts one's reputational capital in the short-term and precludes the impulse to think through the consequences such recordings might have for those involved.

For this reason, the Christchurch sex romp can be read as symptomatic of the normalization of surveillance. It is a product of a monitorial culture in which lateral, peer-to-peer watching and reporting further blurs notions of public and private, particularly as they intersect around entertainment, scandal, and capital. As an example of post-panoptic power, the Christchurch sex romp as a participatory mode of surveillance signals an important shift in how surveillance influences sociality. Interactive, mobile, and digitally networked technologies and hand-held recording devices *enable* the normalization, democratization, and blurring of (1) surveillance, (2) scandal, and (3) the public/private divide. And it may even implicitly encourage such uses. This acclimation to surveillance increases as associated technologies and practices become more ubiquitous, less visible, and less surprising. As surveillance scholars David Murakami Wood and C. William R. Webster argue, "We need to make surveillance strange again, and therefore open to rigorous examination and possibly change."[41] Speaking to their point, it might have actually been more surprising had the sex romp *not* gone viral.

Scandals, much like gossip, have long been thought of as an "informal means of social control."[42] Yet this is a different mode of power and control than disciplinary regimes. Freed from the enclosed space of disciplinary structures, a population is encouraged to "roam free," to forget the increasingly automated, ubiquitous, and invisible surveillant gaze while actively participating in it. In this case, control is one that puts economic motivations at the forefront of the decision-making processes that, in turn, commodifies and valorizes surveillance as entertainment. Post-panoptic perspectives of seductive, non-disciplinary forms of surveillance account for this productive dimension. Value is generated in other ways by a single story's virality as contents are discussed, retweeted, commented upon, and re-circulated by media companies worldwide at minimal cost and labor beyond the original recording and uploading of the captured events. In this instance, surveillance is not about the production of docile bodies or a disciplined subject, but controlling sociality in a way that generates commodities made valuable for capital.

## Notes

1. Beck Eleven, "Sex in this City," *The Press*, February 7, 2015.
2. The band reportedly returned to the set with a tongue-in-cheek version of Kings of Leon's "This Sex is on Fire."
3. "New Zealanders Part of Global Opposition to USA Big Brother Mass Surveillance." *Amnesty International NZ*, accessed September 2, 2015, https://www.amnesty.org.nz/new-zealanders-part-global-opposition-usa-big-brother-mass-surveillance.
4. Fredric Jameson, *The Political Unconscious: Narrative as a Socially Symbolic Act*, (Ithaca: University of Cornell Press, 1981).
5. Clay Calvert, *Voyeur Nation: Media, Privacy, and Peering in Modern Culture*, (New York: Westview Press, 2000).
6. David Lyon, *Surveillance Society*, (Buckingham: Open University Press, 2001).
7. Michel Foucault's work actually draws from the eighteenth-century social reformer Jeremy Bentham's philosophy of the panopticon, Michel Foucault, *Discipline and Punish: The Birth of the Prison*, (New York: Vintage Books, 1977).
8. Foucault, *Discipline and Punish*, 200.
9. Kevin Haggerty and Richard Ericson theorize that post-panoptic forms of surveillance function as an "assemblage," where discrete flows of data are brought together for different purposes and made productive different reasons—be it security, management, entertainment, or profit. Kevin D. Haggerty and Richard V. Ericson, "The Surveillant Assemblage," *The British Journal of Sociology* 51, no. 4 (2000): 605–622.
10. Mark Andrejevic, "Ubiquitous Surveillance," in *Routledge Handbook of Surveillance Studies*, ed. Kirstie Ball et al. (London: Routledge, 2012): pp. 91.
11. Gilles Deleuze, "Postscript on the Societies of Control," *October* 59 (1992): 3–7.
12. Deleuze, "Postscript," 6.
13. James Lull and Stephen Hinerman, *Media Scandals: Morality and Desire in the Popular Culture Marketplace*, (Oxford: Polity): 2.
14. Lull and Hinerman, *Media Scandals*, 3.
15. John B. Thompson, *Political Scandal: Power and Visibility in the Media Age*, (Oxford: Polity, 2000): x–xi.
16. Mark Andrejevic, "The Kinder, Gentler Gaze of Big Brother: Reality TV in the Era of Digital Capitalism," *New Media & Society* 4 no. 202: 251–265.
17. Henry Jenkins, *Convergence Culture: Where Old and New Media Collide*, (New York: NYU Press, 2006).
18. Stephen Green "A Plague on the Panopticon: Surveillance and Power in the Global Information Economy," *Information, Communication & Society*, 2, no. 1 (1999): 26–44.

19. Calvert, *Voyeur Nation*.
20. Calvert, *Voyeur Nation*, 92–93.
21. Calvert, *Voyeur Nation*, 23.
22. Calvert, *Voyeur Nation*, 23.
23. Calvert, *Voyeur Nation*.
24. Rachel Dubrofsky, "Surveillance on Reality Television and Facebook," *Communication Theory* 21 no. 2 (2011): 111–129; Andrejevic, "Big Brother."
25. Dubrofsky, "Surveillance on Reality TV and Facebook," p. 114.
26. David Lyon, *Surveillance Studies: An Overview*, (Oxford: Polity, 2007).
27. Jameson, *The Political Unconscious*.
28. Dubrofsky citing Walters, "Surveillance on Reality Television," 114.
29. There is a notable paradox at play in the way the media spend so much time unpacking the "legal ramifications of public liaisons" that the media themselves effectively made public. This is a key implication that the spectacle of scandal helps obfuscate.
30. "Office Sex Romp Couple May Lose Jobs," *Manawatu Standard*, February 3, 2015.
31. Duncan Garner, "Sex in High Places and the Naked Truth about Social Media," *Dominion Post*, February 7, 2015.
32. "Office Sex Romp".
33. Garner, "Sex in High Places".
34. Susan Hornsby-Geluk, "Spotlight is on this Unsafe Sex," *The Press*, February 10, 2015.
35. Michele A'Court, "Caught Out and Never Forgotten," *The Press*, February 4, 2015.
36. Following conventional reporting norms, mainstream media aggressively sought interviews with the couple, their acquaintances, employer, and witnesses who could provide additional details of the affair. In spectacularizing the event, they shifted coverage to the man's marital and family status, the inconsolability of his wife (e.g., she is "in pieces"; "can't stop crying"); information on the young woman involved, including the status of her Facebook account (reportedly deleted within days of the sandal). The story resurfaced a month later to report neither employee worked at the company anymore, while follow-up stories in March 2015 reported that the woman had left New Zealand to return to her home country in England. "Christchurch Sex Romp Woman Leaves New Zealand," *TVNZ*, March 31, 2015. https://www.tvnz.co.nz/one-news/new-zealand/christchurch-sex-romp-woman-leaves-new-zealand-6273746.
37. Phil Taylor, "Legal Ramifications of Public Liaisons," *New Zealand Herald*, February 7, 2015.
38. Haggerty and Ericson, "The Surveillant Assemblage," 606.
39. Jenkins, *Convergence Culture*.
40. Dubrofsky, "Surveillance on Reality Television," 113.
41. David Murakami Wood and C. William R. Webster, "Living in Surveillance Societies: The Normalisation of Surveillance in Europe and the Threat of Britain's Bad Example," *Journal of Contemporary European Research* 5 no. 2 (2009): 260.
42. Sally Engle Merry, "Rethinking Gossip and Scandal," in Daniel Klein (ed) *Reputation: Studies in the Voluntary Elicitation of Good Conduct*, (Ann Arbor: University of Michigan Press, 1997): 47.

# CHAPTER 11

# Over-Sharing in a Political Sex Scandal

*Gina Masullo Chen, Paromita Pain, and Deepa Fadnis*

When former South Carolina Governor Mark Sanford complained about his ex-wife on Facebook—calling her latest demands in their divorce "preposterous, crazy, and wrong"[1]—he was doing what many of us do: airing grievances online about a relationship gone bad. It was one of several posts in September 2014 that drew hundreds of comments. Some offered support. Others chided him for sharing personal details. What sets his posts apart from ours is that by taking his private battle public, he obliterated what sociologist Jürgen Habermas[2] calls the intimate sphere through the exaggerated sense of closeness that flourishes on social media. As Habermas wrote: "The intimate sphere, once the very center of the private sphere, moved to the periphery to the extent that the private sphere itself became deprivatized."[3]

Sanford's posts made very public his fray with his ex-wife, Jenny, who left him after he tried to hide a visit to his mistress by saying he was hiking the Appalachian Trail. They offer a sobering example of how today's era of hyper-surveillance has blurred the lines between public and private for politicians negotiating sex scandals. Politicians' sex scandals have been public affairs for decades, but the always-on nature of social media heightens this effect, fueling a voyeuristic culture where people cling to every salacious detail of politicians' lives, while blasting politicians for making these tidbits public.

This chapter explores this phenomenon by qualitatively analyzing more than 300 comments members of the public posted on Sanford's Facebook wall in response to a series of posts he wrote about his divorce. We looked for common themes in these comments. Then we interpreted them using Habermas' theory of the public sphere, which argues that a "repoliticized social sphere"[4] emerged that blended the lines between public and private as society industrialized. In much the same way, we argue, social media have

G.M. Chen (✉) • P. Pain • D. Fadnis
School of Journalism, The University of Texas at Austin, TX, USA

© The Editor(s) (if applicable) and The Author(s) 2016
H. Mandell, G.M. Chen (eds.), *Scandal in a Digital Age*,
DOI 10.1057/978-1-137-59545-4_11

131

merged public and private[5] through the technological features of social media that make the distant seem close.[6] This fosters a heightened sense of interpersonal intimacy—called a parasocial relationship[7]—between politicians and other celebrities with those who engage with them online.[8] We begin by providing a brief history of Sanford's situation and how it fits the definition of a political scandal. Next, we discuss the theories of parasocial interaction and the public sphere. We then explain details about the Facebook posts and comments at the heart of this study and explore themes we found, interpreting them using theory. Finally, we offer suggestions for what these findings mean for public discourse and society as a whole.

## MARK SANFORD'S STORY

Sanford's public political demise began in June 2009 when he admitted he had traveled to Argentina to meet his lover, Maria Belen Chapur.[9] This scandal ended his marriage, threatened his governorship, and dashed his presidential aspirations. He finished his second term as governor in 2011 despite claims of ethics violations and attempts at impeachment.[10] He returned to politics after winning a special election to Congress in 2013.[11] Sanford and his wife divorced in February 2010, but their battles raged.[12] In September 2014, Sanford took to Facebook in a series of posts, complaining about what he saw as his ex-wife's unfair demands. In the posts, he speaks directly to his constituents, using the conversational tone of a friend. For example, on September 3, 2014, he posted a statement about her latest legal claim. It read in part:[13]

> As I have expressed countless times, I am sorry for the way I handled the events of 2009, but no degree of acrimony will fix nor change its history. I've come to believe that we all have chapters of life that we wish we might handle differently, but as I'm sure you're well aware by now, my former wife Jenny has moved forward with another legal claim. I refrained from responding in the first 24 hours because response in any form seems to be a no win, but given the level of the claims and accusations, I felt it important to respond.

Later that month, Sanford posted a 2346-word status update that *New York Times* columnist Gail Collins called "mainly a whine about his ex-wife, the divorce settlement, and visitation rules."[14] In the post, Sanford rails against his ex-wife's demands that he undergo a psychiatric evaluation and anger management training while referencing his own self-restraint.[15] In a third Facebook post, Sanford apologizes: "Stepping back from my post of a few days ago let me again apologize for going into the iterations of court actions on the personal sphere."[16]

To understand this moment as the public and private spheres melded, we analyzed 351 comments posted in response to Sanford's posts on September 3 and September 14, 2014. Comments on his September 12, 2014, post could not be analyzed because the post was deleted before comments could be retrieved. All three posts have now been removed from Sanford's Facebook page,[17] and the tone of his page has shifted from any public statements about his personal life. His most recent Facebook posts are professional and revolve heavily around his day-to-day activities in Washington.

Our analysis involved reading through comments again and again, looking for themes in what people were saying. This type of qualitative textual analysis "focuses on the underlying ideological and cultural assumptions of the text. Text is understood as a complex set of discursive strategies that is situated in a special cultural context."[18] This approach allowed us to focus on contextual and implied meaning in the comments and make broader inferences, rather than focus merely on details.[19] This approach views culture as a narrative process in which artifacts are consciously or unconsciously linked to larger societal issues. In this case, the larger societal issue is how the exaggerated intimacy of social media perpetuates the public's rapacious appetite for titillating details of politicians' sex scandals.

## ANALYZING THIS SCANDALOUS MOMENT

Before delving into what our analysis found, it is important to understand why we examined this scandalous moment. It fits the definition of political scandal, defined as a private event that violates social norms where the person committing the misdeed is caught.[20] Scandal scholar Hinda Mandell[21] argues a scandal is not merely a tawdry event but becomes a "hegemonic tool to reinforce social norms and the means by which the general public can hold (temporary) power—in the form of negative public opinion—over an elected official." Politicians must constantly use their symbolic power over the public to persuade, confront, and influence actions and beliefs,[22] but scandal can destroy this resource. Toward the end of the twentieth century, political scandals became a dominant strand of Western media coverage, further exacerbated by the imperatives of the 24-hour news demand, technological developments, and a burgeoning number of electronic outlets.[23] Reputation makes scandal in politics important.[24] Reputation is a resource, a symbolic capital, allowing politicians to build up legitimacy and develop trust among fellow politicians, the electorate, and media professionals.[25] In scandal, a politician's reputation takes the blow.

The public gravitates to scandals because people are naturally hardwired to pay attention to news that involves conflict.[26] Politicians embroiled in scandal receive more media attention. Social media may amplify coverage of scandal,[27] by fostering conditions conducive to the rapid spread of ribald stories, captured in real time and shared through Twitter and Facebook. When the immediacy and heightened interpersonal closeness of social media are thrown in, snippets about a sex scandal in a politician's life may become too enticing for the public to resist. Sanford's Facebook posts offer a vivid example of this. Posts are both private and public and reveal the jaundiced underbelly of a marriage gone wrong. They offer a chance to understand how the public—Sanford's Facebook "friends"—make sense of his personal outbursts on a public stage.

## SOCIAL MEDIA AS A REALM FOR PARASOCIAL RELATIONSHIPS

Facebook provides a fruitful context to understand this dynamic because, as a social-networking site, it offers potential for both mass and interpersonal communication.[28] When we speak out on social media, we are conversing directly with our imagined audience,[29] which in our minds may be a handful of people or hundreds. Our goal with these computer-mediated conversations is to foster or maintain social relationships.[30] When we interact with those in power—celebrities, politicians, athletes—on social media, these seemingly personal conversations can obscure the fact that these people are strangers. In the 1950s, sociologist Donald Horton and R. Richard Wohl[31] proposed that television, radio, and movies created an illusion of intimacy, whereby sports spectators felt as if they were engaging closely with famous athletes, though the athletes had no knowledge of the spectators. They called this a parasocial interaction, where the celebrity "stimulates an informal, intimate, face-to-face conversation with the invisible and remote spectator."[32]

Social media exaggerates this potential for parasocial relationships. In earlier forms of media, parasocial relationships were one-sided: The audience identified with the media character, but the media character had little idea this was going on.[33] Social media, however, offer two-sided interactions. Audience members imagine the actor, athlete, or politician is having a personal relationship with them. At the same time, the celebrity may be actively creating this illusion of intimacy with the follower or fan by sharing personal information through a process called "celebrity as practice."[34] The audience seeks out the celebrity to fill a need for social interaction.[35] Then celebrity interaction with the public on social media influences how closely the public feels to this person.[36] Given this background, it seems logical that Sanford's interactions on Facebook with his virtual "friends" and commenters formed a two-sided parasocial interaction, spurred by his copious revelations of private facts. As he shared his details, members of the public responded with their own sentiments, further bolstering this illusory interpersonal intimacy.

## BLURRED LINES BETWEEN PRIVATE AND PUBLIC

In his seminal work, Habermas[37] argues that Marxism, liberalism, the state's expanding power, and the commercial media weakened the public sphere into a passive mediatized culture of consumption that readily embraces what those in elite society are doing.[38] Habermas'[39] concept of the public sphere implies a public armed with agency to address political scandal and require that those in power be accountable. Rhetorician Gerald A. Hauser[40] expands on this notion, suggesting the public sphere is defined by understanding, not conflict. In Hauser's[41] public sphere, members of the public network through evolving conversations that are part of a larger developing dialogue.[42] In Sanford's example, these conversations are writ large in the computer-mediated public space of Facebook. The public defines the scandal both through conflict and understanding, and their discussions about it form a larger conversation about society as a whole.

Scandals represent a breach of institutional trust[43] where the public views a politician's private foibles as a public affront. The politician's actions come to characterize the failure of the larger institution of government.[44] The scandal also marks the public discourse and through that discourse permeates society. As Hauser[45] explains, "Our daily conversations with co-workers, neighbors, superiors, subordinates, community and church contacts, group members, friends, and family provide countless opportunities to exchange views on public matters." Today, these conversations shift to the virtual water cooler of social media.

The "sociotechnical affordances" of social media foment social saturation, where public and private blur.[46] The norm becomes to share rather than withhold.[47] We argue this forms what Habermas[48] calls a "social sphere," a blended state that grew out of the traditional separation of public and private. He argues that as the market economy grew, this social sphere transformed the relationship between those in power and those without power. The state and society permeated each other, and the intimate sphere—once the hallmark of the private space—shifted. In our current day, politicians and others in power may transverse between the public and private sphere through their parasocial online relationships with supporters, fans, or followers. Those in authority still wield power, but this imagined closeness on digital media creates an illusion of intimacy where the norm is to share private information because the public seems part of this social sphere.

## WHAT THE COMMENTERS ARE SAYING

Three main themes emerge in our analysis of the comments posted in response to Sanford's status updates. The first suggests members of the public felt a form of parasocial relationship with Sanford, feeling closeness toward him based on his revelation of private details. A second theme suggests Sanford's commenters expressed empathy for what he and his ex-wife were going through. A third theme indicates commenters felt Sanford should keep his private life private. Comments reveal a palpable tension between a desire to know and discomfort with knowing private details of a public figure.

## "HANG IN THERE, MARK"

Often, commenters assume a personal tone, using the pronoun "you" and speaking to Sanford's worth as a person—not just a politician—as if he were a friend. "We don't know you personally, but we like and admire you as a person and as a congressman. Try to hold your head up high. We are behind you 100%," commented Linda Munch Wilson.[49] Fueled by Sanford's disclosure, commenters may feel a sense of heightened closeness that social media can foster.[50] They reply to him personally and empathize with his pain as a friend, rather than as a distant constituent. They called Sanford by his first name, increasing the sense of intimacy. "Hang in there, Mark," wrote Roger Pinckney Xi.[51] Commenter Bill Litchfield[52] used a colloquial tone that suggests heightened intimacy: "Mark, I been there buddy with a vindictive ex." Commenters seemed to suggest Sanford's disclosures made him more authentic and that he was speaking to them directly. Laura Johnston[53] wrote in response to Sanford's apology [emphasis added]:

> Your comment to provide your point of view *to me* was OK to express—even though personal. And you got right back to work. You are a good father. You are a good man. So you just continue to keep your head up and continue to speak from your heart. I really find your honestly quite rare and prefer your "Velveteen Rabbit"—like realness to the usual sanitized comments from other politicians.

Commenters suggest Sanford's vulnerability made them feel connected to him and set him apart from other politicians. This proposes a dual-sided parasocial relationship where Sanford shares and actively creates an illusion of intimacy,[54] and the public feels gratified by this disclosure because it fills a need for social interaction.[55] People seek to form and maintain relationships with Sanford using Facebook, much as the general public has been found to use Facebook.[56] The very attributes of the medium—in particular the way Facebook allows people to speak directly to those in power—hides that Sanford is not really a friend to most of these people. Much as Horton and Wohl[57] theorized long ago, the public feels a specific closeness to Sanford, the politician. In a newer twist, the politician furthers this illusion.[58]

## "CONGRESSMAN, I FEEL YOUR PAIN"

For many commenters, the online parasocial interaction drove them to draw on their own experiences to understand Sanford's disclosure. They compare Sanford's situation to their own romantic battles, divorces, and experiences of infidelity, and urged him to draw strength from their words. Ralph Lewis[59] wrote, "Congressman, I feel your pain," and then described his own situation, comparing it to Sanford's. In some cases, commenters speak about their own experience at length. This seems to mirror the experience many have when they are going through a difficult time, and well-meaning friends offer support that turns into a cathartic rehashing of their own plights. For example, Tina Stucki Brauner[60] commented:

> Some battles are not worth entertaining. I had some similar situations with my ex, only he was the one that cheated on me. I moved on, he never could. I put up with years of criticism and name calling no one should have to deal with. I just let it go in one ear and out the other. I would not drop to his level. See I knew he was just jealous that I could move on and be happy. And I wasn't going to let him ruin my happiness. Keep your chin up and keep smiling, eventually it gets better.

Commenters seem to identify strongly with Sanford's troubles. Men compare Sanford's ex-wife to their former partners and identify most strongly with Sanford. As Azriel Berkovits[61] explained: "Since I had to go through something similar, although not the same, I have understanding of your situation and feelings." Women also frequently side with Sanford, though they could relate to his ex-wife's experiences. It appears as if they side with Sanford because they believe his former wife crossed a line they would never transverse. "I have been in your ex-wife's shoes," commented Kathryn W. Cox,[62] "but never would I have gone to the extent she has against my ex." This support is somewhat unsurprising because commenters likely would not follow Sanford's Facebook page if they did not like him. However, not all the women offer support. A few women identify more strongly with Sanford's ex-wife, so they respond to him as they would if he were their own unfaithful husband. "Quit whining already," commented Cathy Haynes.[63] "At sometime or other, you have to pay the price for what you do." Kristie Griffin Strickland[64] was more pointed:

> A conscious decision to cheat, lie and steal is not a mistake. It is a choice! A really selfish choice. If I were your wife I'd want revenge too. The lady planned to spend the rest of her life with you. I'm pretty sure I'd be really mad for a really long time.

Collectively, these comments where women cast themselves into the role of the scorned wife demonstrate a level of parasocial relationship they feel with Sanford. Not only do they feel close to him, they relate to him almost as if he were their spouse.

## "Just Quit Talking About It"

Despite the strong parasocial relationship with Sanford many commenters display, others chafe at his revelations. Their comments suggest anger at Sanford for trampling the divide between public and private. One commenter wrote: "Why would you lower yourself and put this personal information on Facebook of all places."[65] Treina Siegel[66] was blunt: "This should be a PRIVATE Matter for all involved." These commenters bristle at the loss of an intimate space where private details are separate from the public. More than the scandal itself, this blending of private and public spheres breaches their sense of trust[67] with Sanford, whom they saw as personally offending them through his lack of restraint. "Find your voice. Find your issue and become a national spokesman. And again DO NOT COMMENT ON YOUR PERSONAL LIFE," wrote John Campbell.[68] Don Bartlett's[69] comment suggests Sanford should remain mum on personal matters and re-assert his place in the public political sphere:

> If we gave a dam about your personal life we never would have put you back in office, your mistake is even discussing it, especially as my representative. If you want people to put it in the past you need to do the same and not even discuss it publically. If you are going waste your time discussing this publically rather than doing the dam job we hired you to do then shame on us for giving you a second chance. Take your baggage and move on, hell better yet resign! Too much dam drama with you.

Comments such as these suggest a gendered element to the opposition of Sanford's openness. Bartlett's word choice—referring to Sanford's "drama"—conjures a mental model that fits the cultural prototype associated with women, not men.[70] Over-sharing is associated with femininity, so when Sanford reveals too much, he challenges a contemporary definition of what it means to be a man. People balk at this.

The tension between aspiring to be Sanford's confidant yet not wanting to know too much private information was apparent in some comments. Melinda Sian Norris[71] seems to jockey between seeing the situation through Sanford's eyes and through his ex-wife's, while seeing Sanford as both a friend and a politician. She wrote:

> I think this last claim by your ex-wife is a little "out there", but I have to be honest...when you take the position of leader, you are held to a higher level than others and you need to do your best to set a good example for your children as well as your constituents. You dropped the ball with that one, and now suffering the consequences.

These comments suggest some constituents did not value Sanford taking them so far into their confidences. While their frank tone suggests a heightened intimacy with him, their words belie this closeness. As in Hauser's[72] public sphere, their conversations about the scandal appear part of a larger narrative.[73] They long for a firmer line between state and society where the social sphere has not obliterated the intimate sphere.[74]

## POLITICAL SCANDAL IN AN OVER-SHARING CULTURE

Sanford's posts—and the biting or supportive responses they elicit—offer a telling illustration of how our current culture of over-sharing on social media has diminished the line between public and private. Sanford's extramarital betrayal of his ex-wife fits the classic definition of political sex scandal,[75] and, as such, is clearly part of the public debate. Political scandals such as his give the public power over the politician,[76] as people weigh what influence—if any—the scandal should have on a politician's career. The public makes this call by examining the influence the scandal has on the politician's reputation[77] and how much it breaches their trust.[78]

Sanford's case illustrates that social media change the calculus of this dynamic. When he began to vent about his deteriorating relationship on Facebook in public—as if he were privately talking to friends—the attributes of the social network itself allowed the blurring of lines between the public and private, the state and society.[79] Sanford amplified his celebrity status[80] by over-sharing, fostering a sense of social saturation[81] with his Facebook friends. Those friends, seeking to fill their own needs as social beings,[82] were drawn to Sanford by his digital confessions, seeing him like a real friend in a parasocial relationship.[83] The Facebook platform allowed this to happen by perpetuating this illusion of intimacy[84] and acting as an accelerant for public debate[85] that in this case may have been best left in the private sphere. The public was left in a quandary. Some felt moved to relate to Sanford's woes and re-assure him as they would an actual friend. Kelly A. Morelli[86] urged: "Just keep your head up. The haters are going to hate." Another commenter urged Sanford to keep quiet with a colloquial charm that belies their distant relationship. "My grandmother always said 'The dog that barks the loudest is the dog that bites/bit'. Don't be sucked into a bantering of comments because that is what they want," commented Tracy Davis.[87]

## WHAT THIS MEANS FOR SOCIETY

Clearly, these findings suggest that the way we understand scandal is forever altered. Social media have become an agent for the spread of information, discussion, and even activism related to controversy.[88] The rising power of social media is happening at a particular moment when media as a whole are fragmented and polarized.[89] Social media can amplify the coverage of scandal in traditional media, especially when the audience engages personally[90] with the political players by following or friending them. That can provide more balance, but it also interjects the personal into the public space. This allows the public to relate personally to the politician in a parasocial interaction,[91] but it also means the scandal itself may take on a larger life.

Precipitated by the audience's seemingly insatiable appetite for revealing details about politicians' mistakes, social media provides a platform for public debate, but it also extends the conversation about a scandal. People feel as if they know the politicians, so they may feel more empathetic toward them or more hurt by their actions. A politician cheating on his wife is no longer merely a breach of public trust.[92] Instead, the public becomes enmeshed in the politician's scandal, and this changes the influence of the scandal. Social media, with its illusion of intimacy,[93] allows the public to feel the scandal through their own experiences and project onto to the politicians their own beliefs about how it should be handled. This not only blurs the line between public and private but also casts the politician—and the constituency—in a seemingly co-dependent relationship where what one does influences the other. It personalizes the political, making politicians' private foibles more relevant in the public's eyes and casts doubt on the politicians' ability to do their jobs. Ultimately, this may make the public less tolerant of politicians who engage in scandal. As Carolyn Moore David Murdock[94] commented:

> I have gone through a painful divorce in the past, and it interferes with every aspect of one's life. You may not think it is affecting your ability to serve as an effective Congressman, but I assure you it does. Please consider resigning from your Congressional seat, so that someone who has no such personal problems can take over your position.

# NOTES

1. Mark Sanford, September 3, 2014, Facebook status update, "As I have expressed countless times, I am sorry for the way I handled the events of 2009."
2. Jürgen Habermas, *The Structural Transformation of the Public Sphere*, (Cambridge, MA: MIT Press, 1991).
3. Habermas, *The Structural Transformation of the Public Sphere*, 152.
4. Habermas, *The Structural Transformation of the Public Sphere*, 142.
5. Nancy K. Baym and danah boyd, "Social Mediated Publicness: An Introduction," *Journal of Broadcasting & Electronic Media* 56, no. 3 (2012), 320–329.
6. Alice Marwick and danah boyd, "To See and Be Seen: Celebrity Practice on Twitter," *Convergence* 17 (2011): 139–158.
7. Donald Horton and R. Richard Wohl, "Interaction in Audience-Participation Shows," *The American Journal of Sociology* 62 (1956): 579–587.
8. Evan L. Frederick, Choong Hoon Lim, Galen Clavio, and Patrick Walsh, "Why We Follow: An Examination of Parasocial Interaction and Fan Motivations for Following Athlete Archetypes on Twitter," *International Journal of Sport Communication* 5 (2012): 481–502.
9. "Timeline: Mark Sanford's Downfall and Survival," *The State*, March 18, 2010. http://www.thestate.com/incoming/article14380862.html.
10. Paul Steinhauser, Kevin Liptak, and Gregory Wallace, "Mark Sanford, Former South Carolina Governor, Wins GOP Nomination for House Seat," *CNN*, April 2, 2013. http://politicalticker.blogs.cnn.com/2013/04/02/mark-sanford-former-south-carolina-governor-wins-gop-nomination-for-house-seat/.
11. Rachel Weiner, "Mark Sanford Wins South Carolina Special Election," *The Washington Post*, May 7, 2013. http://www.washingtonpost.com/news/post-politics/wp/2013/05/07/mark-sanford-wins-south-carolina-special-election/.
12. "Timeline: Mark Sanford's Downfall and Survival."
13. Mark Sanford, September 3, 2014, Facebook status update, "As I have expressed countless times, I am sorry for the way I handled the events of 2009."
14. Gail Collins, "Sex is the Least of it: Mark Sanford Just Can't Stop Sharing," *The New York Times*, September 17, 2014. http://www.nytimes.com/2014/09/18/opinion/gail-collins-mark-sanford-just-cant-stop-sharing.html?_r=0.
15. Collins, "Sex is the Least of it: Mark Sanford Just Can't Stop Sharing."
16. Mark Sanford, September 12, 2014, Facebook status update, "Stepping back from my post of a few days ago let me again apologize."
17. All Mark Sanford Facebook posts, and the comments posted on these posts, were accessed in fall 2014 before the posts were removed from Facebook.
18. Elfriede Fursich, "In Defense of Textual Analysis," *Journalism Studies* 10 (2009): 240.
19. Donald G. McTavish and Ellen B. Pirro, "Contextual Content Analysis," *Quality & Quantity* 24 (1990): 245–265.
20. John B. Thompson, *The Media and Modernity: A Social Theory of the Media*, (Stanford, CA: Stanford University Press, 1995).
21. Hinda Mandell, "Political Wives and Scandal: Reading Agency in silence at Press Conferences," *Catalan Journal of Communication and Cultural Studies* 4 (2012): 206.

22. Karen Sanders and Maria José Canel, "A Scribbling Tribe: Reporting Political Scandal in Britain and Spain," *Journalism* 7 (2006): 453–476; Thompson, *The Media and Modernity: A Social Theory of the Media*.

23. Howard Tumber and Silvio R. Waisbord, "Introduction: Political Scandals and Media Across Democracies, Volume II," *American Behavioral Scientist* 47 (2004): 1143–1152.

24. Thompson, *The Media and Modernity: A Social Theory of the Media*.

25. Sanders and Canel, "A Scribbling Tribe: Reporting Political Scandal in Britain and Spain."

26. Pamela J. Shoemaker and Steve Reese, *Mediating the Message in the 21st Century: A Media Sociology Perspective*, (New York, NY: Routledge, 2013).

27. Amy Mitchell, Tom Rosenstiel, and Leah Christian, "The State of the News Media 2012: What Facebook and Twitter Mean for News," Pew Research Center's Project for Excellence in Journalism. http://www.stateofthemedia. org/2012/mobile-devices-and-news-consumption-some-good-signs-for-journalism/what-facebook-and-twitter-mean-for-news/.

28. Gina Masullo Chen, "Tweet This: A Uses and Gratifications Perspective on How Active Twitter Use Gratifies a Need to Connect with Others," *Computers in Human Behavior* 27 (2011): 755–762.

29. Marwick and boyd, "To See and Be Seen: Celebrity Practice on Twitter."

30. Chen, "Tweet This: A Uses and Gratifications Perspective on How Active Twitter Use Gratifies a Need to Connect with Others."; Gina Masullo Chen, "Why Do Women Bloggers Use Social Media? Recreation and Information Motivations Outweigh Engagement Motivations," *New Media & Society* 17 (2015): 24–40; Jennifer Bonds-Raacke and John Raacke, "MySpace and Facebook: Identifying Dimensions of Uses and Gratifications of Friend Networking Sites," *Individual Differences Research* 8 (2010): 27–33.

31. Horton and Wohl, "Interaction in Audience-Participation Shows."

32. Donald Horton and Anselm Strauss, "Interaction in Audience-Participation Shows," *American Journal of Sociology* 62 (1957): 579.

33. Horton and Wohl, "Interaction in Audience-Participation Shows."; Hartmann and Goldhoorn, "Horton and Wohl Revisisted: Exploring Viewers' Experience of Parasocial Interaction."

34. Marwick and boyd, "To See and Be Seen: Celebrity Practice on Twitter," 1.

35. Monica Ancu and Raluca Cozma, "MySpace Politics: Uses and Gratifications of Befriending Candidates," *Journal of Broadcasting & Electronic Media* 53 (2009): 567–583.

36. Frederick, Lim, Clavio, and Walsh, "Why We Follow: An Examination of Parasocial Interaction and Fan Motivations for Following Athlete Archetypes on Twitter."

37. Habermas, *The Structural Transformation of the Public Sphere*.

38. C.T. Maier, "Weathering the Storm: Hauser's Vernacular Voices, Public Relations, and the Roman Catholic Church," *Public Relations Review* 31 (2005): 219–227.

39. Habermas, *The Structural Transformation of the Public Sphere*.

40. Gerald A. Hauser, *Vernacular Voices: The Rhetoric of Publics and Public Spheres*, (Columbia, SC: The University of South Carolina Press, 1999).

41. Hauser, *Vernacular Voices: The Rhetoric of Publics and Public Spheres*.

42. Maier, "Weathering the Storm: Hauser's Vernacular Voices, Public Relations, and the Roman Catholic Church."

43. Gary Alan Fine, "Scandal, Social Conditions, and the Creation of Public Attention: Fatty Arbuckle and the 'Problem of Hollywood,'" *Social Problems* 44 (1997): 297–323.

44. Fine, "Scandal, Social Conditions, and the Creation of Public Attention: Fatty Arbuckle and the 'Problem of Hollywood.'"

45. Hauser, *Vernacular Voices: The Rhetoric of Publics and Public Spheres*, 65.

46. Zizi A. Papacharissi, "Without You, I'm Nothing: Performance of the Self on Twitter," *International Journal of Communication* 6 (2012): 1992.

47. Papacharissi, "Without You, I'm Nothing: Performance of the Self on Twitter."

48. Habermas, *The Structural Transformation of the Public Sphere*, 142.

49. In all cases, all Facebook comments are attributed to the name used in the actual comment, and gender of the commenter is assumed based on those names. In the interest of accuracy, grammatical errors and misspellings in comments are retained; Linda Munch Wilson, September 3, 2014, Facebook comment, "We don't know you personally, but we like and admire you as a person and as a congressman. Try to hold your head up high. We are 100% behind you."

50. Marwick and boyd, "To See and Be Seen: Celebrity Practice on Twitter."

51. Roger Pinckney Xi, September 3, 2014, Facebook comment, "Hang in there Mark."

52. Bill Litchfield, September 14, 2014, Facebook comment, "Mark, I have been there buddy with a vindictive ex…"

53. Laura Johnston, September 14, 2014, Facebook comment, "Your comment to provide your point of view to me was OK to express—even though personal."

54. Marwick and boyd, "To See and Be Seen: Celebrity Practice on Twitter."

55. Ancu and Cozma, "MySpace Politics: Uses and Gratifications of Befriending Candidates."

56. Chen, "Tweet This: A Uses and Gratifications Perspective on How Active Twitter Use Gratifies a Need to Connect with Others."; Chen, "Why Do Women Bloggers Use Social Media? Recreation and Information Motivations Outweigh Engagement Motivations."; and Bonds-Raacke and Raacke, "MySpace and Facebook: Identifying Dimensions of Uses and Gratifications of Friend Networking Sites."

57. Horton and Wohl, "Interaction in Audience-Participation Shows."

58. Marwick and boyd, "To See and Be Seen: Celebrity Practice on Twitter."

59. Ralph Lewis, September 3, 2014, Facebook comment, "Congressman I feel your pain."

60. Tina Stucki Brauner, September 3, 2014, Facebook comment, "Some battles are not worth entertaining."

61. Azriel Berkovits, September 3, 2014, Facebook comment, "Since I had to go through something similar, although not the same, I have understanding of our situation and feeling."

62. Kathryn W. Cox, September 3, 2014, Facebook comment, "I have been in our ex-wife's shoes."

63. Cathy Haynes, September 3, 2014, Facebook comment, "Quit whining already."

64. Kristie Griffin Strickland, September 3, 2014, Facebook comment, "A conscious decision to cheat, lie and steal is not a mistake."

65. Janette Edens Hall, September 14, 2014, Facebook comment, "Why would you lower yourself and put this personal information on Facebook."

66. Treina Siegel, September 3, 2014, Facebook comment, "This should be a PRIVATE Matter for all involved."

67. Fine, Scandal, "Social Conditions, and the Creation of Public Attention: Fatty Arbuckle and the 'Problem of Hollywood.'"

68. John Campbell, September 14, 2014, Facebook comment, "Find your voice. Find your issues."

69. Don Bartlett, September 3, 2014, Facebook comment, "If we gave a dam about your personal life we never would have put you back in office."

70. George Lakoff, *Women, Fire, and Dangerous Things: What Categories Reveal About the Mind*, (Chicago, IL: University of Chicago Press, 1990).

71. Melinda Sian Norris, September 3, 2014, Facebook comment, "I think this last claim by your ex-wife is a little 'out there.'"

72. Hauser, *Vernacular Voices: The Rhetoric of Publics and Public Spheres*.

73. Maier, "Weathering the Storm: Hauser's Vernacular Voices, Public Relations, and the Roman Catholic Church."

74. Habermas, *The Structural Transformation of the Public Sphere*.

75. Thompson, *The Media and Modernity: A Social Theory of the Media*.

76. Mandell, "Political Wives and Scandal: Reading Agency in Silence at Press Conferences."

77. Thompson, *The Media and Modernity: A Social Theory of the Media*.

78. Fine, "Scandal, Social Conditions, and the Creation of Public Attention: Fatty Arbuckle and the 'Problem of Hollywood.'"

79. Habermas, *The Structural Transformation of the Public Sphere*.

80. Marwick and Boyd, "To See and Be Seen: Celebrity on Twitter."

81. Papacharissi, "Without You, I'm Nothing: Performance of the Self on Twitter."

82. Ancu and Cozma, "MySpace Politics: Uses and Gratifications of Befriending Candidates."

83. Horton and Wohl, "Interaction in Audience-Participation Shows."

84. Marwick and Boyd, "To See and Be Seen: Celebrity on Twitter."

85. Benjamin R. Warner, Sarah Turner McGowen, and Joshua Hawthorne, "Limbaugh's Social Media Nightmare: Facebook and Twitter as Spaces for Political Action," *Journal of Radio & Audio Media* 19 (2012): 257–275.

86. Kelly A. Morelli, September 3, 2014, Facebook comment, "Just keep your head up."

87. Tracy Davis, September 3, 2014, Facebook comment, "My grandmother always said 'The dog that barks the loudest is the dog that bites/bit'...".

88. Warner, McGowen, and Hawthorne, "Limbaugh's Social Media Nightmare: Facebook and Twitter as Spaces for Political Action."

89. Shanto Iyengar, and Kyu S. Hahn, "Red Media, Blue Media: Evidence of Ideological Selectivity in Media Use," *Journal of Communication* 59 (2009): 19–39; Natalie Jomini Stroud, "Polarization and Partisan Selective Exposure," *Journal of Communication* 60 (2010): 556–576.

90. Mitchell, Rosenstiel, and Christian, "The State of the News Media 2012: What Facebook and Twitter Mean for News."
91. Horton and Wohl, "Interaction in Audience-Participation Shows."
92. Fine, "Scandal, Social Conditions, and the Creation of Public Attention: Fatty Arbuckle and the 'Problem of Hollywood.'"
93. Marwick and boyd, "To See and Be Seen: Celebrity Practice on Twitter."
94. Carolyn Moore David Murdock, September 3, 2014, Facebook comment, "I have gone through a painful divorce in the past."

# CHAPTER 12

# Media's Role in the Rob Ford "Crack-Tape" Scandal

*Gemma Richardson and Romayne Smith Fullerton*

For much of 2013 and 2014, the Canadian public was captivated with the "crack-tape" scandal that engulfed the mayor's office in the country's largest city, Toronto. After the initial news broke that Mayor Rob Ford had been captured on video smoking crack cocaine, and that this video was being shopped around to news outlets by drug dealers looking to make a six-figure payday, *The Toronto Star* and *The Globe and Mail* published stories further detailing Ford's connections to drugs and criminals.[1] While these breaking stories led many to question the mayor's legitimacy to rule, a sizable number of ordinary citizens continued to defend Ford and question not *his* actions, but those of the mainstream media.[2] The backlash culminated in part in an Ontario Press Council (OPC) hearing where the two newspapers were exonerated of acting unethically; however, some continued to blame the messenger.

In this chapter, we will explore the disconnect between ostensibly outstanding examples of investigative journalism exposing illegal conduct in a city's highest elected office and a vocal portion of the public who still argue that much of the media coverage was too personal or nasty. In his book *After Virtue*, philosopher Alasdair MacIntyre argued: "What matters at this stage is the construction of local forms of community within which civility and the intellectual and moral life can be sustained through the dark ages which are already upon us."[3] Working from MacIntyre's premise, we contend that the news media have an obligation to address audiences as citizens who need information to participate in a democracy, not as individuals who want to be entertained or whose private curiosity ought to be teased to sell more products. We will begin with some details on the background to the scandal and highlight the role of

G. Richardson (✉)
Digital Communications and Journalism, Humber College, Toronto, ON, Canada

R.S. Fullerton
Media Studies and Journalism, University of Western Ontario, London, ON, Canada

© The Editor(s) (if applicable) and The Author(s) 2016
H. Mandell, G.M. Chen (eds.), *Scandal in a Digital Age*,
DOI 10.1057/978-1-137-59545-4_12

the media. We will then probe the public's right versus need to know, and we consider whether employing different approaches or frames—a feminist ethics of care approach or a mental health frame instead of a criminal one, for example—might have changed the dynamic between press and audience. While practitioners and academics have long debated the role investigative journalism ought to play in holding those in power accountable, the news coverage of the Rob Ford crack scandal offers a real case study on which to focus. The series of events surrounding the crack-tape scandal indicate that the public is deeply lacking in knowledge of newsroom conduct and is highly skeptical of media coverage of scandal, including digital media capturing outrageous conduct. This distrust extended to investigative journalists who were working in the public interest to expose this troubling behavior in the mayor's office.

## BACKGROUND

Even prior to the crack-tape scandal, Ford was no stranger to negative media coverage. Both *The Toronto Star* and *The Globe and Mail* (the two highest-circulating newspapers in Canada[4] and both based in Toronto) detailed Ford's frequent public missteps before they uncovered his connections to drugs and criminals. He was elected to Toronto City Council in 2000 and made several controversial statements throughout his two terms as councillor. He was charged in a 2008 domestic assault incident involving his wife, but the charges were dropped. He also made his dislike for journalists abundantly clear, and this disdain only intensified after he was elected mayor in 2010. He constantly derided reporters, accused *The Star* of harassing him and his family, refused interviews about city business, and called journalists "maggots" on his weekly radio show. He became known as "the Teflon mayor" because all accusations seemed to just slide right off him. He had faced a lawsuit for defamation, overcame conflict of interest charges in City Hall, and eluded responsibility for photos showing him reading documents while driving and also using his cell phone at the wheel. However, these incidents paled in comparison to his behavior in 2013 and the subsequent media coverage it generated that focused international attention on the city of Toronto.

In May 2013, the American gossip website *Gawker*,[5] followed a few hours later by Canada's largest metropolitan daily *The Toronto Star*,[6] published a story contending that the mayor of Toronto had been recorded on a cell phone video smoking crack and making homophobic and racist comments. Both outlets had received a tip about the video, and *Toronto Star* reporters viewed it multiple times in the backseat of an unnamed source's car. The men with the cell phone recording of the mayor were asking a six-figure price for the video, so both outlets passed. The editor-in-chief of *The Toronto Star*, Michael Cooke,[7] explained in a brief column that the crack video story was the culmination of months of investigation. However, there was a lot of debate among ethics experts, editors, and journalists about why *The Star* chose to run the story immediately after *Gawker* released its version. In addition, the credibility and reliability of the sources who presented the cell phone video were called into question because the men were involved in dealing drugs and remained unnamed. A week after the crack-tape story broke, *The Globe and Mail* ran a long investigative piece on Ford.[8] It turns out the newspaper had been investigating the mayor and his family for months for alleged ties to the illegal drug scene. The article contended that all the mayor's older siblings had ties to drug traffickers; however, the sources remained anonymous, leading to criticism of this newspaper as well.

The crack-tape story was far from the only scandal the mayor would face that year. Over the next few months, while continuing to deny the existence of the video, the mayor received negative coverage for various public missteps, including appearing under the influence at a street festival, appearing in a second cell phone video where he was seen screaming obscenities (and once again appeared under the influence), screaming at spectators of a hockey game, and allegedly pinching a woman's backside at a charity function. All of this fed plenty of material not just to the Canadian mainstream press, but also the American media and late night comedy shows. In fact, a media-monitoring survey released at the end of 2013 noted that the Rob Ford scandal garnered more coverage in the USA than any other Canadian news event this century.[9]

## "FORD NATION" FIGHTS BACK

Despite the numerous examples of highly problematic, and in some instances, illegal behavior, the mayor's popularity did not suffer for quite some time among the people who refer to themselves as "Ford Nation."[10] Just over a week after the crack scandal story broke, a poll of nearly 1400 Torontonians showed that in a hypothetical two-way mayoral election race between Ford and Councillor Olivia Chow, 36% would support him compared to 56% for Chow, which were the same results when the same poll was conducted in early May before the crack-tape scandal surfaced.[11] While residents of Toronto had every right to know that the city's chief executive was acting in such a manner, critics such as Mark Hasiuk of *The Huffington Post*[12] and John Miller, former senior editor for *The Toronto Star* and former chair of the Ryerson University School of Journalism, questioned why a reputable Canadian newspaper like *The Toronto Star* would put its credibility on the line over the authenticity of a cell phone video that allegedly showed the mayor smoking crack and making offensive remarks.[13] Miller criticized *The Star* for seemingly rushing to print the story with anonymous sources and only a last-minute attempt to get Ford to tell his side of the story after *Gawker* broke the news of the crack tape. Members of the public who identified as Ford Nation asserted that after all the acrimonious history between the newspaper and mayor, publishing the details of the cell phone video provided retribution for *The Star*.[14]

In the days following the media coverage around the crack-tape scandal and the subsequent reporting about the Ford family's ties to drug dealers, numerous Canadian media outlets conducted brief interviews on the streets with city residents, and some of these comments offered telling insights into the mindset of those in "Ford Nation." One Ford supporter said to a *Star* reporter: "To me, the media comes out worse in this than Rob Ford does. People are making allegations, using unnamed sources. … It's lazy journalism."[15] Bruce Davis, former campaign manager for another candidate (George Smitherman) who lost to Ford in the 2010 mayoral election told Robyn Doolittle of *The Star*: "I haven't met a single person who has changed their mind (because of the latest controversy)."[16] Davis also said back in 2010 the Smitherman campaign conducted focus group testing where they asked voters about previous Ford controversies and political gaffes. One woman apparently said to them: "If I have to choose between someone who wastes our money and someone who (breaks the law), I'll choose the person who (breaks the law)."[17]

An Ipos Reid poll conducted on behalf of CTV News and CP24 found that half of the 530 residents polled agreed with the mayor and his brother that the allegations were an example of the media's agenda to have him resign from office.[18] Nearly half (49%) of those polled believed Ford was telling the truth that he did not use crack cocaine, while the remaining 51% did not believe him. Just over half of those polled (55%) said they believed the video existed and was real, while 45% contended that Ford was telling the truth when he said the video did not exist.[19]

The coverage of Ford and the subsequent backlash from his supporters resulted in formal complaints being lodged with the Ontario Press Council against *The Toronto Star* and *The Globe and Mail*; all charges were brought by the general public and none came from the Ford family. In fact, Ford himself never threatened to sue for defamation. Five official complaints were filed with the OPC—one about each paper and three jointly—and there were another 40 or so people who phoned into the Council to complain but declined to officially file a complaint. To put this in context, the OPC usually receives on average 100 complaints each year.[20] One of the complaints alleged that the anonymous sources in the *Globe's* story lied about the Ford brothers. The complainant argued that the news should be concrete and proven truth; however, the OPC did not try to determine the truth of either of the newspapers' coverage of Ford. The Council was focused on three particular questions: Were the articles in the public interest? Were adequate efforts made to verify the allegations? Were the Fords given adequate time to respond and were the responses published? The Council made its rulings on whether journalists had followed proper procedures and upheld ethical norms in October 2013.[21] The reporting in both newspapers on Ford was found to be appropriate by the Council, and the complaints were dismissed. The OPC noted that since the mayor was a senior public servant in an important elected position, it was appropriate that he be subjected to more scrutiny than if he were a private person. Therefore, the OPC found that the newspapers acted in the public interest by reporting on his behavior when it appeared he was acting both illegally and extremely inappropriately. The conduct of the mayor could impair his ability to fulfill his public duties, and the Council pointed out the hypocrisy of his involvement in activities he himself had condemned. The OPC also noted that both papers had acted ethically in the use of anonymous sources, but pointed out that the public does not generally know enough about journalistic standards. The Council encouraged the newspapers to operate in a more transparent manner so that citizens could better understand the journalistic norms and standards to which these newsrooms adhere.

In response, *The Globe*'s public editor, Sylvia Stead, outlined why the newspaper chose anonymity for the sources in the Ford family story. In a column on October 19, 2013, she explained that the journalists involved corroborated what the unnamed sources told them by using court documents, social media, and other documents throughout the lengthy 18-month investigation.[22] She reiterated that the Supreme Court of Canada has said that some form of protection is required for the confidential relationship between journalists and their sources.

At the end of October 2013, Toronto police chief Bill Blair called a news conference to announce that police had located the infamous cell phone video on the hard drive of one of the computers seized in a drug-related apartment raid—the same video that Ford had maintained did not exist up until that point. Blair confirmed the video contained the images of Ford as reported by *Gawker* and *The Star*. A few days later, the mayor publicly admitted to using crack cocaine while in one of his "drunken stupors" and apologized, but maintained he would not step down from office. Even after the Toronto police chief confirmed the existence of the crack tape, many members of Ford Nation continued to support him. In November, *The Globe* reported that some of his supporters maintained that the allegations were flimsy at best.[23] They called the coverage of Ford a conspiracy and a media feeding frenzy, saying Ford was just a good guy trying to limit the size of government and save taxpayers money. They said it would take a lot, possibly a criminal conviction, to persuade them to change their minds. A former banker told a *Globe* reporter: "I think the media is out to get [Ford]. He hasn't been charged with anything and they're calling for him to resign."[24]

## PUBLIC DISTRUST IN JOURNALISTS

While we do not debate the legitimacy and importance of the investigative reporting surrounding Ford's ongoing scandals, it matters that a sizable portion of the public called into question the credibility of media outlets in their coverage of the crack-tape scandal. As American media ethics scholar Patrick Plaisance points out, credibility is the only real currency journalists have: "If audiences no longer believe that journalists serve as credible sources of information, their very reason for existence evaporates."[25] It became clear from the criticism of the coverage of this scandal that the public generally did not know about the lengths journalists go to verify sources, corroborate information, and use objective methods in news gathering. Theodore Glasser and James Ettema, who have written about press accountability and investigative journalism, argue that there is a failure to communicate outwardly, a reluctance to talk to the very audiences journalists aim to serve and upon whose support news organizations depend.[26] This parallels the OPC finding in its rulings on the coverage of the crack-tape scandal, as discussed above.

This lack of knowledge about the media by the public also speaks to the larger issues of public distrust in journalists. According to an Ipos Reid poll commissioned by PostMedia News and Global National, trust in journalists was ranked at 31%, putting journalists slightly above lawyers, TV and radio personalities, and national politicians on a scale of trusted professions.[27] This ranking meant journalists were considered less trustworthy than some traditional scapegoats, such as mechanics, chiropractors, and financial advisors. In another Ipos Reid poll conducted for the Canadian Journalism Foundation (CJF), 40% of poll respondents said that the media in Canada use tactics like phone hacking and paying police for tips in pursuit of stories, the same activities that resulted in the 2011 shutdown of the UK tabloid *News of the World*.[28] The chair of the CJF said that the excesses of *News of the World* had unfairly tainted the whole business, meaning that journalists needed "to redouble their commitment to accountability and transparency."[29]

It is also important to consider both the historical and popular culture context for credibility. There have been some very high-profile cases where journalists have fabricated facts and stories—such as the Janet Cooke scandal at *The Washington Post* in the early 1980s where she fabricated her story "Jimmy's World" about an 8-year-old heroin addict.[30] The story initially won a Pulitzer until she finally revealed that the story was a fake when members of the public put pressure on officials to "save Jimmy"; he never actually existed, and Cooke confessed to creating him from a series of composites drawn from many young people she claimed to have met. Among other examples, there was Oprah's pick for her book club—*A Million Little Pieces* by James Frey—that also turned out to be largely made up.[31] There was also Stephen Glass of *The New Republic* who was exposed for fabricating quotations, sources, and even events in a number of magazine articles,[32] and Jayson Blair who resigned from *The New York Times* in 2003 after it was discovered he had plagiarized and fabricated parts of his articles.[33] In recent years in Canada, there were reports that widely read columnists have plagiarized large amounts of information.[34]

## Privacy and the Public's Need to Know

There is longstanding debate about balancing the privacy rights of people with the public's need to know, but this discussion has become more visible in the wake of Britain's Leveson inquiry into press practices and ethics, following the revelation that newspapers owned by Rupert Murdoch had been illegally wire-tapping private phone lines for news tips.[35] While freedom of speech and the press are protected in the Charter of Rights and Freedoms in Canada, just how much information is needed for citizens to make informed decisions is a matter of debate. Information about those who hold public office and wield power affects the public's ability to make decisions on governance. While Ford supporters charged that some members of the mainstream media were pandering to lurid curiosity, pursuing the mayor because people wanted to know the details of his personal life, it is not hard to understand that allegations about Ford using crack cocaine and socializing with drug dealers is information that goes beyond what people *want* to know, and into the public realm of *need* to know. We dismiss the notion that the crack video's content was exclusively a matter of Ford's private life: By taking up public office, all elected officials give up some of their entitlements to privacy. If information about the official's conduct is relevant to the way in which he or she does his or her job, there is public benefit to disseminating this information. In *The Virtuous Journalist*, authors Stephen Klaidman and Tom Beauchamp explain:

> If there is good reason to believe that some fact, situation, or circumstance in his private life has or is likely to have bearing on his public life, there is justification for weighing the public benefit of knowing about it against the potential harm to the official. In short, if an official's actions are relevant to his position of public trust, then the duty of the press to provide the public with information it needs would outweigh the competing duty to avoid harm.[36]

This is especially relevant in secret arrangements, which may not be directly related to official business, but reflect on the moral compass of the official and could also lead to the official becoming vulnerable to blackmail. Elaborating on this point, ethicist Candace Gauthier notes that what are traditionally private concerns, such as a person's sexual conduct or the use of drugs, become issues of character, particularly if the official has lied about these activities or when the activities are illegal.[37] There are of course limits to this—the drug use of an official 30 years ago has little bearing on his or her current activities. While the spectacle taking place in Toronto's City Hall quickly became a lurid curiosity not just for locals, but also international media and American late night hosts and comedians, there were credible and defendable reasons why this scandal needed to be exposed to the public. Philosopher Dale Jacquette reminds us that breaking the law removes everyone, including public officials, "from the realm of morally protected private behavior and makes the action one in which the public in principle has an interest."[38] Ethics scholar Louis Hodges argues that journalists should publish private information about officials, even against their will, if the private activity might reasonably have a significant effect on their official performance.[39] Few would argue that using crack cocaine and cavorting with drug dealers while holding the highest public office in Canada's largest city is a matter of no bearing on the official's performance. So journalists have a duty to report on the private matters of public officials if there is reason to believe these activities will have an impact on their official duties. Information about Ford's drug use and conduct was information the public needed to know. But why then did a significant portion of Torontonians feel that many members of the media were stooping to the lowest common denominator with the coverage of the Rob Ford crack-tape scandal? Perhaps the issue lies not in the "rightness" of the coverage, but in the way in which it was conveyed.

## "Gotcha Journalism" Misses the Point

We contend that far too many of the Ford stories exemplified "gotcha journalism." The reporting positioned much of the mainstream media as pointing a smug and superior finger at the mayor as the criminal that the reporters had known all along he was. This would be irresistible retribution, in light of the history of animosity between the mayor and reporters already outlined. The vast majority of coverage between May and November 2013 (from the time the crack-tape scandal first broke to when the police confirmed the existence of the tape) focused on Ford as a criminal rather than as a human being with a problem.[40] In addition to the thematic focus, most of the coverage relied heavily on the kind of episodic style that crime stories exemplify—what is alleged to have happened, who did what to whom, lots of quotes from police, and in the case of editorials, lots of consideration of what all this seemingly illegal activity might "mean" in the courts and whether Ford could be ousted from office.

Both *The Star* and *The Globe* ran articles in which they consulted numerous communications professionals who all agreed the mayor was bungling the situation further by not addressing the rumors about drug use. But the newspapers did not consult with addictions or mental health specialists to weigh in on the situation. There was no exposé on crack in Toronto; no stories on alcohol or drug addiction, or the economic, social, and psychological fallout from these issues on individuals, families, or the community. When health and addiction issues were mentioned, they were largely relegated to a sentence or two in a story largely about criminal behavior. A week into the scandal, when Ford himself addressed the allegations, *The Globe* pressed sources close to the mayor for details on his addictions. In an article that ran on May 25, 2013, one source told the paper simply, "He drinks too much" but said he did not have knowledge of other substance use.[41] No experts on addictions were asked to weigh in to give context or provide information about addictions in general. A couple of days after this, *The Globe* ran a story about the fund set up by *Gawker* (nicknamed "crackstarter") to raise money to purchase the crack tape and how Canadian addictions and recovery organizations would react to a potential donation since the drug dealer with the video could no longer be contacted.[42] Instead of giving these agencies an opportunity to comment on addiction and recovery issues, the article outlined how they would react to potentially having the "crackstarter" funds donated to their organization. The newspapers seemed to skirt the addictions and mental health issues like this, even when they had qualified sources who could comment and provide context. The few exceptions to the mainly criminal and scandal-focused articles were the stories where sources close to Ford themselves brought up the addictions angle. For example, *The Globe* ran a story on June 8, 2013, about how Ford's former campaign manager would not help the mayor run for re-election unless he entered rehab for substance abuse problems[43]—again no broader discussion was opened on addiction issues in Toronto and the facilities available. Yet while *The Globe* and *The Star* focused mainly on the criminal aspect and the optics of the scandal, *The Toronto Sun* addressed the addiction issue head-on by running a pithy front page directive on May 24, 2013, that stated in bold letters: GO TO 'REHAB.'[44] For the most part, many Toronto columnists had a field day with the scandal. But the style and tone of many of these columnists may have furthered the gulf between journalists and many members of the public. The issue is one of ethics.

People realize that mass media organizations are centers of institutional power, and their editorial and business policies and decisions can be self-serving. Both individual journalist's career ambitions and institutional competition can affect the application of professional codes and ethics guidelines. Supporters of an ethics approach called "communitarianism"—in which the focus is on the community's good as a whole rather than on the individual rights of each citizen—urge journalists to consider morality as holistic, inseparable from considerations of the individual role, and to place at the center of their approaches to journalism a basic human decency: no harm to innocents, telling the truth, honoring promises, generosity, gratitude, and making reparations for wrong action.[45] If motivations and behaviors were refocused in this manner, reporters would operate in the same arena as their audiences—not from above in a position of superiority—and then reporters would not be seen as detached from the community or fixated on self-interest. Such an approach would be a citizens' ethics, implemented by journalists who were humans and citizens first, rather than professionals or practitioners. From this communitarian perspective, journalists would be part and parcel of the citizenry whom they serve, and this connection would permeate their understanding of, and empathy for, people and their concerns for privacy.

In a similar vein, a feminist ethics of care approach, if adopted in such situations, would be one in which journalists would consider everyone as part of a community and everyone, regardless of position, as linked together in a web of connection.[46] From this perspective, media coverage that "others" anyone—that depicts even a public figure as wholly bad or criminal and as someone who ought to be "expelled" from civilized society—is insensitive journalism and unhelpful to the public and its discourse in several related ways. First, this type of media coverage suggests that people are only the sum total of their human fallibilities; that they are incapable of making mistakes and learning from those mistakes; that they must always be held in contempt; and also that communities belong only to those members who are "perfect." This "othering" style of news and storytelling also clearly implies a hierarchy with those at the top—and in the Ford case, it would be the journalists—being those who have never "sinned."

Two American academics, Renita Coleman and Esther Thorson, argue that news media need a different approach to covering crime and violence in order to demonstrate that these phenomena have roots in a variety of economic and social factors.[47] They argue that members of the public can see crime as preventable rather than as inevitable or the personal failure of an individual, when these stories are reported through a public health model. Coleman and Thorson developed this approach in a slightly different context where media coverage focused on alleged perpetrators who were living disadvantaged lives. The public health model places far less emphasis on the role of individuals' motives and intentions, whose responsibilities are often exaggerated in Western culture, while downplaying the role of contextual or societal factors. Coleman and Thorson point out that this personalizing narrative is problematic because the "attribution of responsibility is crucial to social change; whom citizens hold accountable for social problems can determine the kinds of solutions they choose."[48] Proponents of this style of journalism argue that crime reporting must be reframed from a public health perspective so that stories include information that connects incidents of violence to larger social and environmental contexts.[49] This would mean coverage must expose risk factors and include information about prevention in articles on crime and violence. Coleman and Thorson contend that journalists should avoid simplistic frameworks when covering crime and violence, opting instead to construct stories from the perspective of the public health model. The public health model of reporting could be used to inform future investigative reporting, like the detailed and complex investigative work done around the Ford crack-tape scandal. What most media professionals missed in the Ford case was linking how his potential use of crack was not just illegal, but also reflected on his ability to conduct the duties of his office. While all of this may have been implied, using a public health model of reporting would have made the links clear between alleged crack use and the mental health and addictions issues that accompany this type of high-risk drug use. And in a simpler light, it might have made journalists sound sympathetic on a human level rather than vindictive and morally superior.

Our approach does not suggest that bad behavior is always the result of mental illness or addictions, but rather that taking the ethical approaches we have outlined here would result in a deeper investigation into these issues, providing context, and always keeping the focus on the quality of the public conversation. Our premise is that while it is certainly the job of journalists to inform the public (as the eyes and ears of citizens), it is not the job of journalists to shame those who act in ways unbecoming to holding public office. While media shaming of public figures has become standard practice in England, the USA, and Canada, it is not the practice in all democracies. It is worth questioning whether we want or expect media to shame or punish people. Perhaps if journalists were seen to be more neutral, the citizenry would take over these discussions among themselves, and they would decide about punishment, the degree of shaming, and so on.

To conclude, the press must not only serve the public interest and work as a public trust, but also earn its trust. It is important that the reporting styles utilized by the media do not "other" people, or further distance journalists from the public of which they are a part and for whom they work so diligently. It is journalism's mandate to build a better public conversation, and it is one in which everyone ought to be included and feel invested. We need a journalism that includes citizens in discussions about the officials who lead them and focuses clearly on those people not as the sum of their fragilities, but as human beings who make mistakes and whose leadership ought to be re-evaluated—not by the press, but by the people.

## Notes

1. Both newspapers had been investigating these stories about Ford's connections to drugs and criminals for several months prior to the crack-tape revelations.
2. It would seem much of this backlash was directed particularly at the two major newspapers, *The Globe and Mail* and *The Toronto Star*, as these were the only media outlets that were called before the Ontario Press Council to answer to complaints filed against them (as detailed later in this chapter).
3. Aiasdair MacIntyre, *After Virtue* (Notre Dame, Indiana: Notre Dame University Press, 1981), 245.
4. "2014 Daily Newspaper Circulation Data," *Newspapers Canada*. http://www.newspaperscanada.ca/daily-newspaper-circulation-data.
5. John Cook, "A Video of Toronto Mayor Rob Ford Smoking Crack Cocaine," *Gawker*, May 16, 2013. http://gawker.com/for-sale-a-video-of-toronto-mayor-rob-ford-smoking-cra-507736569.
6. Robyn Doolittle and Kevin Donovan, "Rob Ford in 'Crack Cocaine' Video Scandal," *The Toronto Star*, May 16, 2013. http://www.thestar.com/news/city_hall/2013/05/16/toronto_mayor_rob_ford_in_crack_cocaine_video_scandal.html.
7. Michael Cooke, "Rob Ford Crack Scandal: Star Editor's Unanswered Questions," *The Toronto Star*, May 17, 2013. http://www.thestar.com/news/canada/2013/05/17/rob_ford_crack_scandal_star_editors_unanswered_questions.html.
8. Greg McArthur and Shannon Kari, "Globe Investigation: The Ford Family's History with Drug Dealing," *Globe and Mail*, May 25, 2013. http://www.theglobeandmail.com/news/toronto/globe-investigation-the-ford-familys-history-with-drug-dealing/article12153014/?page=all.
9. Alexander Panetta, "Rob Ford Saga Biggest Canadian News Story in U.S. Media This Century: Analysis," *CTV News*, December 4, 2013. http://www.ctvnews.ca/canada/rob-ford-saga-biggest-canadian-news-story-in-u-s-media-this-century-analysis-1.1574128.
10. Ford Nation was the name of the short-lived television discussion program that aired only once on the Canadian Sun News Network featuring Rob Ford and his brother, city councillor Doug Ford. It is also the term widely used (and often self-declared) in Toronto to describe the ardent supporters of the two Ford brothers.
11. Madhavi Acharya and Tom Yew, "Mayor's Popularity Unaffected by Drug Allegations, Poll Shows," *The Toronto Star*, May 27, 2013, A8.

12. Mark Hasiuk, "Rob Ford 'Crack' Scandal Cooked Up By the Worst Kind of Folks," *The Huffington Post*, May 21, 2013, accessed August 18, 2015, http://www.huffingtonpost.ca/mark-hasiuk/rob-ford-scandal_b_3300769.html.
13. John Gordon Miller, "Rush to Print?," The Journalism Doctor, last modified May 17, 2013, http://www.thejournalismdoctor.ca/Blog.php/archived/20130501/crackgate.
14. Catherine Porter, "Ford Nation has Spoken: They Stand By Their Man," *The Toronto Star*, May 28, 2013, A11.
15. Porter, "Ford Nation," A11.
16. Robyn Doolittle, "Mayor Expected to be 'Very Strong' in Election," *The Toronto Star*, June 2, 2013, A11.
17. Doolittle, "Mayor Expected," A11.
18. Andrew Livingstone, "Residents Split on Existence of Crack Video," *The Toronto Star*, June 3, 2013, A8.
19. Livingstone, "Residents Split," A8.
20. Don McCurdy, "Ontario Press Council: Why We Hold Media To Account," *J-source.ca*, last modified September 3, 2013, http://j-source.ca/article/ontario-press-council-why-we-hold-media-account.
21. "OPC Decision: Donley vs. Toronto Star, October 2013," last modified October 16, 2013, http://ontpress.com/2013/10/16/opc-decision-donley-vs-toronto-star-october-2013/.
22. Sylvia Stead, "The Fords, the Facts, and the Use of Anonymous Sources," *The Globe and Mail*, October 19, 2013, F8.
23. Joe Friesen, "The Day After: Are They With Him?," *The Globe and Mail*, November 2, 2013, M1.
24. Friesen, "The Day After," M1.
25. Patrick L. Plaisance, *Media Ethics: Key Principles for Responsible Practice* (Thousand Oaks: Sage, 2009), 27.
26. Theodore L. Glasser and James S. Ettema, "Ethics and Eloquence in Journalism: An Approach to Press Accountability," *Journalism Studies* 9 (2008): 512–534.
27. Dana Lacey, "Trust in Journalists Up in 2010: Poll," *J-Source.ca*, January 4, 2011, accessed August 17, 2015, http://www.projetj.info/article/trust-journalists-2010-poll.
28. "Forty Percent of Canadians Say Journalists Do Things Like Hack Phones, Pay Police for Tips: Poll," *CNW*, last modified October 18, 2011, http://www.newswire.ca/news-releases/forty-percent-of-canadians-say-journalists-do-things-like-hack-phones-pay-police-for-tips-poll-508893901.html.
29. "Forty Percent of Canadians Say."
30. David L. Eason, "On Journalistic Authority: The Janet Cooke Scandal," *Critical Studies in Mass Communication* 3 (1986): 429–447.
31. "A Million Little Lies," *The Smoking Gun*, January 4, 2006, http://www.thesmokinggun.com/documents/celebrity/million-little-lies.
32. Buzz Bissinger, "Shattered Glass," *Vanity Fair*, September 1998, accessed October 7, 2015, http://www.vanityfair.com/magazine/1998/09/bissinger199809.
33. "Correcting the Record," *The New York Times*, May 11, 2003, http://www.nytimes.com/2003/05/11/us/correcting-the-record-times-reporter-who-resigned-leaves-long-trail-of-deception.html.

34. Sean D. B. Craig, "Everyone Hates Plagiarism, Except the Canadian Media," *Vice*, September 24, 2012, http://www.vice.com/en_ca/read/everyone-hates-plagiarism-except-the-canadian-media.

35. In 2011, it was revealed that a number of British newspapers owned by Rupert Murdoch had tapped into or hacked the phones of celebrities, politicians, and even victims of crime and recorded private conversations or messages. These private conversations were then used as part of stories that were published. It was also uncovered that newspaper management authorized payments to police in exchange for tips. This scandal resulted in a public judicial inquiry into the practices and ethics of the British Press, chaired by Lord Justice Leveson.

36. Steven Klaidman and Tom L. Beauchamp, *The Virtuous Journalist* (New York: Oxford University Press, 1987), 104.

37. Candace C. Gauthier, "Understanding and Respecting Privacy," in *Journalism Ethics: A Philosophical Approach*, ed. Christopher Meyers (New York: Oxford University Press, 2010), 223.

38. Dale Jacquette, *Journalistic Ethics: Moral Responsibility in the Media* (Upper Saddle River: Oxford University Press, 2007), 192.

39. Louis Hodges, "Privacy and the Press," in *The Handbook of Mass Media Ethics*, ed. Lee Wilkins and Clifford G. Christians (New York: Routledge, 2009), 282.

40. We examined 175 articles written between May 17 and November 5, 2013 (from the day of the crack scandal first breaking to the days immediately following the revelation by the Toronto Police Chief that the crack tape existed and depicted the Mayor smoking crack), in *The Toronto Star* and *The Globe and Mail*.

41. Elizabeth Church, "'I Do Not Use Crack Cocaine,' Ford says," *The Globe and Mail*, May 25, 2013, A15.

42. Kathryn Blaze Carlson, "Gawker Meets $200,000 Fundraising Goal to Purchase Alleged Ford Video," *The Globe and Mail*, May 28, 2013, A7.

43. Adam Radwanski, "Ford's Former Campaign Manager Indicates He Won't Return Unless Mayor Enters Rehab," *The Globe and Mail*, June 8, 2013, A15.

44. "Go to Rehab," *The Toronto Sun*, May 24, 2013, A1.

45. See, for example, the work of Clifford Christians, John Ferre, and Mark Fackler (1993; 2012) and Clifford Christians and Michael Traber (1997).

46. See, for example, the work of Carole Gilligan (1982) or Nel Noddings (1984).

47. Renita Coleman and Esther Thorson, "The Effects of News Stories that Put Crime and Violence into Context: Testing the Public Health Model of Reporting," *Journal of Health Communication* 7 (2002): 401–425.

48. Coleman and Thorson, "Public Health Model," 404.

49. Lori Dorfman, Esther Thorson, and Jane Ellen Stevens, "Reporting on Violence: Bringing a Public Health Perspective into the Newsroom," *Health Education and Behaviour* 28 (2001): 402–419.

# PART III

# Digital Surveillance

# CHAPTER 13

# Scandal at the Top in TV News

*Susan Keith*

US journalism was rocked in February 2015 by the revelation that one of its most respected broadcast figures, Brian Williams, anchor and managing editor of *NBC Nightly News with Brian Williams*, had repeatedly told a story about what happened to his news team during the 2003 US-led invasion of Iraq that was not true.[1] Less than a month later, another widely known television figure, Bill O'Reilly, host of the Fox News conservative opinion show "The O'Reilly Factor," was accused of lying about his experiences during wartime, when he was a CBS journalist assigned to cover the 1982 conflict between the UK and Argentina over ownership of the Falkland Islands.[2] Williams recanted his accounts but was suspended for six months without pay[3] and demoted to anchoring breaking news reports "on busy news days" on the cable channel MSNBC at a lower salary.[4] He began the MSNBC assignment on September 22, 2015, with coverage of Pope Francis' trip to the USA.[5] O'Reilly, who denied that he had mischaracterized his combat involvement, was supported by Fox News Chairman and CEO Roger Ailes and continued in his pundit role[6]—even though other journalists said O'Reilly had exaggerated his war reporting experiences.[7]

Although the facts of the Williams and O'Reilly controversies are different, the two cases are significant to how we think about journalism in the twenty-first century. They raise important questions about journalists' reliance on memory and journalism's increasing culture of self-promotion—often in realms beyond journalism—which invites various types of surveillance once carried out *by* journalists rather than *against* them. This chapter will argue that the controversies should be read in context of the contraction of journalism as an occupation, the shrinking of audiences for legacy news outlets, and the rise of partisan media in a country accustomed for decades to at least a veneer of objectivity.

S. Keith (✉)
Department of Journalism and Media Studies, Rutgers University, New Brunswick, NJ, USA

© The Editor(s) (if applicable) and The Author(s) 2016
H. Mandell, G.M. Chen (eds.), *Scandal in a Digital Age*,
DOI 10.1057/978-1-137-59545-4_13

161

## The Williams Case

Williams' fall from his network's top position centered on how he retold events that he first reported on in 2003, when, as an NBC News correspondent, he traveled with a US Army unit in an air mission over Iraq. In a March 26, 2003, segment on NBC's *Dateline* newsmagazine show filed from Kuwait City, Williams explained that the Chinook helicopter he was traveling in had "been ordered to land in the desert." Once on the ground, he reported, "we learned the Chinook ahead of us was almost blown out of the sky" by a rocket-propelled grenade that "punched cleanly through the skin of the ship but, amazingly … didn't detonate." Williams reported that the crew of the Chinook was too shaken to be interviewed, but video with his report showed visuals of the hole left by the RPG. Williams said his team members were then grounded for two nights by a "massive sandstorm" while a unit from the US Army Third Infantry sent to watch over them stood guard "the whole time."[8]

Nearly 12 years later, Williams—who had been promoted from correspondent to "NBC Nightly News" anchor in 2004—told a different story as he honored one of the infantrymen who had guarded his team in the Iraqi desert. In a two-minute segment toward the end of the newscast on January 30, 2015, Williams explained that the night before he had taken retired Command Sergeant Major Tim Terpak—with whom he had stayed in touch—to a New York Rangers game at Madison Square Garden, where Terpak was honored for his military service. During the segment, Williams said that in the 2003 incident, "the helicopter we were traveling in was forced down after being hit by an RPG" and the NBC news team was "rescued, surrounded and kept alive" by Terpak's unit. During the segment, the Madison Square Garden public address announcer could also be heard lauding Terpak for being "responsible for the safety of Brian Williams and his NBC News team after their Chinook helicopter was hit and crippled by enemy fire."[9]

When NBC posted the video of the newscast on Facebook, comments left by Facebook users were, at first, mostly positive. "Just when I thought that I couldn't love Brian Williams any more," one Facebook user wrote. Another commenter wrote "Priceless. Brian Williams, one of the very few newspeople I trust. Thank you." The first questions about whether Williams was telling the truth seemed to emerge in the Facebook comments on January 31. Soon, a number of posters who said they were veterans wrote that it was not the Chinook that Williams had been traveling in, but another helicopter, that had been forced down. A poster identified as Chris Simone commented on January 31: "Such a liar! I was the Pilot in Command of the CH-47 flying Brian Williams into Iraq during the invasion. He was on my aircraft and we were NOT shot down. That was a sister ship and a friend of mine."

*Stars and Stripes*, a US Department of Defense newspaper, investigated, and on February 4, published a story in which three of the Facebook critics present in Iraq—Sgt. First Class Joseph Miller, the flight engineer on the aircraft that carried the journalists; Lance Reynolds, the flight engineer on the plane that was hit; and Mike O'Keeffe, a door gunner on the damaged Chinook—asserted that Williams' plane had not been hit.[10] The same day, Williams conceded in a Facebook post, "I was indeed on the Chinook behind the bird that took the RPG in the tail housing just above the ramp. ... I think the constant viewing of the video showing us inspecting the impact area—and the fog of memory over 12 years—made me conflate the two." He also told his "NBC Nightly News" audience on February 4, 2015, that "I made a mistake in recalling the events of 12 years ago" and called it "a bungled attempt" to honor military veterans.[11] Reaction on Facebook was swift. One user wrote below the video from the January 30 broadcast, "Send Brian Williams back to Iraq to report on what is going on over there now ... maybe he can really get shot at or shot down."

## THE O'REILLY FACTOR

A few weeks later, a story in the progressive magazine *Mother Jones* asserted that O'Reilly, the conservative opinion show host, had also told stories about his international reporting that were not true. The article, by Washington correspondent David Corn and senior editor for politics and national security Daniel Schulman, said that O'Reilly, had, for years, "recounted dramatic stories about his own war reporting that don't withstand scrutiny—even claiming he acted heroically in a war zone that he apparently never set foot in."[12] Corn and Schulman pointed to four instances in which O'Reilly had referred to his coverage with statements they said implied his presence in the Falkland Islands during the 1982 conflict, such as "I've reported on the ground in active war zones from El Salvador to the Falklands" and "I've covered wars, okay? I've been there. The Falklands, Northern Ireland, the Middle East"[13]—although O'Reilly, like most other US journalists, covered the Falklands from Buenos Aires and Uruguay.[14] Even in the Argentinian capital, the article reported, O'Reilly had exaggerated the level of violence he experienced, referring to a protest by thousands over the Argentinian junta's surrender as "a major riot" where "many were killed"— though no report of fatalities was included in the *CBS Evening News* coverage based on his reporting[15] or in coverage by *The New York Times*.[16]

O'Reilly—who had expressed sympathy for Williams in a February 9, 2015, appearance on ABC's *Jimmy Kimmel Live*[17]—responded with attacks on Corn, a former Fox News contributor,[18] and on the CNN and *New York Times* reporters covering the issue.[19] On his February 20, 2015, show, O'Reilly told his cable audience, "I never said I was on the Falkland Islands, as Corn purports. I said I covered the Falklands War, which I did."[20] Whether that claim was true, the *Tampa Bay Times*' Politifact political fact-checking site pointed out, turned on how one interpreted the preposition "in":

> Under some circumstances, "in" can mean "during," as in "What did you do in the war, Daddy?" Daddy might have slogged through the swamps of Vietnam or he might have worked a desk in a Pentagon office. On the other hand ... O'Reilly strongly implied that he had been with soldiers in combat "in the Falklands War." Even experienced listeners have stumbled over his meaning.[21]

Whether the protests in Buenos Aires constituted a "war zone" was, in the most generous reading, open to interpretation, though several of O'Reilly's former CBS colleagues said the protests were not that dangerous.[22] "[What] he's trying to do is build it up into a more frightening and deadly situation than it was," said Eric Engberg, a former CBS correspondent in Argentina, to CNN's Brian Stelter. "It wasn't a combat situation by any sense of the word that I know. There were no people killed."[23]

Although the combat reporting claim was only one of several career-related statements by O'Reilly that critics have questioned[24]—along with assertions that he witnessed bombings in Northern Ireland and murders in El Salvador, which Fox admitted in March 2015 were false[25]—he continued to have the support of the network. Viewers also continued to watch; he scored his largest audiences to that point in 2015 just after the accusations.[26] As one observer put it: "Being accused of fabulism by liberal news outlets like *Mother Jones* ... doesn't harm O'Reilly's credibility, because O'Reilly's credibility is dependent on exploiting a sense of victimization among his audience. ... The first thought isn't *Bill O'Reilly is a liar*. It's *The world is out to get Bill O'Reilly*."[27]

## MEMORY AND THE BROADCASTER

It is worth considering, however—as few sources did when the incidents occurred[28]—the role of remembering in the Williams and O'Reilly incidents, since, as sociologist and memory scholar Jeffrey K. Olick notes, "like everyone else, journalists clearly depend on memory in their work."[29] Although O'Reilly staunchly maintained that his memories were accurate, Williams referred on Facebook to "the fog of memory over 12 years" and told his TV audience that he had "made a mistake in recalling."[30] Both incidents are based on autobiographical memories, which vary, as one group of British psychologists studying the genre[31] write:

> Some personal memories seem like copies because they are vivid and contain a considerable amount of irrelevant detail. However, some personal memories are not accurate, and, rather than being raw experiences, they sometimes incorporate the interpretations that are made with hindsight, which suggests they are reconstructed.[32]

More specifically, the memories in these cases can be seen as the type labeled "episodic memory" by Canadian psychologist and cognitive neuroscientist Endel Tulving.[33] This type of memory is focused on the self, as opposed to "semantic memory," which covers general knowledge about the world. So for Williams and O'Reilly, the semantic memory would be that they took trips to Iraq and South America, respectively, while what happened to them there would be the subject of episodic memory. In his later work, Tulving has noted that episodic memory comes with what he called "autonoetic consciousness" or "recollective experience," a sense of oneself "in the past and other associated images, feelings or other memory details"[34] not present in other types of autobiographical memory. Researchers also have theorized that interference effects play a role in forgetting, with things that happen before or after an event influencing how it is remembered. The general principle is that "an event that occurs after (or before) some event may later be retrieved as if it were the event of interest."[35]

These conceptions of autobiographical memory suggest that one must at least consider the possibility that Williams and O'Reilly meant to recount their involvement in conflict situations accurately but misremembered as their memories were subjected to building a sense of themselves, associated with other images and feelings about the role of the broadcast newsman. In addition, one might consider the role of interference, at least in the Williams case. In the original March 26, 2003, NBC "Dateline" report of his time in Iraq, Williams did *not* suggest he was on the Chinook helicopter hit by the RPG. According to published excerpts,[36] that story remained fairly consistent in reports in other media outlets in 2003 and in a 2005 interview Williams did with NBC newsman Tim Russert, though a 2003 NBC book on the invasion was ambiguous about which helicopter was hit. *Operation Iraqi Freedom: The Insider Story*, a photo-heavy volume with a forward by television journalist Tom Brokaw, said that "The NBC team went along for the ride, occupying the third of four Chinook choppers" and then later noted that "the grenade entered the helicopter's open tail" without specifying which helicopter had been hit.[37]

In March 2007, however, an Associated Press (AP) story about Williams' return to Iraq with retired US Army General Wayne Downing, who had been with him on the 2003 mission, said Williams' helicopter had been shot down. The story, which did not quote Williams directly, placed Williams in the attacked Chinook, referring to the episode "when Williams' helicopter was forced down by insurgent fire."[38] A few months later, in a July blog post that noted Downing's death, Williams gave an accurate account of the trip.[39] Almost immediately, however, ambiguity entered his accounts, with the anchor using the first-person plural pronoun "we" as the object of the RPG attack.[40] Soon after, press releases for speeches Williams gave began to use ambiguous terms.[41] A release published by Notre Dame—with, no doubt, information from NBC News—announcing that Williams would be the university's 2010 commencement speaker is illustrative. The release said: "Just days into the war, Williams was traveling on a U.S. Army Chinook helicopter mission when the lead helicopter was shot down by a rocket-propelled grenade." That sentence did not assert whether Williams was in that lead helicopter, but the next sentence—"Williams spent three days and two nights in the Iraqi desert south of Najaf, with a mechanized armored tank platoon of the Army's Third Infantry Division providing protection"[42]—might have tended to suggest a cause-and-effect relationship that could have led to the conclusion that Williams was on the ground because *his* Chinook had been shot down.

Subsequently, Williams' accounts of the event became even more dramatically different from his 2003 reporting, using the first-person singular "I" to identify who was fired upon. On actor Alec Baldwin's public radio show, *Here's the Thing* on March 4, 2013, Williams said, "I've done some ridiculously stupid things ... like being in a helicopter I had no business being in in Iraq with rounds coming into the airframe."[43] Later that month, Williams was more specific on *The Late Show with David Letterman,* telling the NBC host, "Two of the four helicopters were hit, by ground fire, including the one I was in."[44]

It is impossible to know, of course, whether Williams' claims about misremembering are true, especially in light of a May 2015 report in *Vanity Fair* magazine that he had trouble explaining to NBC News President Deborah Turness what had happened.[45] And it may be a reach to suggest that ambiguity in NBC's *Operation Iraqi Freedom* book or a shift in narrative in a single AP story could constitute interference sufficient for such a substantial change in memories, especially as there is no evidence that Williams even saw the AP story. However, as mass communication scholar Mark West notes,[46] it is also unwise to completely dismiss the notion that journalists' memories can be significantly altered. As Yale University academic neurologist Steven Novella has written, "[G]iven what we know about memory it is reasonable to give Williams the benefit of the doubt. It is absolutely possible, even likely, that it is his memory that has shifted over the years, in a fashion consistent with memory research."[47]

## SURVEILLANCE OF THE WATCHDOGS

However, one construes the role of memory in the Williams and O'Reilly incidents, the episodes point to both the news media and the public engaging in the surveillance of the journalism field in the way that journalism has long engaged in surveillance of government.[48] In the Williams incident, in particular, we see this watchdog role being reversed, with a journalist becoming the subject of scrutiny. Tracing how it happened reveals a fascinating web of interdependencies in the twenty-first-century media environment. In this case:

- A mainstream media outlet, NBC News, posted video prepared for the legacy medium of broadcast on an online social media site, Facebook.
- Military members or veterans who were users of the site pointed out what they viewed as inaccuracies, serving as watchdogs on traditional media—but doing so on a social media platform.
- The military members' claims were first reported in traditional media in *Stars & Stripes,* a daily newspaper serving members of the military that has sometimes chafed under the control of the US Department of Defense, its owner.[49]

In a way, the Williams situation presented a case of what we might call both citizen surveillance and a quasi-governmental entity acting as watchdogs on mainstream media.

In the O'Reilly case, it was not citizens but journalists who sparked the scrutiny of a member of the media. That surveillance could be seen as the type of intermedia criticism sought by the Hutchins Commission in its 1947 report, *A*

*Free and Responsible Press,* which articulated as one dimension of social responsibility that the press engages in "vigorous mutual criticism."[50] Because of the political orientations of the outlets involved, however—*Mother Jones* on the left and Fox News on the right—the act of reporting on O'Reilly also can be viewed as a result of political polarization of at least some US media outlets.

## A COMPLICATING FACTOR: THE JOURNALIST AS BRAND

Public surveillance of journalists has been encouraged by broadcast journalism's promotion, over the past 50 years, of news as a brand,[51] with the focus in the USA on the individual anchor attempting to provide journalistic authority in a ritualized way, five nights a week.[52] (This type of promotion has also extended into the world of cable opinion broadcasting dominated in the USA by Fox News and MSNBC, where some of the highest-rated shows center on a single figure, such as Bill O'Reilly, articulating opinion nightly.) The public is invited to look at the local or national news anchor as not only the person delivering the news but also, in many cases, as the eponymous person whose name is branded as news, as in *The NBC Nightly News with Brian Williams.* That invites both adoration and scrutiny not only of news content but also of the news figurehead as a personality—something that was evident in the reaction to Williams' aggrandizement of his Iraq role.

To ensure that these symbolic individuals remained unsullied, US networks once limited their connections with other, less-factual, aspects of the network's operations. For example, CBS News President Richard S. Salant wrote in 1976 of "the overriding importance peculiar to our form of journalism of drawing the sharpest possible line—sharp perhaps to the point of eccentricity—between our line of broadcast business, which is dealing with fact, and that in which our associates on the entertainment side of the business are generally engaged, which is dealing in fiction and drama."[53]

Over the past 20 years, however, as television news audiences have contracted, the anchor's brand has been extended beyond the confines of news. Anchors and reporters have played themselves—once controversially, now routinely—on a variety of fictional series, including the politics-based "House of Cards,"[54] or appeared in non-journalistic roles on talk shows.[55] O'Reilly has portrayed himself hosting fictional versions of his show in the films *Iron Man 2* and *Transformers: Dark of the Moon.*[56] Williams appeared as himself on the fictional NBC series *30 Rock,* hosted *Saturday Night Live,* and made lighthearted appearances on *The Daily Show with Jon Stewart* and *The Tonight Show Starring Jimmy Fallon.* News reports also said Williams was interested in succeeding Jay Leno or David Letterman in their late-night shows or seeing his short-lived *Rock Center* prime-time news show evolve into a variety show.[57]

It is important to see this orientation away from so-called "serious" news—as well as the overall controversy surrounding Williams and O'Reilly—in the light of the contraction of journalism as an occupation. Although journalists have long been quick to point out missteps by other journalists—think of the scrutiny of *The New York Times* after reporter Jayson Blair was found to have made up sources and plagiarized articles or the rhetoric that followed CBS News' flawed reporting on Benghazi—there seems to be something more embedded in coverage of Williams and O'Reilly than mere *schadenfreude* or attempts to draw boundaries between ethical and unethical journalistic practice. As the number of journalism jobs available in the USA has declined over the past 15 years,[58] transgressions of norms by any journalist—but especially those at the top levels of the craft—have come to hold higher stakes. It is easier for a smaller number of journalists still left to be tarred by the unethical actions of a few—even if some of those people, like O'Reilly, are more political pundits than journalists.

The Williams and O'Reilly cases offer important instructional value for journalists and journalism educators. First, they point out that journalists need to acknowledge the limitations of memory not only in their reporting but also in later recollections of their roles in historical events—especially if their positions reward off-the-cuff sharing of personal anecdotes. Second, the cases provide further evidence that network and cable news/opinion channel efforts to engage audiences by promoting the personalities of anchors and hosts can create a culture where self-aggrandizement is not sufficiently challenged. And that, in turn, can result in intense scrutiny of journalists by audiences trained to focus their gaze on the newsperson, instead of the news.

## NOTES

1. Travis J. Tritten, "NBC's Brian Williams Recants Iraq Story After Soldiers Protest," *Stars & Stripes*, February 4, 2015, http://www.stripes.com/news/us/nbc-s-brian-williams-recants-iraq-story-after-soldiers-protest-1.327792.
2. David Corn and Daniel Schulman, "Bill O'Reilly Has His Own Brian Williams Problem," *Mother Jones*, February 19, 2015, http://www.motherjones.com/politics/2015/02/bill-oreilly-brian-williams-falklands-war.
3. Emily Steel and Ravi Somaiya, "Brian Williams Suspended from NBC for 6 Months Without Pay," *The New York Times*, February 10, 2015.
4. John Koblin and Emily Steel, "Brian Williams Gets New Role at Lower Salary," *The New York Times*, June 18, 2015.
5. James Warren, "Pope Departs as a Restrained, Effective Brian Williams Returns," *Poynter.org*, September 28, 2015, http://www.poynter.org/news/mediawire/375274/pope-departs-as-a-restrained-effective-brian-williams-returns/.
6. Tom Kludt, "Bill O'Reilly Has Full Support from Fox News Chief," *Money.CNN.com*, February 23, 2015, http://money.cnn.com/2015/02/23/media/bill-oreilly-roger-ailes-falklands/.
7. Ben Dimiero and Hannah Groch-Begley, "All the Journalists Disputing Bill O'Reilly's Falklands War Tales," *MediaMatters.org*, February 24, 2015, http://mediamatters.org/research/2015/02/24/all-the-journalists-disputing-bill-oreillys-fal/202647.

8. Dateline, March, 26, 2003, archived at Curtis Houck, "Brian Williams Admits to Falsely Saying He Was Shot Down Over Iraq in 2003 [Updated]," *Newsbusters.org*, February 4, 2015, http://newsbusters.org/blogs/curtis-houck/2015/02/04/brian-williams-admits-falsely-saying-he-was-shot-down-over-iraq-2003.

9. "NBC Nightly News," *NBC*, January 30, 2015, https://www.facebook.com/video.php?v=10153110016813689.

10. Tritten, "NBC's Brian Williams Recants Iraq Story After Soldiers Protest."

11. "NBC Nightly News," *NBC*, February 4, 2015.

12. Corn and Schulman, "Bill O'Reilly Has His Own Brian Williams Problem."

13. Corn and Schulman, "Bill O'Reilly Has His Own Brian Williams Problem."

14. Even the British reporting contingent was limited to 28 journalists. Renée Dickason, "La BBC, Imperméable à la Propagande? De la Guerre des Malouines aux Guerres du Moyen-Orient," *Vingtième Siècle: Revue d'Histoire* 80 (2003), 71–81; John Jewell, "Remembering the Falklands—the Worst-Reported Conflict of the Century," *Walesonline.co.uk*, April 4, 2012, updated March 27, 2013, http://www.walesonline.co.uk/news/wales-news/remembering-falklands—worst-reported-conflict-2046922.

15. Corn and Schulman, "Bill O'Reilly Has His Own Brian Williams Problem."

16. Richard J. Meislin, "Thousands in Buenos Aires Assail Junta for Surrendering to Britain," *The New York Times*, June 16, 1982.

17. "Jimmy Kimmel Live," *ABC*, February 9, 2015.

18. Erik Wemple, "The Massive Lefty Conspiracy Against Bill O'Reilly," *The Washington Post*, February 26, 2015, https://www.washingtonpost.com/blogs/erik-wemple/wp/2015/02/26/the-massive-lefty-conspiracy-against-bill-oreilly/.

19. Margaret Hartmann, "Bill O'Reilly Threatened a New York Times Reporter Over His 'War Zone' Controversy," *NYMag.com*, February 24, 2015, http://nymag.com/daily/intelligencer/2015/02/bill-oreilly-threatens-new-york-times-reporter.html; Andrew Kirell, "O'Reilly Lashes Out at *Mother Jones* and CNN's Brian Stelter: 'Far-Left Zealots' Smearing Me," *mediaite.com*, February 20, 2015.

20. "Bill O'Reilly's Talking Points Memo 2/20/15: A Response to Mother Jones," February 21, 2015, accessed September 1, 2015, http://nation.foxnews.com/2015/02/20/bill-oreillys-talking-points-memo-22015-airing-tonight-8pm-et.

21. Jon Greenberg, "Bill O'Reilly: 'I never said I was on the Falkland Islands,'" *Politifact.com*, March 3, 2015, http://www.politifact.com/punditfact/statements/2015/mar/03/bill-oreilly/oreilly-i-never-said-i-was-falkland-islands/.

22. Brian Stelter, "CBS Staffers Dispute Bill O'Reilly's 'War Zone' Story," *Money.CNN.com*, February 23, 2015, http://money.cnn.com/2015/02/22/media/cbs-staffers-oreilly-argentina/.

23. "Reliable Sources," Ex-CBS Staffers Dispute O'Reilly's Claims, *CNN*, February 22, 2015, http://www.cnn.com/videos/tv/2015/02/22/ex-cbs-staffers-dispute-oreillys-claims.cnn.

24. Gabriel Arana, "Fox News Doesn't Care if Bill O'Reilly is a Liar," *HuffingtonPost.com*, March 5, 2015, http://www.huffingtonpost.com/2015/03/05/fox-news-oreilly-liar_n_6810916.html; Rob Quinn, "Now in Question: O'Reilly's LA Riots Stories."

25. Paul Farhi, "Bill O'Reilly Cites Conflict that He Witnessed. How Much of That is True?," *WashingtonPost.com*, February 27, 2015, https://www. washingtonpost.com/lifestyle/style/is-bill-oreilly-making-things-up-or-just-bloviating/2015/02/27/bd5e7f66-bea4-11e4-b274-e5209a3bc9a9_ story.html; Matt Wilstein, "O'Reilly Apparently Contradicted Himself on Witnessing Nun Killings; Bill Responds," *Mediaite.com*, February 25, 2015, http://www.mediaite.com/tv/oreilly-apparently-contradicted-himself-on-witnessing-nun-killings-fox-responds/.

26. Lisa de Moraes, "Bill O'Reilly Scores His Best Ratings of 2015," *Deadline. com*, March 4, 2015, http://deadline.com/2015/03/bill-oreilly-ratings-2015-controversy-1201386281/.

27. Justin Peters, "Why Bill O'Reilly Won't Share Glenn Beck's Fate," *Slate.com*, February 26, 2015, http://www.slate.com/articles/news_and_politics/politics/2015/02/why_fox_isn_t_willing_to_fire_him_like_glenn_beck.html.

28. For an exception, see Brian Adam Jones, "How Brian Williams' War Memories Could Have Failed Him," *TaskandPurpose.com*, February 9, 2015, http://taskandpurpose.com/brian-williams-war-memories-failed/.

29. Jeffrey K. Olick, "Reflections on the Underdeveloped Relations Between Journalism and Memory Studies," in Barbie Zelizer and Keren Tenenboim-Weinblatt (Eds.) *Journalism and Memory* (New York: Palgrave Macmillan, 2014), p. 29.

30. "NBC Nightly News," *NBC*, February 4, 2015.

31. Helen L. Williams, Martin A. Conway, and Gillian Cohen, "Autobiographical Memory," in Gillian Cohen and Martin A. Conway, *Memory in the Real World*, pp. 21–90 (New York: Psychology Press, 2008).

32. Williams, Conway, and Cohen, "Autobiographical Memory," p. 23.

33. Endel Tulving. "Episodic and Semantic Memory," in Endel Tulving and Wayne Donaldson (Eds.), *Organization of Memory*, pp. 382–402. (New York: Academic Press, 1972).

34. Williams, Conway, and Cohen, "Autobiographical Memory," p. 22.

35. Endel Tulving and Fergus I. M. Craik, *The Oxford Handbook of Memory* (New York: Oxford University Press, 2000), p. 154.

36. "A Shifting Story," *Stripes.com*, February 4, 2015, http://www.stripes.com/news/us/nbc-s-brian-williams-recants-iraq-story-after-soldiers-protest-1.327792; Lauren Carroll, "Timeline of Brian Williams' Statements on Helicopter Attack," *Politifact.com*, February 5, 2015, http://www.politifact.com/punditfact/article/2015/feb/05/timeline-brian-williams-statements-iraqi-helicopte/; Tom Kuldt and Brian Stetler, "How Brian Williams' Iraq Story Changed," *Money.CNN.com*, February 20, 2015, http://money.cnn.com/2015/02/05/media/brian-williams-iraq-timeline/.

37. Marc Kusnetz, William M. Arkin, General Montgomery Meigs retired, and Neal Shapiro, *Operation Iraqi Freedom: The Inside Story* (Kansas City: Andrews McMeel Publishing), pp. 69–70.

38. Associated Press, "NBC's Brian Williams Arrives in Iraq," *USAToday.com*, March 4, 2007, http://usatoday30.usatoday.com/life/television/news/2007-03-04-brian-williams-iraq_N.htm.

39. Brian Williams, "The Long Gray Line," *DailyNightly. NBCnews.com*, September 27, 2007, http://dailynightly.nbcnews.com/_news/2007/09/27/4372931-the-long-gray-line. The blog post was republished, with a new introduction, in September 2007 after Downing was memorialized at West Point.

40. Kuldt and Stetler, "How Brian Williams' Iraq Story Changed."

41. Kuldt and Stetler, "How Brian Williams' Iraq Story Changed."

42. Dennis Brown, "'NBC Nightly News' Anchor Brian Williams to Deliver 2010 Notre Dame Commencement Address," *News.ND.edu*, January 14, 2010, http://news.nd.edu/news/14368-nbc-nightly-news-anchor-brian-williams-to-deliver-2010-notre-dame-commencement-address/.

43. Carroll, "Timeline of Brian Williams' Statements on Helicopter Attack."

44. Variety staff, "Watch: Brian Williams Tell his Story to Letterman in 2013," *Variety.com*, February 4, 2015, http://variety.com/2015/tv/news/watch-brian-williams-tell-iraq-story-to-letterman-in-2013-1201424379/.

45. Byran Burrough, "The Inside Story of the Civil War for the Soul of NBC News," *Vanity Fair*, May 2015, http://www.vanityfair.com/news/2015/04/nbc-news-brian-williams-scandal-comcast.

46. M.D. West, "Brian Williams and the Perils of the Use of Autobiographical Memory in Research," *Journal of Mass Communication & Journalism* 5 (2015), doi: 10.4172/2165-7912.1000255.

47. Steven Novella, "Did Williams Lie?," *Neurologicablog*, February 6, 2015, http://theness.com/neurologicablog/index.php/did-williams-lie/.

48. Pippa Norris, *Driving Democracy: Do Power-Sharing Institutions Work?* (New York: Cambridge University Press, 2008).

49. Cindy Elmore, "Stars and Stripes: A Unique American Newspaper's Historical Struggle Against Military Interference and Control," *Media History* 16, no. 3 (2010), 301–317.

50. Commission on the Freedom of the Press, *A Free and Responsible Press* (Chicago: University of Chicago Press, 1947).

51. Patrick Hughes, "Brand News," *Social Alternatives*, April 1992, 41–45; Terry O'Reilly, "Branding the News," *CBC Radio*, May 5, 2012, http://www.cbc.ca/player/Radio/More+Shows/Age+of+Persuasion/ID/1610597298/; Helle Sjøvaag, "Revenue and Branding Strategy in the Norwegian News Market: The Case of TV 2 News Channel," *Nordicom Review* 33, no. 1 (2012), 53–66.

52. Matt Carlson, "Rethinking Journalistic Authority: Walter Cronkite and Ritual in Television News," *Journalism Studies* 13, no. 4 (2012), 483–498.

53. Quoted in Hillary Profita, "Outside Voices: Gordon Joseloff Suggests CBS News Look to its Past to Map the Future," *CBSNews.com*, July 28, 2006, http://www.cbsnews.com/news/outside-voices-gordon-joseloff-suggests-cbs-news-look-to-its-past-to-map-the-future/.

54. Michael Hiltzik, "Real TV News Stars Rush to Prostitute Themselves on 'House of Cards,'" *LATimes.com*, March 24. Retrieved from http://articles.latimes.com/2014/mar/24/business/la-fi-mh-tv-journalists-20140324.

55. Glen Tickle, "Jimmy Fallon Asks Real News Anchors to Deliver Fake Good News on 'The Tonight Show,'" *Laughingsquid.com*, August 25, 2014, http://laughingsquid.com/jimmy-fallon-asks-real-news-anchors-to-deliver-fake-good-news-on-the-tonight-show/.

56. Sean Ian Mills, "Why Does Bill O'Reilly Play Himself as a Geek Villain?," *Henchman-4-Hire*, July 14, 2015, http://henchman4hire.com/2011/07/14/why-does-bill-oreilly-play-himself-as-a-geek-villain/.

57. Burrough, "The Inside Story of the Civil War for the Soul of NBC News."; Gabriel Sherman, "(Actually) True War Stories at NBC News: The Trouble Didn't Start with Brian Williams," *New York Magazine*, March 8, 2015, http://nymag.com/daily/intelligencer/2015/03/nbc-news-brian-williams-deborah-turness.html.

58. The number of local television news jobs has remained relatively stable, but the number of jobs at newspapers and their digital operations fell more than 41 % between 2000 and 2015. "Local TV: Newsroom Staff Levels," State of the News Media 2015, www.journalism.org, http://www.journalism.org/media-indicators/local-tv-newsroom-staff-levels/; American Society of News Editors, "2000 Census," April 12, 2000, http://asne.org/content.asp?pl=121&sl=172&contentid=172; American Society of News Editors, "2015 Census," July 18, 2015, http://asne.org/content.asp?pl=121&sl=415&contentid=415.

# CHAPTER 14

# Political Cartoon Framing of the NSA Snooping Scandal

## Joan L. Conners

The world learned about US National Security Agency (NSA) tactics on June 5, 2013, through a news report published in the UK's *Guardian*. Four days later, Edward Snowden's identity was revealed as the NSA whistleblower who downloaded a reported 1.5 million NSA files before fleeing from the USA to Hong Kong, on his way to asylum in Russia. The American public learned how the NSA had been monitoring their Internet activity, collecting smartphone user data. And world leaders learned that the NSA had been monitoring them as well. In the midst of this, the debate over security versus privacy grew, and US President Barack Obama spoke to both, professing that nobody was listening to American's phone calls, but also justifying the use of particular monitoring tactics by the NSA. Unlike other scandals described and analyzed in this collection, the NSA snooping scandal involves a number of parties—citizens, President Obama, Edward Snowden, and the NSA, to name a few. The attention brought to this scandal resulted in court rulings against—and then in support of—the NSA in its collection of phone data, as well as demands for reform of NSA tactics.

Through unfolding media coverage of this case, the public became aware of what information the American government might be gathering on them. But the NSA snooping scandal remains a complicated story to follow, differing from the more titillating, easy-to-digest narratives of sex scandals—for instance. Therefore, how has media framed this confusing scandal? Specifically, this analysis will explore how the NSA snooping case was framed in the visual commentary medium of political cartoons. While this visual form is quite distinct from news reports about this case, political cartoons work to encapsulate an opinion in a snapshot, often through just one visual image. They reflect an

J.L. Conners (✉)
Communication Studies, Randolph-Macon College, Ashland, VA, USA

© The Editor(s) (if applicable) and The Author(s) 2016
H. Mandell, G.M. Chen (eds.), *Scandal in a Digital Age*,
DOI 10.1057/978-1-137-59545-4_14

173

opinion about the current event, but often try to explain an issue or event in that reflection as well.

In this chapter, I will present a brief overview on how mass media has framed political scandals in the past, and specifically how political cartoon representations have framed this scandal. I will also present a brief timeline of the NSA snooping scandal before proceeding to an analysis of how political cartoons framed this case, focusing on the most prominent themes and the implications of such portrayals.

## MEDIA FRAMING OF POLITICAL SCANDAL

What is framing? Sociologists William A. Gamson and Andre Modigliani are often identified as first defining a frame as a "central organizing idea or story line that provides meaning to an unfolding strip of events. The frame suggests what the controversy is about, the essence of the issue."[1] While the analysis discussed here will consider how cartoons have framed a particular scandal rather than how news stories framed it, the notion of framing can apply to a broad range of media messages. According to media and public affairs scholar Robert M. Entman, a specific focus may be involved in a frame, saying "to frame is to select some aspects of a perceived reality and make them more salient in a communicating text, in such a way as to promote a particular problem definition, causal interpretation, moral evaluation, and or treatment recommendation for the item described."[2] Therefore, framing may involve subjectivity, but even if one sees an objective framing of an event, it may still address some aspects of a news event while ignoring others. Based on that definition, interpretation and evaluation frames may be particularly relevant in the case of media framing of scandal.

It is worth briefly revisiting Watergate, the watershed scandal that refers specifically to the 1972 break-in of the Democratic National Committee headquarters and more broadly to the scheming and illegal machinations of President Richard Nixon and his administration, involving wiretapping and blackmail, which ultimately resulted in the president's resignation. The comparison is necessary because the Watergate political scandal closely mirrors media attention on the NSA snooping scandal. Unlike political sex scandals, which may involve only a few people, Watergate and the NSA snooping case both involve multiple parties, individuals, as well as agencies. Watergate is also a political scandal (not a political sex scandal) that was the focus of research about political cartoon representations.

Research analyzing political cartoon imagery of Watergate demonstrates a variety of approaches in evaluating political cartoons about scandal and their potential impact. For example, politics researcher Colin Seymour-Ure identifies a change in British cartoons about the USA around the time of Watergate. Cartoon images of the American president became more critical in the 1960s and 1970s, as cartoons stripped "away the mystique of the presidency and the White House."[3] Cartoon imagery of presidents became cruder in British media.

Seymour-Ure suggests a number of factors may have contributed to such a shift: "Along with public tolerance of these images, and greatly strengthening their effect, was a cultural change in the USA toward far greater inquisitiveness about the president's character. Watergate, again, may mark the change. Journalists and official inquiries crawled all over the Nixon White House."[4]

While Seymour-Ure's analysis provides a broader scope of Watergate's impact on cartoon imagery of presidents, other research specifically examined cartoon representations of President Richard Nixon. Media researchers Mary E. Wheeler and Stephen K. Reed studied cartoon images of Nixon before and after Watergate. They found that undergraduates rated cartoon images of Nixon published after Watergate less favorably than those published prior to the scandal becoming public. They concluded that the change in tone of the caricatures reflected "the change in public opinion that occurred during this time period."[5] Furthermore, they found that non-Watergate cartoons published after Watergate were rated as more negative than those published before Watergate, perhaps reflecting a more widespread shift in public opinion post-Watergate. They suggest that a more detailed examination of the presidential caricatures themselves might determine what features changed, and what features in a caricature are associated with more favorable versus unfavorable images. The former is in essence what scholars Mitchel Goldman and Margaret A. Hagen's analysis explored, in their study of caricatures (and photographs) of Richard Nixon published in 1972 and 1973 in the midst of the Watergate scandal. They found facial features of Nixon, such as the size of his nose or jowls, were distorted to a greater degree in images from 1973, while such features did not physically change significantly in photographs taken then. They concluded that "the choice of *what* to caricature is determined largely by characteristics of the subject's face, while the *degree* of caricature is determined by the individual artist's style and bias."[6] The analysis conducted below does not focus on specific features exaggerated in cartoon imagery. Instead, I focus on how cartoon imagery presents various parties involved in or impacted by the NSA snooping scandal. However, Goldman and Hagen's discussion of what features are distorted in caricature will be revisited in my analysis.

## TIMELINE OF THE NSA SNOOPING SCANDAL, 2013–2014

The following timeline outlines the period for which political cartoons were collected:

May 20, 2013   Edward Snowden leaves for Hong Kong, after downloading a reported 1.5 million NSA files

June 5, 2013   The first story on Edward Snowden's leaks is published by the UK's *Guardian*; Glenn Greenwald interviewed Snowden in Hong Kong on June 1

June 9, 2013   Snowden's identity is revealed as the source of the NSA leaks

August 1, 2013   Snowden is granted temporary asylum by Russia

September 7, 2013    Public learns that NSA has access to smartphone user
    data
October 24, 2013    Public learns of NSA's surveillance of world leaders,
    including German Chancellor Angela Merkel
December 16, 2013    Federal District judge issues preliminary injunction to
    stop NSA collection of phone data
January 3, 2014    FISA (Foreign Intelligence Service Court) upholds NSA's
    collection of phone data practice
January 17, 2014    President Obama gives speech on recent NSA disclosures
    and calls for reform

Given Entman's three qualifications for a "high-magnitude" scandal,[7] the
NSA snooping scandal would meet those criteria and warrant further analysis. First, the scandal had considerable *duration*, given the timeline presented
above. Second, the scandal had *prominence*, in receiving prominent attention
in news coverage as well as commentary via news and social media. Third, the
scandal has *resonance*, about which Entman says a scandal "must be framed as
such, not just through the use of that word, but through evocative, symbolic
language and images that connote the president's or candidate's guilt of mis-
representation causing some degree of harm to Americans."[8] While the NSA
case goes beyond the focus of presidential scandals of Entman's analysis, these
criteria still apply to this scandal; in particular the third criteria of resonance.
After all, the embodiment of scandal through symbol and image suggests that
an analysis of political cartoons is quite appropriate to complicate media coverage of this multifaceted news episode.

## How Did Political Cartoons Portray the NSA Scandal?

Cartoon images were collected from www.cagle.com, an online cartoon collection site. From a collection of current event cartoons labeled "NSA Snooping"
230 images were published between June 7, 2013, just two days after the first
story based on Snowden's leaks was published, and January 24, 2014, following a speech by President Obama on NSA practices. A qualitative thematic
analysis was conducted, and the most prominent themes that emerged are discussed below. While a sample of this size might lend itself to a quantitative analysis, there was no particular sampling frame used to select these images—they
were categorized as such through the online cartoon collection. Additionally,
rather than fit these images into discrete categories based on specific details or
qualities that might be part of a quantitative content analysis, and report the
percentages of such representations, this analysis allowed themes to emerge
from reading and re-reading these images. Beyond identifying the parties represented in the image (e.g., the NSA as an organization or President Obama
as an individual), each image was noted for the overall theme demonstrated,
and any prominent visual details presented. From there, themes that repeatedly

arose in cartoon images were highlighted for further analysis to examine commonalities and distinctions among them.

## EARS AND EYES OF BIG BROTHER

Surveillance of the public was portrayed in a variety of ways in cartoon images, most of which commented on the inappropriate nature of such monitoring. Images featured individuals' phone conversations being intercepted, or online computer behavior being monitored, by the NSA, or President Obama, or some mysterious third party. Some images were humorous in terms of the conversations overheard—for example, Obama listening in on a "Jake from State Farm" phone call asking what he was wearing (by Randy Bish, *Pittsburgh Tribune Review*, June 19, 2013). Others were much more sinister, with a dark ominous figure listening to a conversation, for example, Steve Benson's image (*Arizona Republic*, June 11, 2013).

Many cartoon images portrayed "big brother" surveillance through the use of oversized ears as listening devices, or eyes to monitor individuals in private situations. Such imagery persisted throughout this scandal, from the first reports when the public learned of NSA surveillance tactics in June 2013, to Obama's address to the nation in January 2014 in which he attempted to defend the need for NSA surveillance while also announcing changes to restrict particular forms of data gathering. In an image by Bob Englehart of the *Hartford Courant* from January 17, 2014 (see Fig. 1), Obama is at a podium speaking, and his ears are large satellite devices. The technological transformation of Obama's ears was common during this snooping scandal. For example, syndicated cartoonist Bill Day's image (June 9, 2013) contains no words, just an image of Obama with satellite dish ears. In other images, such as Weyant's World drawn by Chris Weyant for *The Hill* (June 16, 2013) and John Cole's cartoon for the *Scranton Times-Tribune* (June 13, 2013), Obama's ears are oversized to enhance his listening abilities.

The exaggeration of Obama's ears is nothing new to political cartoons of US politicians or political candidates. For example, Hill found that President Jimmy Carter's smile was found frequently exaggerated in cartoon images.[9] Such portrayals demonstrate Goldman and Hagen's distinction between *what* to caricature and *degree* of caricature discussed earlier in this chapter.[10] President Obama's ears are likely exaggerated in cartoons related to completely different topics, as part of the process of a humorous caricature, but in the context of the NSA snooping scandal, his ears are transformed further for the visual message emphasized by them. Not only are Obama's ears oversized for listening in on private conversations, but others as well; for example, Mike Luckovich features one cartoon image of the NSA as an anonymous figure with oversized ears for surveillance in one image (*Atlanta Journal-Constitution*, Aug. 4, 2013), and another of his cartoons (Nov. 1, 2013) featured the NSA as a monster with oversized ears and more than one dozen eyes.

Surveillance by sight, often through an all-seeing eye, was also a common image conveying a "Big Brother" role by the NSA. While the ears for surveillance were featured on someone specific, such as President Obama, the eyes of surveillance in cartoons were usually just that—a large eyeball monitoring the situation. For example, a cartoon by Nate Beeler (*Columbus Dispatch*, June 10, 2013) features a huge eyeball looking into a home simultaneously through a window, the TV, a laptop screen, and a cell phone, with them saying "You can trust government!" Following the President's speech about NSA reforms in January 2014, Beeler features the same eye to which Obama has applied mascara while saying "There. Made some changes. Happy now?" (*Columbus Dispatch*, Jan. 24, 2014). The extent to which people are unaware of such snooping is also demonstrated by the spying eye, as in Rick McKee's (*Augusta Chronicle*, Nov. 1, 2013) cartoon of a man wrapping himself in a towel after a shower, saying, "You know, hon, with all these NSA spying stories, it's nice to know there's at least one place I can still go for some privacy." In the scene, the shower drain has been replaced by an eyeball.

Similarly, in revealing that, the NSA had been spying on foreign heads of state, Pat Bagley's (*Salt Lake Tribune*, Oct. 30, 2013) cartoon features President Obama saying to German Chancellor Angela Merkel, "Ya know, I hadn't really noticed that before." Merkel is pointing to a figure behind him in the Oval Office, who is wearing a trench coat labeled NSA, with two huge ears and one large eyeball comprising the head of this monitoring creature. In these portrayals, the eyes are not exaggerated on a known person, such as the ears of President Obama; rather, the eye is independent of a recognizable individual, and is instead an anonymous "Big Brother" figure spying on people.

Besides featuring the NSA and Barack Obama in surveillance activities, popular icons such as Santa Claus and the Statue of Liberty also frequently appeared in these political cartoons. In December 2013, many cartoons represented Santa Claus as being employed by, or monitored by, the NSA. His "naughty and nice" list would be particularly valuable for NSA purposes, and as we all learned from the song "Santa Claus is Coming to Town," which was the basis for Gary Varvel's image (*Indianapolis Star*, Dec. 11, 2013), "he sees you when you're sleeping, he knows when you're awake" (see Fig. 2). This co-opting of Santa Claus by cartoonists to demonstrate the extent of possible NSA surveillance reflects prior findings on the frequent use of literary and cultural allusions in political cartoons.[11]

Other images that suggest "Lady Liberty is Listening" appeared frequently soon after the NSA scandal broke in the news, and in particular around July 4, 2013, less than one month after the first report based on Edward Snowden leaks. The adaptation of this popular symbol underlies questions of liberty versus security regarding NSA tactics; to feature Lady Liberty in the surveillance of others suggests security has won out over liberty. For example, one image by David Fitzsimmons (*Arizona Daily Star*, June 10, 2013) has multiple surveillance gadgets popping out of the Statue of Liberty; a cartoon by Mike Keefe (*Denver Post*, June 20, 2013) has tourists commenting to each other that it is "spooky how her eyes seem to follow you everywhere," with Lady Liberty's eyes labeled NSA and IRS. Similarly, Michael Ramirez's (*Investor's Business Daily*, July 4, 2013) "Taking Liberty" cartoon features the Statue of Liberty's torch replaced by a satellite dish, connected to headphones she is wearing. Uncle Sam appears similarly in many cartoon images, but is featured in a broader range or roles, being involved in surveillance tactics (as a "peeping Sam" portrayed by Dave Granlund's nationally syndicated cartoon of June 7, 2013), witnessing snooping by the NSA or President Obama, or being investigated by the NSA.

This Big Brother theme is just one identified in cartoons about the NSA snooping scandal, but it dominated this collection of images, and was demonstrated in a variety of approaches as noted above—overhearing ears, spying eyes, as well as through the use of popular icons implied to be caught up in NSA surveillance tactics.

## PRESIDENT OBAMA AND BUSH SIMILARITIES

Cartoon images offered parallels between Obama and George W. Bush for their policies on surveillance, since many of the NSA tactics in 2013 were approved as part of the Patriot Act, which passed in 2001 following the 9/11 terrorist attacks during President George W. Bush's administration. For example, a cartoon by J.D. Crowe (*Huntsville Times*, June 10, 2013) titled "I Spy BushObama," which reminds us of the childhood game "I spy with my little eye, something that ...," features Bush morphing into Obama. The exaggerated ears for surveillance continued in images featuring both Obama and Bush. In Steve Sack's cartoon (*Minneapolis Star Tribune*, June 7, 2013), both Bush and Obama have oversized ears labeled "surveillance program," and Obama says to Bush "I feel your pain." Both are buried up to their chest in paperwork labeled "Criticism." Similarly, Mark Streeter's cartoon (*Savannah Morning News*, June 8, 2013) features both presidents, with exaggerated ears, appearing out of the earpiece or mouthpiece of a phone labeled "NSA phone tracking." Bush is shown saying "Can he hear you now?" similar to the phrase made popular in Verizon cell phone advertisements ("Can you hear me now?"), and Obama says "hello?" While most of these images portray Bush and Obama equally involved in surveillance policies, Monte Wolverton's image (Cagle cartoons, June 10, 2013) of Bush operating a drone featuring Obama's face suggests that Bush is behind the policies. In the cartoon Bush says "Look at my new toy that I controlify remotely! I call it the Obama administration!"

These political cartoons continue to link President Barack Obama directly to the NSA surveillance scandal, but they position him in relation to President George W. Bush in ways that suggest the policies of Bush are continuing with Obama, or perhaps that Bush is controlling aspects of Obama's surveillance policies of his administration. The similarity in their portrayals, continuing with the exaggerated ears of surveillance, connects to the previous theme, as well as suggests commonality between these two presidents of different political parties when it comes to security policies.

### Unwitting US Citizens

The final theme that arose in many cartoon images regarding the NSA spying scandal was the role of US citizens when they learned of surveillance tactics by the US government against them. In most images, citizens appear quite innocent, not involved in any way in the surveillance tactics; in some cartoons, citizens appear shocked and surprised when learning of such practices. In other images, they are portrayed as ignorant or unconcerned about such tactics. Citizens are often depicted as are unaware of such practices even when they are made public; furthermore, they are portrayed as not terribly concerned about surveillance practices and the potential violation on their own privacy. Titling this theme as citizens who are "unwitting" encompasses all of this—unsuspecting, ignorant, as well as innocent.

News media coverage of NSA surveillance tactics brought such practices to the public's attention. Many cartoons took that awareness a step further, depicting citizens developing a new consciousness about the extent of their surveillance. For example, Randy Bish's cartoon (*Pittsburgh Tribune Review*, June 7, 2013) features a person who is reading the paper about government surveillance practices. He sneezes, to which his computer replies "Bless you" and his cell phone says "Gesundheit." Similarly, a cartoon of a cell phone user asking Verizon Wireless' question "Can you hear me now?" hears five responses (Bruce Plante, *Tulsa World*, Jan. 22, 2014). Many similar cartoon images portray one's digital devices wrangled into such monitoring, including cell phones, home computers, Google glass, and online video games.

Another portrayal of citizens suggested that people's previous paranoia of such practices was justified given the disclosure of NSA surveillance methods. Adam Zyglis (*Buffalo News*, July 5, 2013) portrays the "monster under your bed" of government data mining, confirming the validity of our childhood fears. Other cartoons, such as those by syndicated cartoonist Chip Bok (Jan. 16, 2014), and Gary Varvel (*Indianapolis Star*, Aug. 21, 2013) feature citizens as patients on the couch in a therapy session, learning that their paranoid delusions of government surveillance were true all along. While some of the other images here are humorous as well as thought-provoking, these cartoons confirm our own fears rather than poke fun at what the NSA is actually doing.

Some images of citizens portray them as truly innocent, going on about their lives with little awareness of such surveillance tactics (e.g., Monte Wolverton of Cagle Cartoons, featured an image of a person in his "home sweet home" on a computer, with three NSA agents dressed in black surrounding his home). However, other cartoon images regarding the NSA scandal portray citizens as apathetic. Syndicated cartoonist Dave Granlund demonstrates this apathy with an image of an elderly couple reading the news about NSA practices, about which one suggests the government can help her find where she left her glasses (June 6, 2013). A lack of concern is demonstrated in a conversation in a cartoon by Rick McKee (*Augusta Chronicle*, June 12, 2013) in which a man on a park bench says he was telling a buddy the other day that he has nothing to hide and is not worried if the NSA is tracking his phone calls, to which the other person in the scene, an NSA agent, replies "yes, I know." Apathy is also represented in a Bruce Plante (*Tulsa World*, June 19, 2013) cartoon image of two men in a bar discussing "what's the worst that can happen" if you do not have anything to hide or if the NSA stopped spying. In response to one asking the other "well, whaddya gonna do," they both order another round of drinks as their response. In a variety of portrayals of apathy, these cartoon images suggest it is worse to be unconcerned than it is to be unaware of such surveillance tactics by one's government.

## Concluding Thoughts

The NSA snooping scandal provided ample material for political cartoonists in late 2013 and early 2014. This analysis discovered prominent themes that were frequently featured in cartoonists' visual imagery, most noteworthy was the variety of ways NSA tactics were portrayed as contemporary "Big Brother" activities. Listening to conversations, monitoring new technology, and watching people in the privacy of their homes were regular portrayals of NSA tactics. Activities such as big data mining are not easily translatable to a single-image cartoon that has little text, which might explain why more observational activities were featured so often. And such monitoring is more personal and perhaps perceived as more intrusive than data aggregating would be. Even though more sophisticated techniques were used by the NSA, cartoons simplified such tactics into images that readers could easily digest and understand.

While the NSA was often portrayed as an anonymous intelligence agent, President Barack Obama was regularly portrayed along with the NSA, either aware of or participating in surveillance activities. If the agency was embodied more in an individual director, perhaps similar to the role of Attorney General, or a more public head of another federal agency, we might see someone else identified instead of Obama. And instead of featuring an anonymous generic agent, cartoons might have caricatured that individual, in addition to, or perhaps instead of, Obama. The comparison of Obama to President George W. Bush crossed partisan lines and also implies this was not a short-term practice by the NSA, but rather one developing over the years that had just come to the public's awareness.

The public was portrayed in a variety of ways in political cartoons, as innocent victims in such surveillance, becoming aware of NSA tactics and worried about them, and as apathetic upon learning how their actions or communication routines might be monitored. This breadth of portrayals reflects different aspects of the "unwitting citizen," more so than how an "outraged citizen" might have been framed. The "unwitting" portrayal is particularly disconcerting when we consider that at the time the NSA snooping scandal was leaked, we have never before had so much personal information so easily shared. Between photos, texts, posts, and embarrassing Google searches in our browser history, we have massive amounts of information about ourselves out there, for others to access, collect, and use in some way. When an incident such as the NSA's use of Verizon cell phone data makes national news, for example, the public might get momentarily worried. Otherwise, it seems as though none of us are reading those user agreements when we set up a new online account about how our information might be used. Or we cannot even bear to consider the potentially devastating consequences if our private information is breached so we just click "accept" without pondering the risks too carefully.

Perhaps, as we were all just beginning to learn about the scope of NSA intelligence gathering, understanding needed to precede outrage. There was not clear and widespread public outrage when NSA surveillance tactics were made public. The debate between the need for such tactics for security purposes versus the potential violations of privacy may underlie such portrayals of the public in cartoon images as well.

Political cartoonists were certainly interested in this scandal, as reflected in the number of cartoons over a short period of time—even if cartoonists portrayed the American public as less-than-engaged in these events. In contrast, polls conducted by the Pew Research Center show people were aware, and many were concerned. While cartoonists portrayed Americans frequently as unaware or uncaring, the Pew Center found 87 % of Americans were cognizant of federal surveillance programs, and 22 % said they changed how they use technology in some way following the leaks of NSA tactics.[12] They also found 54 % of Americans disapproved of the government's collection of data as part of anti-terrorism tactics, while 42 % approved of such practices. So while political cartoons did not consistently portray US citizens as concerned, public opinion research reports that most people had at least a baseline understanding of the NSA issues at play, and quite a few were disapproving of them.

Finally, this analysis of framing does not assume what sociologist Ari Adut considers a constructivist perspective on media and scandal, that media play a major role in the making of a scandal.[13] Rather, the media have a role in framing a scandal, which may influence how the public envisions a scandal, but it does not operate as a "hypodermic needle" direct effect on media audiences. The media's frames of a scandal, including those in political cartoons as examined in this analysis, contribute to the shaping of opinion about a scandal.[14] Those opinions are also shaped by non-media factors, including personal experience, knowledge we gain in discussing such issues with others, as well prior beliefs on issues of security and privacy. The perspectives expressed by political cartoonists in their work contribute to that discussion, as do news reports, editorial columns, and commentary in social media. Political cartoonists express those perspectives in a creative "snapshot" of a visual embodiment of opinion, and this analysis discovered patterns existed in those opinions and visuals in portraying the NSA surveillance scandal.

# Notes

1. William A. Gamson and Andre Modigliani, "The Changing Culture of Affirmative Action," In *Research in Political Psychology, Volume 3 ed.* Richard D. Braungart, *Research in Political Psychology, Volume 3*, (Greenwich, CT: JAI, 1987): 143.
2. Richard M. Entman, "Framing: Toward Clarification of a Fractured Paradigm," *Journal of Communication* 43 (1993): 52.
3. Colin Seymour-Ure, "Farewell, Camelot! British Cartoonists' Views of the United States since Watergate," *Journalism Studies* 8 (2007): 734.
4. Seymour-Ure, "Farewell, Camelot!" 734.
5. Mary E. Wheeler and Stephen K. Reed, "Response to Before and After Watergate Caricatures," *Journalism Quarterly* 52 (1975): 136.
6. Mitchel Goldman and Margaret A. Hagen, "The Forms of Caricature: Physiognomy and Political Bias," *Studies in the Anthropology of Visual Communication* 5 (1978): 36.
7. Robert M. Entman, *Scandal and Silence: Media Responses to Presidential Misconduct*, (Malden, MA: Polity Press, 2012): 34.
8. Entman, *Scandal and Silence*, 34.
9. Alette Hill, "The Carter Campaign in Retrospect: Decoding the Cartoons," In *Rhetorical Dimensions in Media: A Critical Casebook*, ed. Martin J. Medhust and Thomas W. Benson (Dubuque, IA: Kendall/Hunt Publishing Co., 1984): 182–203.
10. Goldman and Hagen, "The Forms of Caricature," 30–36.
11. Medhurst, Martin J., and Michael A. DeSousa, "Political Cartoons as Rhetorical Form: A Taxonomy of Graphic Discourse," *Communication Monographs* 48 (1982): 197–236.
12. Pew Research Center (2015, May 29). "What Americans Think About NSA Surveillance, National Security and Privacy," May 29, 2015. http://www.pewresearch.org/fact-tank/2015/05/29/what-americans-think-about-nsa-surveillance-national-security-and-privacy/.
13. Ari Adut, *On Scandal: Moral Disturbances in Society, Politics, and Art*, (New York: Cambridge University Press, 2008): 13.
14. Hans M. Kepplinger, Stefan Geiss, and Sandra Siebert, "Framing Scandals: Cognitive and Emotional Media Effects," *Journal of Communication* 62 (2012): 659–681.

# CHAPTER 15

# Evolution of a Modern Sports Scandal

*Brian Moritz*

In many ways, the dominant storyline of 2014 for the NFL was not the sustained excellence of the New England Patriots and their dramatic last-second Super Bowl victory over the Seattle Seahawks or the continued record-setting career of Denver Broncos quarterback Peyton Manning.

Rather, the season's dominant storyline belonged to a player who did not gain a yard, score a touchdown, or make a tackle. The dominant storyline of the season belonged to player who did not play in 2014.

The dominant storyline of the 2014 NFL season belonged to Ray Rice.

The one-time Baltimore Ravens star running back, two years removed from winning a Super Bowl championship, was arrested in February 2014 on domestic violence charges after assaulting his then-fiancée in an Atlantic City casino. Rice was indicted on felony charges, which were later dropped after he entered a pre-trial diversionary program.

One thing that made the Rice incident different from others involving athletes was that footage of it was captured by surveillance cameras inside the casino and subsequently leaked to the website TMZ. An initial video showed Rice dragging his unconscious fiancée out of an elevator. Months later, after Rice had been suspended two games by the NFL, a second video emerged from inside the elevator that showed Rice punching his fiancée. The graphic nature of the second video prompted the NFL to suspend Rice indefinitely and the Ravens to terminate his contract. Rice's suspension was later lifted after he appealed in federal court.

That second video also changed the tenor of the scandal and subsequent coverage. Rather than being a scandal about an athlete accused of beating a woman, it became a scandal about institutional failure. The NFL and commissioner Roger Goodell became the focus of the coverage and criticism.

B. Moritz (✉)
Digital Media and Online Journalism, SUNY Oswego, Oswego, NY, USA

H. Mandell, G.M. Chen (eds.), *Scandal in a Digital Age*,
DOI 10.1057/978-1-137-59545-4_15

Goodell received the brunt of the criticism for statements that were perceived as dishonest, and a specter of cover-up surrounded the league's actions after Rice's arrest.[1] There was, it appeared, a transference of scandal from Rice to Goodell. In essence, by the end of the year, the Ray Rice scandal had little to do with Ray Rice himself. Instead, it focused on Roger Goodell and his conduct as commissioner. A player's arrest led to "the biggest crisis confronting a commissioner in the NFL's 94-year history."[2]

This chapter will trace the evolution of the Ray Rice scandal through media coverage. The purpose is to understand the evolution of a scandal in modern media and how the framing and focus of a scandal can change over time. It will examine how the initial coverage of the story reflected standard tropes of media coverage of arrested athletes and race relations in sports.[3] It will use Joshua Gamson's[4] model of media scandal coverage to demonstrate how an individual scandal becomes an institutional one through the media.

In addition, this chapter will demonstrate that one of the reasons the narrative of the scandal shifted from Rice to the NFL and Goodell can be understood through the social construction of news, an area of media sociology that includes journalists' routines, values of newsworthiness, and the study of journalist-source relationships.[5] This chapter will present the argument that the publication of the second surveillance video (the one showing the full altercation) fundamentally changed the nature of the scandal. It introduced a vein of institutional malfeasance and dishonesty from those in charge of the NFL and was a strong example of deviance—all strong news values by journalists.[6] In short, journalists' routines and the social construction of news led to the evolution of the Ray Rice scandal from an athlete accused of domestic violence into a much larger story.

To do so, the chapter employs a methodology based in grounded theory,[7] in which theories are rooted in data, and the research process involves the concurrent collection and interpretation of data. In this case, Google and database searches were conducted for news stories and blog posts with the search terms "Ray Rice" and "Ray Rice suspension" for the time between his arrest on February 16, 2014, and the end of that year. Themes were culled from stories found in these searches, and articles were selected for relevance to the themes.

## Beginnings of the Scandal: Arrest and First Video

On February 16, 2014, *The Baltimore Sun* ran its first story on Rice's arrest. "Ravens running back Ray Rice arrested after incident in Atlantic City" read the headline. It was a straightforward news account, relying on a statement released by Atlantic City police as well as quotes from Rice's attorney and a statement from the Baltimore Ravens' public relations director. Rice's attorney said the assault was "a very minor physical altercation,"[8] and the story also quoted the police that the altercation "was recorded by video surveillance, according to a statement from police. Footage appeared to show both parties involved in a physical altercation."

At the time, nothing was special or unique about this story. Sadly, an athlete being arrested is not uncommon. *USA Today* reported that between 2000 and 2014, there were 772 arrests of NFL players—an average of nearly 55 per calendar year.[9] Rice was a popular player in Baltimore, where he had played since being drafted in 2008. He had been selected to the NFL's Pro Bowl three times, played on a Super Bowl champion, and was active in the community.[10] But Rice was coming off one of his least productive seasons as an NFL running back and was by no means a national star. TMZ, which for several years had been covering athlete's off-field proclivities on a sports-only website, ran just three stories about Rice prior to his arrest—one about him hoping to play well after the 2011 NFL lockout and another after he was burglarized in May 2013.

Rice's arrest was certainly news, but it was by no means a scandal at this point. The story had no controversial or salacious element that made it stand out among other athlete arrests. Three days after the first reports of his arrest, TMZ released the first bombshell in this story. The site published a 49-second clip of surveillance video from inside the casino lobby that showed Rice dragging Janay Palmer's unconscious body out of an elevator and dropping her on the floor. This video was filmed moments after the alleged assault.[11]

The presence of the initial video gave Rice's arrest a little more attention than other stories of athlete arrests, but not significantly. Between the release of the video on February 19 and the end of July, when the NFL held a disciplinary hearing, Rice's arrest was not a big story. Virtually all stories in that time dealt with estimating the amount of time Rice would be suspended[12] or the effect that Rice's suspension would have on his career and on the Ravens.[13]

For the shocking nature of the video, it did not create an immediate scandal. Rice's story, in fact, did not follow the classic model of media coverage of pro athletes. Sports media scholar David Leonard[14] noted that most media coverage of athlete arrests, and most scholarly research about said arrests, tends to start from a place of lawless athletes being out of control, a sports world that is "overflowing with criminals" and "a spectacle." Leonard argued that the perception put forth by this media coverage and academic scholarship of "America's athletes are out of control"[15] is inaccurate and in fact often has racial bias. Coverage of arrests tends to conflate an arrest with criminal activities, and that coverage of athletes and crimes often reinforces racial stereotypes of black males. Sports researcher Richard E. Lapchick[16] proposed a systematic coupling of athletes and crime that revolves around racial stereotyping. The primary argument is that the arrests of black athletes are treated as indicative of a larger problem of "thug athletes," while the arrests of white athletes are treated as isolated incidents, not as indictments of a larger class.

The Rice story followed the familiar pattern of athlete arrests. The Ravens held a press conference with Rice and Palmer sitting next to each other to apologize to the media and (by proxy) the fans for what had happened. The Ravens were widely criticized for this press conference. Putting Rice and Palmer on stage next to each other in a public setting—abuser and victim sitting side by side— was seen as insensitive at best and insulting at worst. Palmer also apologized for "any role I played" in the assault—a line that the Ravens' public relations staff tweeted out—in another move that caused controversy.[17] "Ray Rice's effort at damage control Friday didn't appear to control much of the damage … a tearful Rice provided plenty of self-pity to go along with his apologies."[18]

## INITIAL SUSPENSION

On July 25, eight days after a disciplinary hearing at NFL offices in New York City, Commissioner Roger Goodell announced that Rice would be suspended for the first two games of the upcoming season.

The two-game suspension was widely panned.[19] "Roger Goodell wrist slaps Ray Rice in suspension" read the headline in *The Philadelphia Inquirer*.[20] "This is yet another signal that the NFL doesn't care nearly enough about domestic violence. This may be the best signal yet."[21] Several commentators noted the disconnect between Rice's two-game suspension for domestic violence and Cleveland Browns' receiver Josh Gordon's yearlong suspension for marijuana use.[22]

> Message received, Roger Goodell. Loud and clear. When it comes to running afoul of the law and NFL rules, 'tis worse—far worse—in the league's eyes to take some Adderall or smoke some marijuana than it is to, say, allegedly knock your fiancée out cold and then drag her unconscious body from a casino elevator.[23]

However among other members of the elite sports media, the suspension was viewed as adequate. Adam Schefter, ESPN's lead NFL reporter, reported on the air that some of his sources in the league were wondering if the suspension was too harsh.[24] On *Pardon the Interruption*, one of ESPN's daily sports-news debate shows, hosts Michael Wilbon and Jason Whitlock both said they agreed with the suspension length, citing a lack of full knowledge of what happened inside the elevator and the fact that Rice's case had been adjudicated with no conviction. They also criticized the social-media lynch mob that called for a greater penalty.[25]

One of the main reasons elite sports media members defended the suspension as appropriate was the existence of a second video—one taken inside the elevator that preceded the video TMZ had released. Peter King of Sports Illustrated and the MMQB (Monday Morning Quarterback)—widely seen as the most plugged-in NFL reporter—reported that league officials had seen the video:

> There is one other thing I did not write or refer to, and that is the other videotape the NFL and some Ravens officials have seen, from the security camera inside the elevator at the time of the physical altercation between Rice and his fiancée.[26]

That report provided reasoning to defend the NFL. The logic went: They have seen more than we have, they know what really happened; we can trust them to make the correct decision. This reporting was based almost entirely on anonymous sources—that is, sources whose identity is known to the reporter but whose identities are not published.[27] The Ray Rice story did not go away after the announcement of his punishment. In fact, the suspension escalated attention to the story and began to evolve the narrative. Before the suspension, the story focused on Rice, his actions, the mechanics of his case in the legal system, his future as a player, and the suspension's effect on the Ravens. After the suspension, the narrative evolved into Goodell's decisions and reputation as commissioner, as well as the NFL's attitude toward domestic violence.

This evolution in the story—from focusing on Rice's actions and the legal system to the NFL's reaction to and handling of domestic violence by its players (and the league's institutional attitude toward women)—reflects sociologist Joshua Gamson's findings in how mainstream media cover scandals.[28] Part of this can be seen in the evolution of media scandals. In looking at three sex scandals involving male public figures who were involved with prostitutes (Jimmy Swaggart, Hugh Grant, and Dick Morris), Gamson described how the narratives of those stories evolved from a scandalous act (or acts) into something larger. For Swaggart, it became a story of the individual and institutional hypocrisy of televangelists. For Grant, it became a story of his public versus private image along with potential relationship troubles with his movie-star girlfriend. For Morris, his sex scandal became a story of disloyalty and hubris. In all three cases, Gamson documents how the initial scandalous act becomes about something larger—and often institutional in nature. "The emergence of a scandal story is tightly tied to its institutional location."[29] Writing specifically about Swaggart's fall from grace, Gamson noted: "In the end, the mass mediated scandal story became one not of an individual's sexual transgressions but of an institutional environment that encouraged inauthenticity and thus hypocrisy."[30]

Similar to these stories, the story of Rice's arrest for domestic violence became about something larger and more institutional than the actions of one player. After Rice's initial suspension and leading into the start of the NFL season, Rice's story became a story about domestic violence and the NFL.[31] A month after the suspension and just before the start of the regular season, Goodell announced a new, stricter policy against domestic violence, increasing the suspension to six games for a first offense.

The story hung over the NFL as the regular season began the week of September 7, 2014. Rice was cheered by fans in Baltimore during pre-season games, and several fans continued to wear Rice's replica jersey to the games— including several female fans.

That changed in the early hours of September 8.

## THE SECOND VIDEO

In the early morning hours of September 8, 2014, TMZ published a new story. "Ray Rice—ELEVATOR KNOCKOUT ... Fiancée takes crushing punch."[32] The post featured the previously unpublished video from inside the elevator during the fight between Rice and Palmer. The video was graphic and stunning. It showed Rice punching his fiancée, causing her to hit her head on the elevator's handrail and knocking her unconscious.

> This is what a two game suspension looks like—Ray Rice delivering a vicious punch to his fiancée's face, knocking her out cold ... What was the NFL thinking when it wrist-slapped Rice with such feeble punishment?[33]

This video changed the nature of the scandal. Again, it was the surveillance of a gossip website that changed the course of the conversation. Countless professional athletes had been arrested for domestic violence. None before had the actual act of domestic violence captured on surveillance video.

The graphic nature of the second video removed all shadows of doubt from this case. The arguments that "we don't really know what happened in that elevator," that "she attacked him first," and that "Palmer was knocked out not by the punch but by falling and accidentally hitting her head" were all obliterated in that three-minute clip. The raw and ugly truth of this domestic violence case was clear for everyone. Within hours of that clip's release, the Ravens had severed all ties with Rice, and the NFL had suspended him indefinitely.[34]

However, the brutal clarity of those tapes raised other questions. Had the NFL seen this tape before TMZ's release? Had the NFL seen this tape before levying the widely derided two-game suspension in July? If so, why did the NFL suspend him for so few games then and so many games once the tape was made public? If not, why did the NFL—a multi-billion dollar corporation with a vast security department and connections with local and national law enforcement—not have this tape?[35] It is notable that in that initial post of the second video, TMZ raised the question not of Rice's behavior or actions but of the NFL's response. The first sentence of this update referred to the two-game suspension Rice received, not to his actions. "Ray Rice isn't an ex-Raven today because the NFL finally saw the second tape. He's an ex-Raven because we finally saw the second tape, and we were repulsed by the images."[36]

Similar to the sex scandals Gamson[37] wrote about, the Ray Rice story became about something larger and more institutionally based than the criminal actions that caused it. Like the sex scandals that developed into larger narratives about hypocrisy, image repair, and loyalty,[38] the Ray Rice story evolved into a larger narrative of the NFL's institutional malfeasance.

The alleged malfeasance on the NFL's part stemmed from its decision to suspend Rice indefinitely. In announcing the move on September 8—just hours after TMZ published the video—the NFL said that the move was based on new video evidence.[39] However, according to stories published over the summer, Goodell had initially decided on a two-game suspension in part because he had seen the inside-the-elevator video.[40] Now, the NFL was claiming that it had not seen it. The Associated Press, citing an anonymous law-enforcement source, reported that the NFL had received the tape and officials at the league had seen it prior to its public release—"It's bad" a league employee reportedly said to a law-enforcement official.[41] The fact that Goodell was now saying he had not seen the video raised questions that either Goodell's investigation was incomplete or incompetent. In a long investigative piece on ESPN, Don VanNatta Jr. wrote that more than 20 interviews with 11 sources painted:

> a picture of a league and a franchise whose actions—and inaction—combined to conceal—or ignore—the graphic violence of Rice's assault. When evidence of it surfaced anyway, the NFL and the Ravens quickly shifted gears and simultaneously attempted to pin the blame on Rice and his alleged lack of truthfulness with Goodell about what had happened inside the elevator.[42]

Goodell's actions led to calls for him to lose his job as NFL commissioner, from both media outlets and from the National Organization of Women.[43] They also resulted in a congressional investigation.[44] Keith Olbermann repeated his calls for Goodell's resignation.[45] "If he had not seen the elevator tape—a claim being made Monday afternoon—why not? That's an indictment of Goodell's abilities and thought process. How could a website get access to this shocking information and not the commissioner, Ravens officials or the highly skilled NFL investigators?"[46] The narrative of this story had completely changed, from an arrested athlete to one of a potential institutional cover-up and misconduct.

## Social Construction of the Ray Rice Scandal

One reason for this evolution comes from Gamson's model of scandal coverage. Scandals tend to turn into stories about larger issues.

Another reason for the evolution can be seen through the lens of the social construction of news, which is a loosely coupled theoretical notion from media sociology. To professional journalists, news is something that exists in the world, and it is a reporter's job to go out there and find it. The sociological view holds that news is not something that exists in the world but is instead a social construct.[47] Sociologist Gaye Tuchman[48] found that news is not a reflection of reality (as the traditional journalistic ethos holds) but instead a construction of reality, which is made by journalists through their norms, attitudes, practices, and routines.[49] Sociologist Herbert J. Gans[50] wrote that news construction is a complex interplay of journalists' attitudes and practices and organizational goals and constraints.

The social construction of news is not meant to suggest that reporters make up the news, like fiction. The concept simply means that news is created daily by a socially agreed-upon collection of norms, values, and practices that journalists call newsworthiness. Media sociologist Michael Schudson[51] defined several elements of news, including the fact that it is usually event-driven, negative, process-driven (rather than results driven), and reflects the world and points of view of official sources. Media scholar Pamela J. Shoemaker[52] defined news values as including deviance, timeliness, proximity, and impact. Shoemaker's work has defined deviance as one of the core news values journalists use in deciding whether an event is newsworthy or how newsworthy an event is. Shoemaker and colleagues[53] found that deviance—something outside the normal boundaries of everyday life—indicates newsworthiness. A story headlined "Plane lands safely after routine flight" would hardly qualify as news. A story headlined "Plane crashes; hundreds feared dead" would most certainly be news. Many news values Shoemaker[54] identified can be seen in sports pages as well, whether it is proximity (local sports get more coverage); timeliness (games and events happening today are more newsworthy than next week's game); or deviance (a game that is expected to be close is, instead, a blowout).

Certainly, the evolution of the Ray Rice scandal is an example of deviance. Within the specific context of the sports landscape in 2014, a pro athlete arrested for domestic violence had some level of deviance (it is outside what we consider good or normal behavior, but it is not totally unheard of). A player arrested for domestic violence when the immediate aftermath of the assault was captured by surveillance video is even more out of the ordinary, and, therefore, more deviant. That player being suspended for only two games, which led to a public outcry, increased the deviance. The publication of a second surveillance video that showed the graphic nature of the assault and the subsequent season-long suspension also increased its deviance. Every new development in the Ray Rice story increased the story's overall deviance. A player being arrested is a story. The NFL potentially botching an investigation into the arrest is a much bigger story. There is far more deviance in the potential botched investigation by the NFL and questionable actions by the commissioner than there is in a player being arrested. The more the story evolved, the more it turned from a routine-player arrest story into an example of what Tuchman[55] referred to as a "What A Story!" This is a level of Tuchman's typification in which a story is so juicy, so incredible, so out of the ordinary that it trumps all other news values (the name comes from the tendency of reporters and editors to literally yell "What a story!" when hearing about it).

The Rice scandal also evolved due to the way it was reported, which involves journalists' reliance on sources. This is a critical feature of the social construction of news. Gans[56] called the journalist–source relationship the central relationship of journalism. Journalism is, in many ways, dependent upon sources. Reporters typically are not present when a car accident happens or when a murder takes place or when a decision on which football player to draft in the first round is made. Therefore, they rely on sources for information. While these sources can include documents (both public and private) and databases, sources are primarily people. Media scholar Leon V. Sigal[57] noted that journalism can be defined as what a source says happened or what will happen. Gans[58] compared the journalist–source relationship to a dance and that the source is always leading. Without sources, journalists have little or no news to report.

Who these sources are is important to consider as well. Scholars[59] have noted that journalists rely more on official sources—primarily official government sources—than anyone else for their news. This reliance on sources occurs for several reasons. For one, government sources are socially sanctioned, and they have power and access to information. If a police officer gives details about a crime, there is a certain social acceptance given to that description over an ordinary person's description—or especially the accused's version of events.[60] Official sources also hold a place of privilege for reporters because they are regular, reliable sources of news. Government officials hold regular press conferences. Courts are open to the public, and transcripts are available. Average people do not typically have the time or ability to stage a press conference about an event that matters to them. Government officials do have that time and ability, which makes them reliable sources of information that becomes news. Gans[61] noted that reporters are interested in efficiency of news gathering—not out of nefarious, capitalistic reasons but simply so they can easily complete their stories by deadline. Official sources provide this regular source of news that is socially sanctioned.

This is also true in sports journalism. Sports journalists tend to use star athletes, coaches, and administrators as sources in stories.[62] Sportswriters are reliant upon access to athletes, which leads to a culture that promotes more positive than critical coverage.[63]

In this story, if TMZ's coverage was the spark that started the story, then the elite NFL reporters' coverage and their use of and reliance on official NFL sources led to its evolution.

Let us start in July, with the two-game suspension that drew criticism. Writing on his website, King (the reporter for *Sports Illustrated*) reported that the NFL had seen the inside-the-elevator video.[64] Next we move to September, after the elevator video was released and the NFL suspended Rice for the season, claiming the video was new information.[65] This contradicted King's report from three months earlier that the NFL had seen the video.

This detail helped change the tenor of the story as well. This created the perception of dishonesty. Had the NFL seen the video or not? If they had not seen the video, why not? In an open letter to his site's readers, King explained his reporting:

> Earlier this summer a source I trusted told me he assumed the NFL had seen the damaging video that was released by TMZ on Monday morning of Rice slugging his then-fiancée, Janay Palmer, in an Atlantic City elevator. The source said league officials had to have seen it. This source has been impeccable, and I believed the information. So I wrote that the league had seen the tape. I should have called the NFL for a comment, a lapse in reporting on my part. The league says it has

not seen the tape, and I cannot refute that with certainty. No one from the league has ever knocked down my report to me, and so I was surprised to see the claim today that league officials have not seen the tape.[66]

In sports blogging and social-media circles, King was widely criticized for his reporting on this story. On Deadspin, a popular sports blog often critical of King's reporting and his cozy relationship with league officials, Tim Marcharman wrote:

This is an incredible statement. In the most generous gloss of it, King is admitting to having casually transformed a third party's assumption that the NFL had seen the video into a factual assertion that it had actually done so, and to having done this at a time when it was convenient to the NFL's interests for the public to think that league officials were diligently investigating the case against Rice. This is the sort of thing no college newspaper reporter would ever do, to say nothing of the best-connected reporter in the game. (A less generous reading suggests that King is covering for his source, which would be incredible in its own way.)[67]

King was not the only reporter to have his sourcing be an issue. ESPN's Adam Schefter, that network's popular and plugged-in NFL reporter, criticized the league on the air for misleading him and fellow reporters. Deadspin writer Tom Ley[68] wrote that Schefter all but called NFL officials liars.

The potential of sources lying to reporters—or passing along incomplete or incorrect information—threatens the core relationship of journalism. Because journalists rely on sources as part of their professional routines, a dishonest source drastically inhibits the ability of the reporters to do their jobs. The risk of this happening increases with the use of unnamed sources, as happened in the lead-up to the second Iraq War in the early 2000s.[69]

Sources lying, or passing along incomplete or incorrect information, also increases the sense of deviance around the story. Lying suggests a possible cover-up or conspiracy, or institutional wrongdoing—both of which are more salacious and interesting stories than a player's arrest. In a sense, the very nature of reporting on the Ray Rice story, combined with the way news is constructed, led to the evolution of this story from one of the arrest of an athlete to one of a potential league-wide conspiracy and a threat to the job status of the most powerful man in American sports.

## CONCLUSION

This chapter traced the evolution of the Ray Rice scandal. What once would have been a story of an athlete's arrest—the type of story that is widely covered and studied[70]—took on multiple lives over the course of several months. The presence of video surveillance of the domestic violence,[71] particularly the video that showed the actual assault, changed the story narrative. Ironically, the graphic video of the actual assault did not bring additional criticism of the perpetrator (at least in sports media coverage) but instead changed the focus of the story to the institution of the NFL—a pattern familiar in media coverage of scandals.[72] The social construction of news—specifically, news values of deviance and journalists' reliance on sources—also led to the evolution of the scandal. Because of these factors, by the end of the year, the Ray Rice scandal was about Roger Goodell and the institution of the NFL. The scandal evolved to the point that Ray Rice was only a tangential part of the scandal itself.

## NOTES

1. Don Van Natta Jr. and Kevin Van Valkenburg, "Rice Case: Purposeful Misdirection by Team, Scant Investigation by NFL," *ESPN.com.*, 2014. http://espn.go.com/espn/otl/story/_/id/11551518.
2. Van Natta and Van Valkenburg, "Rice Case: Purposeful Misdirection by Team, Scant Investigation by NFL."
3. David Leonard, "A World of Criminals or a Media Construction? Race, Gender, Celebrity, and the Athlete/Criminal Discourse," in *Handbook of Sports and Media*, eds Arthur A. Raney and Jennings Bryant (New York, NY: Lawrence Erlbaum, 2006): 523–542.; C. Richard King and Charles Fruehling Springwood. *Beyond the Cheers: Race as Spectacle in College Sport*, (Albany, NY: State University of New York Press, 2001).
4. Joshua Gamson, "Normal Sins: Sex Scandal Narratives As Institutional Morality Tales," *Social Problems* 48, no. 2 (2001): 185–205.
5. Christopher William Anderson, *Rebuilding the News: Metropolitan Journalism in the Digital Age*, (Philadelphia, PA: Temple University Press, 2013); Herbert J. Gans, *Deciding What's News: A Study of CBS Evening News, NBC Nightly News, Newsweek, and Time*, (Chicago, IL: Northwestern University Press, 1979); Michael Schudson, *The Sociology of News*, (New York, NY: W.W. Norton, 2011); Pamela J. Shoemaker and Stephen D. Reese, *Mediating the Message in the 21st Century: A Media Sociology Perspective*, (New York, NY: Routledge, 2013).
6. Shoemaker and Reese. *Mediating the Message in the 21st Century: A Media Sociology Perspective*.
7. Kathy Charmaz and J.A. Smith, "Grounded Theory," *Qualitative Psychology: A Practical Guide to Research Methods* (Thousand Oaks, CA: Sage, 2003): 81–110.
8. Justin Fenton, "Ravens Running Back Ray Rice Arrested After Incident in Atlantic City," *The Baltimore Sun*, February 16, 2014. http://articles.baltimoresun.com/2014-02-16/sports/bal-ravens-running-back-ray-rice-arrested-after-incident-in-atlantic-city-20140216_1_ray-rice-chad-steele-ravens.
9. USA Today. USA Today | Sports | NFL. (2015). *USAtoday.com.* http://www.usatoday.com/sports/nfl/arrests/2015/all/all/.
10. Fenton, "Ravens Running Back Ray Rice Arrested After Incident in Atlantic City."

11. TMZ, "Ray Rice—Dragging Unconscious Fiancée … After Alleged Mutual Attack," *TMZ.com*, 2014. http://www.tmz.com/videos/0_c5nk3w3n/.

12. A.J. Perez, "Race Rice, Ravens Continue to Wait on Possible Suspension By NFL," *NJ.com*, July 9, 2014. http://www.nj.com/rutgersfootball/index.ssf/2014/07/ray_rice_ravens_continue_to_wait_on_possible_suspension_by_nfl.html

13. A. Wilson, "What's Next for Baltimore Ravens Running Back Ray Rice?" *The Baltimore Sun*, 2014; J. Zrebjec, J., Ray Rice's Likely Suspension Could Force Ravens to Embrace Running Back by Committee, *The Baltimore Sun*, 2014.

14. Leonard, "A World of Criminals or a Media Construction? Race, Gender, Celebrity and the Athlete/Criminal Discourse."

15. Leonard, "A World of Criminals or a Media Construction? Race, Gender, Celebrity and the Athlete/Criminal Discourse."

16. Richard E. Lapchick, "Crime and Athletes: New Racial Stereotypes," *Society* 37 (2000): 14–20.

17. Barry Petchesky, "Ray Rice: 'Sometimes In Life, You Will Get Knocked Down,'" *Deadspin.com*, May 23, 2014. http://deadspin.com/ray-rice-sometimes-in-life-you-will-get-knocked-down-1580795933.

18. Bart Hubbuch, "Ray Rice's 'Apology' was a Complete Debacle," *New York Post*. http://nypost.com/2014/05/23/ray-rice-apology-a-pitiful-scene-with-a-frightful-metaphor/.

19. Mike Freeman. "Short Rice Ban Shows NFL Doesn't Care," *Bleacher Report*. 2014. http://bleacherreport.com/articles/2139861-ray-rice-suspension-shows-just-how-much-nfl-cares-about-domestic-violence; Michael Klopman. "NFL Star's Suspension Makes Sense To NO ONE," *HuffingtonPost.com*. 2014. http://www.huffingtonpost.com/2014/07/24/ray-rice-suspension-backlash_n_5617445.html; Clay Travis, "Ray Rice Suspension: When Violence is More Acceptable Than Slurs, We Have a Problem," 2014. *Foxsports.com*. http://www.foxsports.com/college-football/outkick-the-coverage/ray-rice-suspended-two-games-for-knocking-out-his-fiancee-072414.

20. Mike Sielski, Roger Goodell Wristslaps Ray Rice in Suspension, *Philadelphia Inquirer*, July 26, 2014. http://articles.philly.com/2014-07-26/sports/52031598_1_janay-palmer-ray-rice-roger-goodell.

21. Freeman, "Short Rice Ban Shows NFL Doesn't Care."

22. Chris Burke, "Lenient Penalty for Ray Rice Troubling Proof of Where NFL's Priorities Lie," *Sports Illustrated*, July 24, 2014. http://www.si.com/nfl/2014/07/24/ray-rice-suspension-roger-goodell-baltimore-ravens; Jeremy Gordon, "Josh Gordon, Ray Rice and the NFL's Complex Morality Court," *The Wall Street Journal*, August 29, 2014. http://blogs.wsj.com/dailyfix/2014/08/29/josh-gordon-ray-rice-and-the-nfls-complex-morality-court/; Sielski, "Roger Goodell Wristslaps Ray Rice in Suspension."

23. Burke, "Lenient Penalty for Ray Rice Troubling Proof of Where NFL's Priorities Lie."

24. Greg Howard, "Does The NFL Think Ray Rice's Wife Deserved It?" *Deadspin.com*, July 31, 2014. http://deadspin.com/does-the-nfl-think-ray-rices-wife-deserved-it-1612138248.

25. PTI. Pardon the Interruption, 2014.

26. Peter King. "What the Heck Happened to Jordan Gross?," *mmqb.si.com*, July 29, 2014. http://mmqb.si.com/2014/07/29/jordan-gross-weight-retirement-panthers/.
27. Matt Carlson. *On the Condition of Anonymity: Unnamed Sources and the Battle for Journalism*, (Champaign, IL: University of Illinois Press, 2011).
28. Gamson, "Normal Sins: Sex Scandal Narratives as Institutional Morality Tales."
29. Gamson, "Normal Sins: Sex Scandal Narratives as Institutional Morality Tales."
30. Gamson. "Normal Sins: Sex Scandal Narratives as Institutional Morality Tales."
31. Freeman, "Short Rice Ban Shows NFL Doesn't Care."
32. TMZ, "Ray Rice—Dragging Unconscious Fiancée ... After Alleged Mutual Attack."
33. TMZ, "Ray Rice—Dragging Unconscious Fiancée ... After Alleged Mutual Attack."
34. Ken Belson, "Ray Rice Cut by Ravens and Suspended by N.F.L.," *The New York Times*, September 8, 2014. http://www.nytimes.com/2014/09/09/sports/football/ray-rice-video-shows-punch-and raises-new-questions-for-nfl.html?_r=0.
35. Ken Belson, "N.F.L. Continues to Face Questions Over Video of Ray Rice," *The New York Times*, September 9, 2014. http://www.nytimes.com/2014/09/10/sports/football/ray-rices-wife-defends-him-and-criticizes-the-media.html.
36. Don Banks, "His Job Is Safe, His Credibility Is Shot," *mmqb.si.com*, September 10, 2014. http://mmqb.si.com/2014/09/10/roger-goodell-credibility-ray-rice-bountygate.
37. Gamson, "Normal Sins: Sex Scandal Narratives as Institutional Morality Tales."
38. Gamson, "Normal Sins: Sex Scandal Narratives as Institutional Morality Tales."
39. Belson, "Ray Rice Cut by Ravens and Suspended by N.F.L."
40. Peter King, "What the Heck Happened to Jordan Gross?," *mmqb.si.com*, July 29, 2014. http://mmqb.si.com/2014/07/29/jordan-gross-weight-retirement-panthers/; Petchesky. "Ray Rice: 'Sometimes In Life, You Will Get Knocked Down.'"
41. John Breech, "AP: NFL Executive Was Sent Copy of Ray Rice Video in April," *cbssports.com*, September 10, 2014. http://www.cbssports.com/nfl/eye-on-football/24704465/ap-nfl-executive-was-sent-copy-of-ray-rice-video-in-april.
42. Van Natta and Van Valkenburg, "Rice Case: Purposeful Misdirection by Team, Scant Investigation by NFL."
43. *Kansas City Star*, "Fire NFL's Roger Goodell for Inexcusable Handling of Ray Rice Assault Case," *Kansas City Star*, September 8, 2014. http://www.kansascity.com/opinion/editorials/article1927674.html; Bill Plaschke, "NFL, Roger Goodell Repeatedly Dropped the Ball in Ray Rice Case," *Los Angeles Times*, September 8, 2014. http://www.latimes.com/sports/nfl/la-sp-ray-rice-nfl-plaschke-20140909-column.html.
44. Jim Corbett, "Congress Probes NFL Commissioner Roger Goodell on Ray Rice Case," *USA Today*, September 10, 2014. http://www.usatoday.com/story/sports/nfl/2014/09/10/roger-goodell-congress-letter-john-conyers-ray-rice/15394317/.

45. Samar Kalaf, "Keith Olbermann: Roger Goodell Needs To Be Fired," *Deadspin.com*, September 20, 2014. http://deadspin.com/keith-olbermann-roger-goodell-needs-to-be-fired-1633251418.

46. *Kansas City Star*, "Fire NFL's Roger Goodell for Inexcusable Handling of Ray Rice Assault Case."

47. Dan A. Berkowitz, *Social Meanings of News: A Text-Reader*, (Thousand Oaks, CA: Sage 1997); Shoemaker and Reese. *Mediating the Message in the 21st Century: A Media Sociology Perspective*.

48. Gaye Tuchman, *Making News: A Study in the Construction of Reality*, (New York, NY: Free Press, 1980).

49. Mark Fishman, *Manufacturing the News*, (Austin, TX: University of Texas Press, 1980).

50. Herbert J. Gans, *Deciding What's News: A Study of CBS Evening News, NBC Nightly News, Newsweek, and Time*, (Evanston, IL: Northwestern University Press, 1979).

51. Schudson, *The Sociology of News*.

52. Pamlea J. Shoemaker, *Communication Concepts 3: Gatekeeping*, (Newbury Park, CA: Sage, 1991).

53. Pamela J. Shoemaker, Tsan-Kuo Chang, and Nancy Brendlinger, "Deviance as a Predictor of Newsworthiness: Coverage of International Events in the U.S. Media," *Communication Yearbook* 10, no. 348 (1987): 65.

54. Shoemaker, *Communication Concepts 3: Gatekeeping*.

55. Tuchman. *Making News*.

56. Gans, *Deciding What's News: A Study of CBS Evening News, NBC Nightly News, Newsweek, and Time*.

57. Leon V. Sigal, *Reporters and Officials*, (Lexington, MA: D.C. Heath, 1973).

58. Gans, *Deciding What's News: A Study of CBS Evening News, NBC Nightly News, Newsweek, and Time*.

59. Sigal, *Reporters and Officials*; Gans, *Deciding What's News: A Study of CBS Evening News, NBC Nightly News, Newsweek, and Time*; Fishman, *Manufacturing the News*; Tuchman, *Making News*.

60. Fishman, *Manufacturing the News*.

61. Gans, *Deciding What's News: A Study of CBS Evening News, NBC Nightly News, Newsweek, and Time*.

62. David Rowe, "Sports Journalism: Still the 'Toy Department' of the News Media?," *Journalism* 8, no. 4 (2007): 385–405.

63. Mark Douglas Lowes, *Inside the Sports Pages: Work Routines, Professional Ideologies, and the Manufacture of Sports News*, (Toronto, Canada: University of Toronto Press, 1999).

64. King, "What the Heck Happened to Jordan Gross?"

65. Belson, "Ray Rice Cut by Ravens and Suspended by N.F.L."

66. King, "On Reporting Ray Rice."

67. Tim Marchman, "Peter King Issues Statement On His Ray Rice Reporting, Self-Immolates," *Deadspin.com*, September 8, 2014. http://deadspin.com/peter-king-issues-statement-on-his-ray-rice-reporting-1632044670.

68. Tom Ley, "Adam Schefter Is Fed Up With The NFL," *Deadspin.com*, September 8, 2014. http://deadspin.com/adam-schefter-is-fed-up-with-the-nfl-1631937239.

69. Carlson, *On the Condition of Anonymity: Unnamed Sources and the Battle for Journalism.*

70. Leonard, *A World of Criminals or a Media Construction? Race, Gender, Celebrity and the Athlete/Criminal Discourse.*

71. TMZ, "Ray Rice—ELEVATOR KNOCKOUT … Fiancée Takes Crushing Punch."

72. Gamson, "Normal Sins: Sex Scandal Narratives as Institutional Morality Tales."

# CHAPTER 16

# Feminist Over-Sharing in the Wake of the Ray Rice Scandal

## *Erin Matson*

Four days after the arrest of Baltimore Ravens star Ray Rice, the online tabloid TMZ released a video showing him dragging the unconscious body of his fiancée from an elevator in Atlantic City. One month passed. Rice was indicted on aggravated assault charges, and the next day the couple married. Janay Palmer became Janay Rice on March 28, 2014.

For six months, the state of New Jersey and the National Football League vied to forgive Ray Rice as painlessly as possible. He was accepted in a pretrial intervention program typically reserved for victimless crimes. The NFL hosted a press conference with the couple, both husband and wife apologized, and he was suspended for two games.

Then TMZ released a second, full video about half a year later on September 8, 2014, showing Ray knocking Janay unconscious before dragging her body from the elevator. That day, Ray was cut by the Ravens. He was also suspended indefinitely by the NFL, a decision that was later overturned on appeal. The story exploded into the scandal of the year; nine months later, the video had been played more than 11 million times on YouTube.

On September 9, 2014, one day after the second video release, Janay posted a statement on Instagram:

> I woke up this morning feeling like I had a horrible nightmare, feeling like I'm mourning the death of my closest friend. But to have to accept the fact that it's reality is a nightmare in itself. No one knows the pain that the media & unwanted options from the public has caused my family. To make us relive a moment in our lives that we regret everyday is a horrible thing. To take something away from the man I love that he has worked his ass off for all his life just to gain ratings is a horrific. THIS IS OUR LIFE! What don't you all get. If your intentions were

E. Matson (✉)
Arlington, VA, USA

© The Editor(s) (if applicable) and The Author(s) 2016
H. Mandell, G.M. Chen (eds.), *Scandal in a Digital Age*,
DOI 10.1057/978-1-137-59545-4_16

to hurt us, embarrass us, make us feel alone, take all happiness away, you've suc-
ceeded on so many levels. Just know we will continue to grow & show the world
what real love is! Ravensnation we love you![1]

In America, the domestic violence love story typically hides in plain sight.
More than one in three women will experience rape, stalking, or physical violence by an intimate partner during their lifetimes.[2] And yet the woman with
the black eye in the checkout line is ignored; the man shouting threats is the
white noise of the apartment complex.

Too often, the polite thing to do when someone in the immediate vicinity is
struggling with domestic violence is to "mind your own business." This is what
a large group of dancing people did when we had to step outside a wedding we
were attending, when my then-husband threatened to kill me in the parking
lot. Only one person, a friend from high school, came looking for me later. He
said he did not know what was happening, but it bothered him. And he cried.

I stayed for another year.

For ten years, I kept silent about my experiences in an abusive marriage. I
did not want to be judged for staying, for the messiness of it all. I loved my
then-husband and tried to make it work. I did not want people to question my
credentials as a feminist and a strong woman, much less my actions and my
sanity.

The day after Janay Rice posted on Instagram in September 2014, I shared
my story with domestic violence. It was not flattering, and I was not a perfect
victim. As I wrote then:

"The reason why I am speaking up now is simple. I believe that violent relationships flourish under those conditions, when women are made to feel ashamed
for having 'imperfect' stories of abuse. We are made to feel that if we admit a
problem, we are then branded with it—that it is a reflection upon us. We are
made to feel that scrutiny of our actions in these situations will lead to public
scorn and private danger. What we need most from our friends and family is
social support that will not further isolate us when we stay, and that can be
ready quickly when we choose or are forced to leave. In the moment, that rarely
feels possible.

What Janay Rice has said in the last few days makes a lot of sense to me."[3]

I wasn't alone.

## #WHYISTAYED

In the course of the 48 hours between the release of the Ray Rice video and
the publication of my story, 92,000 personal accounts of domestic violence
flooded Twitter using the #WhyIStayed hashtag. Beverly Gooden, a domestic
violence advocate and survivor, started it by sharing her own story, in part
because she was frustrated by criticism of Janay Rice on social media.

"I wanted everyone to know that I understood what it was like, that I experienced it," Gooden told me. "It's okay to bide time to figure out what you're going to do. It seemed like no one was saying that was okay."

She was surprised by the response. "I first was thinking that the people that I followed would have a small conversation about it," Gooden told me. "No one pays attention to my tweets." As others began to share her tweets and chime in, she came to see why. "It's really difficult to be vulnerable, especially coming from a place where you've been in pain; it [the hashtag] spoke to the beauty of knowing you have someone who has your back. ... If you were a survivor and you saw a lot of people talking about something you've experienced, it gives you a sense of not just community, but familiarity."

Kirin Kanakkanatt, who served as a national field coordinator for LGBTQ advocacy group GetEQUAL, participated in the hashtag—the first time she had shared her story so publicly—and echoed Gooden's analysis.

Unable to sleep the night of September 8, 2014, she grabbed her phone. "I saw the hashtag. ... and I was compelled to say something," Kanakkanatt told me. "It felt like I was on Twitter in a room full of feminist women saying these things. Feeling anonymous on the Internet emboldened me." She tweeted:

#whyistayed: He told me no one will ever love you like I do
#whyileft: I realized that no one should ever 'love' me like he did.[4]

She went to bed, and later that day realized her story had been retweeted hundreds of times and shared on Buzzfeed. She had mixed feelings about the attention. On the one hand, she felt good because "people weren't throwing garbage at me, it was cool," but on another, "major publications asked really personal questions," trying to find her abuser's name and credentials so they could find him. Because of her perceived celebrity status, Kanakkanatt said she got talked into sharing details that were terrifying for her to share.

She continues to feel ambivalence. "It depends on the day and how far away I feel from that abuse." She said some days she feels happy when people are still retweeting her story. "Other days I wish it would turn off. ... Some days I get to relive the glory of it, and some days I have to relive the traumaness and scariness of it."

Yet from a macro level, #WhyIStayed pushed back against the taboo that empowers domestic violence by re-centering the cultural conversation on the psychological and emotional experiences of those who actually experienced it. In its wake, Gooden made several national media appearances, writing in a post, "Why We Stayed," for the On the Ground blog in *The New York Times*:

Many victims of domestic violence think they are alone. This past month showed them that they're not alone. We are all right here, listening. A critical element of policy change is building up voices that will be the leaders of that policy change. But that can't happen if the owners of those voices are afraid to speak out. ... We are not letting others shame us anymore. We will not accept the social disapproval any longer.[5]

Hashtag activism refers to the decentralized and open production of online post-ings, frequently on Twitter, around a specific topic by using a common hashtag, like #WhyIStayed. Anyone can contribute, and all are welcome to speak their piece. In effect, hashtag activism and online sharing that focus on the personal disclosure of experiences seen as taboo are purposefully seeking to overturn notions of what is considered scandalous. Many of the women leading these campaigns are explicit in their aims to create community, erase stigma, and foster social change.

## ABORTION STORYTELLING ONLINE

Two months after the Ray Rice scandal and the emergence of #WhyIStayed, the reproductive rights group Advocates for Youth hosted the first live-streamed abortion speak-out in November 2014. Women, advocates, abortion provid-ers, faith leaders, and others shared their abortion stories.

"Because abortion is so stigmatizing, the simple act of sharing an abortion experience in a public setting such as the Internet is pretty unprecedented," said Julia Reticker-Flynn, director of Youth Organizing & Mobilization for Advocates for Youth. "We were really impressed with the people willing to do it. We knew it took a lot of courage to share, and were also impressed with how the community stood up and supported people as they shared their stories."

Abortion is a common but largely taboo experience for women. Those who wish to restrict abortion rights often portray abortion as scandalous—or worse. Advocates for Youth's 1 in 3 Campaign, named for the roughly one in three women who will have abortions during their lifetimes, aims to upend that. "What we would love to see is a culture in which no politician would ever even imagine introducing legislation that would restrict abortion access because they would just know that would create an uproar and be against the basic human rights of people in this country," Reticker-Flynn told me. "There's also a vision that people [and] the experience would not be shamed."

The campaign promotes story sharing online and offline, having produced a book, a play, and toolkits for speak-outs on college campuses. More than 800 people have shared a personal story with the campaign. A 1 in 3 Campaign website uses first names only, just one of many precautions the campaign takes to protect individuals from harassment.

Some advocates, however, have been more vocal about their experiences online—not just in the relative safety of an eight-hour video but in searchable text that shows up on Google—while using their full names.

Renee Bracey Sherman, author of *Saying Abortion Aloud: Research and Recommendations for Public Abortion Storytellers and Organizations*, has shared her abortion story many times over the past four years. She received targeted online harassment and death threats that led her to stay in her apart-ment for days in 2014. Using her full name has also impacted her personal life.

"I think that everybody Googles everybody these days," Bracey Sherman told me. "I've definitely been on a date where somebody Googled me and that was interesting. Then the conversation was everything about that [abortion], not the normal things you would talk about to get to know someone over coffee."

She added: "It's changed my life both positively and negatively. Positively it's given me a space to flourish ... and given me a role in the movement ... it's given me connections," she said, even with strangers. "We don't feel alone, and they know I've got their back. I do this work because I want them to know that they shouldn't be feeling isolated."

Bracey Sherman first shared her story in September 2011 on a blog run by Exhale, an organization that uses an apolitical, "pro-voice" approach to address the emotional health and wellbeing of men and women following abortion. She wrote:

> I hope that in the future, the abortion debate moves from above the heads of the people it affects, down to a conversational level, where women and family members who have experienced abortion can talk about how to best support each other.[6]

Yet, the public evolution of Bracey Sherman's storytelling and political consciousness raises questions on ownership of a story once it is online. Two years later, she published a commentary titled "Why I Share My Abortion Story, But Am Not Pro-Voice" in which she detailed how she had come to feel compelled to share her abortion story within explicitly political contexts and frames, writing:

> I don't believe in order to share your abortion authentically, you have to move to the sidelines and become apolitical. And if that is what some people want to do, that's great. That's their choice. But it's unethical for them to tell me that (is) how I should share my story. Because it's just that: mine.[7]

## "The Personal Is Political" Predates the Internet

Second-wave feminism, a time period encompassing the boom that took place in the women's liberation movement in the 1960s and 1970s, purposefully used story sharing to draw connections between the personal experiences of women and the politics of gender-based oppression.

Consciousness-raising (CR) groups met in-person, typically in gatherings of 10 to 20. "Women would gather, and without judgment and with support would, one at a time, tell the story of their experience," Heather Booth told me. Booth is president of Midwest Academy and founder of the Women's Radical Action Program at the University of Chicago, one of the first CR groups in the country.

"The great insight that came out of it was that you'd hear stories in the early days of how we often felt things were our fault ... but when you heard one story after another, that others were also having the same experience, you realized that the personal was political," she said. "It wasn't just a personal issue but a social issue, and socially shared, and if it was a social issue it needed a social solution."

"I definitely think it's a kind of CR," Booth said of #WhyIStayed and online abortion story sharing. "In some ways, it's even more far-ranging in that it can involve so many more people," she said.

"There may be some benefits of not being in the same room, for example, someone in a current abusive relationship who can't get out of the house could be part of it online," she said. Yet she also referenced drawbacks: "I do think there are special things that happen when people are in the same physical space."

This view was echoed by several of the online activists as well, who tended to see their online efforts as just one piece of a broader movement to put the experiences and needs of women at the center of the culture and policy debates that surround them.

And so it may be that, despite intergenerational divides within feminism that often separate second-wave activists from younger activists, #WhyIStayed and live-streamed abortion speak-outs could be viewed as an extension of the 1960s dorm rooms and living rooms where women dared to tell the truth about their own lives before they took to the streets and demanded more.

## ONLINE STORY SHARING: A HASHTAG, AN OVER-SHARE, OR SOMETHING BIGGER?

Within the feminist community, hashtag activism carries a hotly contested connotation. Some dismiss it as "slacktivism" or even damaging, as *The Nation* did in a January 2014 cover story covering what it called "Feminism's Toxic Twitter Wars." Others note the importance of online activism in elevating the voices and experience of women of color, a theme echoed by Kirin Kanakkanatt surrounding her decision to share her story on #WhyIStayed.

"I think especially women of color had a moment, that's what I felt [at the time]. I'm a woman of color and I was in a relationship with a man of color, and I was like, oh word, we can talk about this," she said.

Steph Herold is managing director of the Sea Change Program, an organization that combats abortion stigma. Prior to co-founding that organization, Herold started the #IHadAnAbortion hashtag in 2010.

"I would do things differently," she told me. "I didn't have this awareness about the gravity of what I was asking people to do. ... It was too simple. Individuals are not the solution in and of themselves to systemic problems. ... I think that's the nature of the hypervisibility of the Internet. ... It's on there, it's not finished; it's a lot of unformed thoughts."

Yet, Herold remains active in strategies that use contact between people who have had abortions and others in the aim to change culture and policy. "Being able to speak truth to power is an element of every successful social movement, and people are looking for that person-to-person connection, and storytelling has the power to get people out of their heads and into their hearts," she said.

With the increasing breakdown of barriers of what is thought to be online life and real life, it may be useful to question whether the online/offline distinction is valid, or will remain so with future generations. In any case, it remains radical for a woman to tell the truth about her own life, whether she speaks up in a room or types her story into the void.

I found this to be true when sharing my own story with domestic violence. I felt free after my editors hit publish; I had not realized until then just how much burden I had carried with the secret. Some readers said I made them more sympathetic to women in violent relationships, while others who had had similar experiences told me they felt less alone. These were the reasons I felt called to share my story after the Ray Rice scandal exploded into a national victim-blaming discussion that I did not like. Yet I was surprised by how much the act of sharing my story transformed *me*.

Whether responding to social scandals or expectations that they should feel ashamed, women like me are using the Internet to continue a feminist tradition of supporting one another and changing social systems (and even ourselves) by taking the risk of sharing our own stories, on our own terms.

## NOTES

1. Aaron Wilson, "Janay Rice breaks her silence, describes situation as 'horrible nightmare,'" *The Baltimore Sun*, September 9, 2014.
2. *National Intimate Partner and Sexual Violence Survey*. Centers for Disease Control. 2010.
3. Erin Matson, "Why I Stayed in an Abusive Marriage for Two Years," *RH Reality Check*, September 10, 2014. http://rhrealitycheck.org/article/2014/09/10/stayed-abusive-marriage-two-years/.
4. Kanakkanatt Kirin, Tweet, September 9, 2014. https://twitter.com/kirin_rosemary/status/509207894131507200.
5. Beverly Gooden, "Why We Stayed," *The New York Times*, October 13, 2014. http://kristof.blogs.nytimes.com/2014/10/13/why-we-stayed/.
6. Renee Bracey Sherman, "Why I Share My Abortion Story, But Am Not Pro-Voice," *RH Reality Check*, July 9, 2013. https://exhaleprovoice.org/blog-post/similar-experiences-never-same.
7. Bracey, "Why I Share My Abortion Story."

# CHAPTER 17

# Conclusion: Predicting a New Scandal Environment in the Twenty-First Century

## Gina Masullo Chen and Hinda Mandell

Scandal has always riveted our attention. Thousands of years after Eve ate the fruit of knowledge, disobeying God, and sealing her scandalous fate in the Biblical story,[1] we still repeat this tale, as a warning of what happens when one does what one should not. Millennia later, hundreds of women were defamed as witches for exhibiting what was considered scandalous behavior—dancing with the devil or flying—and burned in public spectacle in Europe's witch craze from the 1300s to 1600s,[2] which preceded and dwarfed the Salem witch trials in America.[3] Crowds of onlookers could not help but watch, as the scandal-engulfed women burned to their death. Witnessing as others' missteps lead to their undoing seems an intrinsically human obsession. We want to look away. But we cannot. We need to see those in trouble get their due.

Like the townspeople who witnessed the fictional Hester Prynne—a scarlet "A" for adultery embroidered on her breast—march to the scaffold to be publicly punished for her sins, we want to witness people wear their digital scarlet letters of shame, so we can set apart their misdeeds from our own and think: I would never do something like that. As media scholar Pamela J. Shoemaker explains, humans are biologically "hardwired to survey their environment and to prefer news about deviant or otherwise threatening events."[4] This tendency to focus on what does not belong served early humans well, saving them from bloody death at the hands of predators so they were able to pass on their genes—and this predilection—to all of us today.

G.M. Chen (✉)
School of Journalism, The University of Texas at Austin, Texas, USA

H. Mandell
School of Communication, Rochester Institute of Technology, Rochester, New York, USA

This book confirms that our fascination with the foibles of others has not abated. If anything, the digital age has intensified this interest, changing the calculus of the conversation regarding news and blurring the lines between public and private. Digital media, in fact, "complicate the very nature of public life."[5] Today's politicians, celebrities, and even members of the public fail—and then share (or over-share) their transgressions through the instant, always-on digital culture in which we now live. The public, much like those of an earlier time, look askance but then lap it all up, tempted by every salacious snippet, perpetuating a cycle of diminished public discourse. We shrug our shoulders and roll our eyes, suggesting these titillating scandals are beneath us. We plead for more dignified news. But then we cannot stop watching, reading, or sharing the deviant, the nasty, the scandalous.

The public scaffolds and branding irons of the past may be gone, but "modern media are far more effective than scaffolds for holding people up for public scrutiny, and the American public's readiness to judge the sins of others remains as strong as it was 350 years ago."[6] We do not have scarlet letters today. But we have viral tweets, Facebook posts, and digital footprints that preserve forever when those in power have done something that they wish they had not. Communication scholar Zizi A. Papacharissi argues that technology has created a "new way to counter powerlessness by allowing individuals to propose new spaces, upon which newer, more empowering habits and relations may be cultivated."[7] We agree but also submit that technology offers a new digital space for malfeasance and indiscretion. This "repoliticized social sphere"[8] merges the public and private and makes almost every detail fair game for public consumption.

In this chapter, we first synthesize what this book has documented about the changing nature of scandal and its fluid relationship with news, social media, and the public in our digital age. Next, we consider how technology has changed both our understanding of scandal and our appetite to consume it. Finally, we predict what the future may hold for scandal in our increasingly digital world.

## What We Understand About Scandal Today

At its core, our fascination with scandal is the same today as it was in millennia past. However, our access to news about scandal has heightened. In Chap. 3, Neal Allen asserts that the public's appetite for gossip and scandal swelled because of digital tools and social media platforms[9] that make every lascivious characteristic of a scandal both easily discoverable and available all the time. That also means that scandals, such as Chappaquiddick—where Senator Edward M. Kennedy left a young woman for dead after a car crashed into a pond in 1969[10]—likely would have turned out very differently today. That scandal, while remembered nearly 50 years later, did little to destroy Kennedy's career, an outcome inconceivable today when the mere accidental sharing of private pictures on Twitter led to the downfall of New York Congressman

Anthony Weiner. As Joshua Gamson[11] points out in Chap. 7, Weiner's case lacked the personal and physically intimate exchanges of prior scandals, but virtual sex was enough to sound the death knell of his career. It is only in today's world where a photograph of a professor posing topless among friends could burst into the public sphere and create a scandal[12] or where two office co-workers engaged in coitus inside an insurance building after hours could jump from private indiscretion to public titillation in a matter of days.[13]

What we have found through this book is that the line between public and private has not only shifted or blurred but may actually cease to exist. Papacharissi[14] notes that even thinking of public and private spheres as a binary may be flawed because the private realm is always defined in contrast to what is public. Thus, the difference between the two becomes elusive.[15] Once information becomes public, it stops being private.[16] In a sense, our need to draw a line between the spheres shapes where we think the line should go.[17] We feel this imaginary line between spheres must exist, so we know when conduct or news has overstepped it. Yet where this line stands can shift, depending on what other news is drawing the public's attention that day. Certainly, our ancestors would be shocked to see what we consider public today, compared to their days. Much like women's dresses of days gone by that covered all but the hands and face, their private sphere was large and engulfing. Much of what we consider public today would have been scandal if revealed back then. Think of even a typical news report on TMZ,[18] the American online gossip site, which reports daily on celebrities' weight gain, drug use, or sexploits. Most of this content is not scandalous today, because it has become so commonplace in the chasm of our public sphere.

Our book also shows that the sense of being watched at all times goes hand in hand with the widening of the public sphere or even elimination of the distinction between public and private. This digital surveillance, which we define as the all-seeing eyes of everyone at all times to examine what is posted online, creates a context where the American people were initially outraged—and later became apathetic—toward revelations that the National Security Agency was monitoring their Internet and cellphone activity.[19] In a world where everything is public, it becomes less alarming that anything ceases to be private. Similarly, once the graphic video that showed one-time Baltimore Ravens star running back Ray Rice brutally attacking his then-fiancée surfaced, the story shifted from Rice himself to the National Football League's handling of the case.[20] It was as if once the private relationship ceased to be private, the public owned the story, and the line between the spheres disappeared. It would be naïve to think technology is to blame for all this change. Scandal has always left us transfixed. The line between public and private has moved many times in the past.

But technology—and its misuse—may desensitize us, making us less alarmed when confronted with damaging facts about another person. With the frequency with which scandals occur and the speed at which news about them buzzes across the globe, we may adopt a "ho-hum" attitude. Oh, this again. Yet we worry that this "ho-hum" attitude may be a mistake. When we see human frailty, even of those in power, it seems troubling that this does not faze us. It vexes us that the stories and scandals are so plentiful in our minds, that we easily lose track of who did what to whom or what politician or athlete was caught in what form of indiscretion this week. Scandal by its very nature is deviant news[21] because it violates norms and moral codes and involves secrets that once revealed provoke outrage and damage to reputation.[22] Yet, when we are barraged by digital media reports of scandal all the time, does scandalous news cease to be as deviant? Can something we witness 24 hours a day still arouse our attention in the same way? Imagine the early humans in Shoemaker's hardwired-for-news analogy[23] who knew to hide, triggered by the gentle crack of a branch beneath the approaching tiger's paw. What if hundreds or thousands of branches were breaking all the time? Could that person have any chance at noticing the one cracking branch that might save a life, or would all the similar sounds blur together? We suggest that that may be where we are heading with scandal news today.

## What the Future Holds

So what does this mean for scandal in the future? While we are not prescient enough to try to predict the future, we know for certain that the speed of technology will increase in the days beyond. Our media technology has shifted from computers to laptops to mobile devices in what seems like the blink of an eye. Top news site are now getting more of their traffic from smartphones than desktop computers,[24] meaning people can find information even more quickly than they could a mere few years ago. That will only increase with time, as improved technology makes our world more connected and more able to quickly spread the electronic pulses of information that translate into words, pictures, and videos online. News organizations are experimenting with data visualizations and virtual reality[25] to tell stories—with more detail and a greater sense of "being there" than the media we know today. The result is it will be even easier in the future to find out lewd details about politicians, celebrities, athletes, and others in power and spread them. There will be more venues to share this information than we can imagine—all aimed at satisfying our seemingly insatiable and often prurient need to know. Even those caught up in scandals may be tempted to cross the ever-altering line between public and private and over-share, as detailed in Chap. 11 about the aftermath of former South Carolina Governor Mark Sanford's adultery scandal.[26] And the speed with which these venues of the future will spread information will make our tweets and Facebook status updates seem as antiquated as snail mail is today.

We are in the midst of an age that media pundit Jeff Jarvis calls "publicness,"[27] which he defines as the act of making things public by revealing them online. He argues that this publicness opens us to new experiences and information that enrich our lives. We do not disagree. However, we do wonder when it will all stop. It is possible, as Mark Ward Sr.[28] writes in Chap. 5, that audience fragmentation will mute interest in some types of scandals while amplifying the frenzy over others. It is also likely the news consumer will eventually be over-saturated with tawdry news, and the bar for scandal will rise. A mere offensive tweet may not qualify as a scandal but be ignored as a peccadillo not worthy of attention. A professor's partially nude picture, which made news today as told in Chap. 9,[29] might be disregarded as a story because it is not scandalous enough. In the rapid speed of news, a politician's or athlete's mistake may be more quickly forgotten unless it involves criminal action or death.

The public also may yearn for more details—more private facts—rather than be sated with the morsels of scandal that constitute news today. Like a drug addict who must continually up the dose to get a fix, perhaps our public of the future will need more and more licentious tidbits to find a scandalous story worthy of notice. We argued earlier that the line between public and private might not even exist anymore. Yet, if we concede that the line still exists today, we predict it will not in the future. After all, the increasing demands for lurid details will not stop with our interest in those who hold power. We predict a trickle-down effect where the same lust for personal details will be demanded of us everyday folk. In scandal, the media have already established the precedent of reporting on private details associated with wrongful or boundary-crossing actions and shaming the transgressor in the process. So what?!, you might say. That person of elite status did something dumb or illegal and should be punished through public humiliation. But we already see evidence of a "scandal creep"—where scandal processes are applied to the actions of everyday people to exploit juicy tidbits of their private lives. Exhibit A represents a woman live-tweeting the breakup of an unsuspecting young couple on an airplane—for her own amusement—in August 2015.[30] Sure, the couple was in the midst of a private moment in a public space, but we do not think they expected their breakup to become news on BuzzFeed and other online sites.[31] Therefore, we would argue that our scandal culture, aided by our toolbox of digital technology, has crept into the mundane of everyday lives belonging to private citizens.

It is clear that mediated publicness does not—and will not in the future—leave unchanged what we mean by privacy.[32] It is plausible that a private world will be gone or so narrow in the future that it bears little resemblance to what we consider private today. The era of publicness may come full circle. But we are more hopeful. Jarvis writes that the challenge for society in today's publicness is "to find a new balance between our roles as free individuals and as members of a public who join together to build better, more open, more generous, and more accountable companies, markets, communities, governments, schools, relationships, and lives."[33] We agree and hope for the same for our future. However, in order to live with decency in a more open society that is bolstered by human connections online and off, we will have to check our expectations regarding the type of personal information we *need* to know about others, versus what we have become accustomed to *wanting* to know. After all, curiosity killed the cat. Let us not find out what an excess of prurience can do to humans, our media, and our networking systems.

# NOTES

1. Gen. 3: 1–19.
2. Lyndal Roper, *Witch Craze: Terror and Fantasy in Baroque Germany*, (New Haven, CT: Yale University Press, 2004);
3. Jess Blumber, "A Brief History of the Salem Witch Trials," *Smithsonian.com*, October 23, 2007. http://www.smithsonianmag.com/history/a-brief-history-of-the-salem-witch-trials-175162489/?no-ist.
4. Pamela J. Shoemaker, "Hardwired for News: Using Biological and Cultural Evolution to Explain the Surveillance Function," *Journal of Communication* 46, no. 2 (1996), 44.
5. Nancy K. Baym and danah boyd, "Social Mediated Publicness: An Introduction," *Journal of Broadcasting & Electronic Media* 56, no. 3 (2012): 1.
6. Margaret Brantley, "Introduction," in *The Scarlett Letter*, Nathaniel Hawthorne, (New York, NY: Simon & Schuster, 2004), viii.
7. Zizi A. Papacharissi, *A Private Sphere: Democracy in a Digital Age*, (Malden, MA: Polity Press, 2013), 15.
8. Jürgen Habermas, *The Structural Transformation of the Public Sphere*, (Cambridge, MA: MIT Press, 1991), 142.
9. J. Richard Stevens, "Scandal's Role in Creating a Surveillance Culture," in *Scandal in a Digital Age*, eds. Hinda Mandell and Gina Masullo Chen, (New York, NY: Palgrave Macmillan, 2016).
10. Grant Cos, "Chappaquiddick Revisited: Scandal and the Modern Mediated Apologia," in *Scandal in a Digital Age*, eds. Hinda Mandell and Gina Masullo Chen, (New York, NY: Palgrave Macmillan, 2016).
11. Joshua Gamson, "Scandal in the Age of Sexting," in *Scandal in a Digital Age*, eds. Hinda Mandell and Gina Masullo Chen, (New York, NY: Palgrave Macmillan, 2016).
12. Diana Blaine, "The Topless Professor in the Digital Age," in *Scandal in a Digital Age*, eds. Hinda Mandell and Gina Masullo Chen, (New York, NY: Palgrave Macmillan, 2016).
13. Kathleen M. Kuehn, "Privacy in Public and the Digital Witness," in *Scandal in a Digital Age*, eds. Hinda Mandell and Gina Masullo Chen, (New York, NY: Palgrave Macmillan, 2016).
14. Papacharissi, *A Private Sphere: Democracy in a Digital Age*.
15. Papacharissi, *A Private Sphere: Democracy in a Digital Age*.
16. Papacharissi, *A Private Sphere: Democracy in a Digital Age*.
17. Papacharissi, *A Private Sphere: Democracy in a Digital Age*.
18. TMZ.com. http://www.tmz.com/.
19. Joan L. Conners, "Political Cartoon Framing of the NSA Snooping Scandal," in *Scandal in a Digital Age*, eds. Hinda Mandell and Gina Masullo Chen, (New York, NY: Palgrave Macmillan, 2016).
20. Brian Moritz, "Evolution of a Modern Sports," in *Scandal in a Digital Age*, eds. Hinda Mandell and Gina Masullo Chen, (New York, NY: Palgrave Macmillan, 2016).
21. Shoemaker, "Hardwired for News: Using Biological and Cultural Evolution to Explain the Surveillance Function."
22. John B. Thompson, *Political Scandal: Power and Visibility in the Media Age*, (Cambridge, MA: Blackwell Publishers, 2000).

23. Shoemaker, "Hardwired for News: Using Biological and Cultural Evolution to Explain the Surveillance Function."

24. Gina Masullo Chen, "Media's Future is Mobile, With Many Points of Access," *Fort-Worth Star Telegram*, June 2, 2015. http://www.star-telegram.com/opinion/opn-columns-blogs/other-voices/article22952529.html; Amy Mitchell, "State of the News Media, 2015," *Pew Research Center*, April 29, 2015. http://www.journalism.org/2015/04/29/state-of-the-news-media-2015/.

25. Erin Polgren, "Virtual Reality is Journalism's Next Frontier," *Columbia Journalism Review*, November 19, 2014. http://www.cjr.org/innovations/virtual_reality_journalism.php.

26. Gina Masullo Chen, Paromita Pain, and Deepa Fadnis, "Over-Sharing in a Political Sex Scandal," in *Scandal in a Digital Age*, eds. Hinda Mandell and Gina Masullo Chen, (New York, NY: Palgrave Macmillan, 2016).

27. Jeff Jarvis, *Public Parts: How Sharing in the Digital Age Improves the Way We Work and Live*, (New York, NY: Simon & Schuster, 2011), 1.

28. Mark Ward Sr., "Televangelism, Audience Fragmentation, and the Changing Coverage of Scandal," in *Scandal in a Digital Age*, eds. Hinda Mandell and Gina Masullo Chen, (New York, NY: Palgrave Macmillan, 2016).

29. Blaine, "The Topless Professor in the Digital Age."

30. Sophia Rosenbaum, "Passenger Live Tweets Couple's Epic Breakup on Plane," *The New York Post*, August 24, 2015. http://nypost.com/2015/08/24/new-yorker-live-tweets-couples-epic-breakup-on-plane/.

31. Kevin Smith, "A Guy Allegedly Broke Up With His Girlfriend On A Plane Before it Even Took Off," *BuzzFeed*, August 24, 2015. http://www.buzzfeed.com/kevinsmith/airplane-breakup-nightmare-live-tweets#.miagzGzYy.

32. Baym and boyd, "Social Mediated Publicness: An Introduction," 320–329.

33. Jarvis, *Public Parts: How Sharing in the Digital Age Improves the Way We Work and Live*, 14.

# Index[1]

[1] Note: Page number followed by 'n' refers to endnotes.

© The Editor(s) (if applicable) and The Author(s) 2016
H. Mandell, G.M. Chen (eds.), *Scandal in a Digital Age*,
DOI 10.1057/978-1-137-59545-4

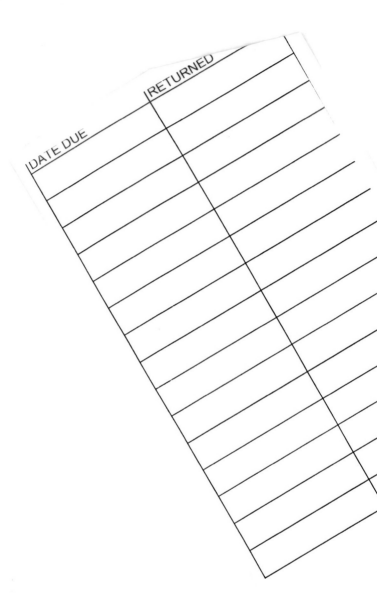

DATE DUE | RETURNED

38475949R00137